Musical Visitors to Britain

Over the centuries Britain has attracted many musical visitors. This book tells the stories of the many composers who visited – a varied and often eccentric collection of individuals. The earliest were invited by royalty with musical tastes; some were refugees from religious and political oppressions; others came as spies, a few to escape from debt and even murder charges. However, the main motive was a possibility of financial reward.

The rise in the nineteenth century of the celebrity composer, who was often also a conductor, is also traced. With the development of new forms of transport, composers were able to travel more extensively, both from the Continent and from the USA. New opportunities were also presented by the opening of public halls, where concerts could be held, as well as the growth of music festivals. In the twentieth and twenty-first centuries the aeroplane has enabled a regular influx of composers, and the book ends with a consideration of the universalising of music as well as the impact of new forms, such as jazz.

Musical Visitors to Britain is a fascinating book which is aimed to appeal to both the general reader and those with a special interest in music history.

David Gordon is one of the leading harpsichordists in the UK, and performs with violinists Andrew Manze, Nigel Kennedy and the baroque orchestra English Concert, specialising in improvisation. He is also a jazz pianist, and has given many workshops on aspects of Renaissance, baroque and jazz improvisation. He composes, and his output includes modern-day paraphrases of works by the seventeenth-century composers Purcell and Paisible.

Peter Gordon is Emeritus Professor of Education at the University of London Institute of Education and is former Head of the Department of History and Humanities. He is the author of many books on different aspects of nineteenth- and twentieth-century British social, political, educational and family history, and is General Editor of the Woburn Education Series. He is also a Fellow of both the Society of Antiquaries and the Royal Historical Society.

1 Frontispiece: Haydn crossing the English Channel, 1 January 1791

Musical Visitors to Britain

David Gordon and Peter Gordon

Routledge
Taylor & Francis Group

LONDON AND NEW YORK

First published 2005
by Routledge
2 Park Square, Milton Park, Abingdon, Oxon OX14 4RN

Simultaneously published in the USA and Canada
by Routledge
270 Madison Ave, New York, NY 10016

Routledge is an imprint of the Taylor & Francis Group

© 2005 David Gordon and Peter Gordon

Typeset in Sabon by
Florence Production Ltd, Stoodleigh, Devon
Printed and bound in Great Britain by
The Cromwell Press, Trowbridge, Wiltshire

British Library Cataloguing in Publication Data
A catalogue record for this book is available from the British Library

Library of Congress Cataloging in Publication Data
A catalog record for this book has been requested

ISBN 0–7130–0238–7 (Hbk)
ISBN 0–7130–4052–1 (Pbk)

Contents

vi *Contents*

Illustrations

Acknowledgements

The authors would like to acknowledge with thanks the following for their kind permission granted for the use of illustrations: the British Library, the Royal Academy of Music, Penguin Books, David and Charles, the Handel House Trust and Hodder Arnold. We are grateful to a number of individuals who have been of especial help, particularly Janet Snowman (Royal Academy of Music), Jane Cockcroft (Handel House Museum), Professor Robert Hume, Tessa Gordon and Evelyn Nallen, as well as the staffs of the British Library, the University of Cambridge Library, the London Library and the University of London Library.

Introduction
Seeking pastures new

An artist and his art tell a story, and part of that story is who he is, and where he is from. Musicians, like any other performers, are usually more fêted abroad than at home. In a profession that relies heavily on tags and trademarks, simply being foreign gives an identity to that performer. If that foreignness also represents some cultural ideal, however vague and however wrongly associated, that performer has a huge advantage over his indigenous counterparts. Similarly, there are many advantages for the musician abroad. Music, being a wordless art, travels very well. A new environment is very often stimulating for an artist, and to be heard 'with new ears' can clarify a musician's thinking. If he is successful abroad, or in reality if he merely survives there, he brings back an enhanced reputation when he returns home. Life on tour can be glamorous, and even if it is not, is often lucrative. Music performance and travel are old bedfellows.

Britain has been the magnet for foreign musicians for many centuries. Given the span of time covered, we have had of course to be selective and have chosen to concentrate on one particular category, composers, though until the later part of the eighteenth century almost all composers were also performers. Indeed, Pelham Humfrey, a leading English Restoration composer, said of the unpopular Catalan Luis Grabu, Master of the King's Music, that he 'understands nothing nor can play on any instruments and so cannot compose'.[1] Even in the 1720s, advertisements for a new Handel opera make no mention of the composer's name,[2] and Handel himself played harpsichord in all performances of his operas, just as Haydn directed his symphonies from the keyboard. From the nineteenth century, composers had become the superstars of the musical world, and Britain was an important destination for a great many of these musicians. It will become clear in what follows that there was a whole range of motives for coming to Britain.

The possibility of access to royalty, bestowing prestige on the individuals and, in some cases leading to employment in their service, was a big incentive for would-be visitors. Until 1690, when William III reorganised the musical household, the court was at the centre of musical life. Generations of foreign musicians have sought to make their mark in England by performing for the royal family. This was especially so where there were musical monarchs. Edward I played host to some of the leading French composers of the time, while Henry VIII, who was both a composer and a performer on lute and organ, made a point of importing musicians from Venice. Not all were well received, however, and a harpsichordist, Zuan de Leze, was so disappointed with his reception that he hanged himself.[3] Mary Tudor's marriage to Philip II of Spain brought the brilliant Spaniard Antonio de Cabezón to England in 1554. Cabezón was the greatest keyboard-player of the sixteenth century, and had a profound influence on the English school of virginal composers such as Tallis, Byrd and Bull. The Italian Alfonso Ferrabosco settled in England and entered the service of Elizabeth I, whilst his son of the same name was employed by James I and Charles I. Charles also employed some of the finest French violinist–composers in his court string band, and his son Charles II, anxious to emulate the French court under Louis XIV, encouraged musicians from France and Italy to come to these shores.[4] A number eventually settled here. Perhaps the best known is George Frederick Handel, who became a British citizen, and whose music was championed by the Hanoverian monarchs. Johann Christian Bach, the youngest son of the great Johann Sebastian, was employed as tutor to the royal children, and the Mozarts eagerly sought audiences before George III and Queen Caroline. One of the later musical monarchs, Queen Victoria, summoned most of the leading composers of her day, ranging from Rossini and Mendelssohn to Liszt and Saint-Saëns. Such occasions could give rise to difficulties, such as when Carl Nielsen was in London in April 1923 to conduct a concert of his own music. He was granted an audience with the Queen Mother, Alexandra, a Danish compatriot, at Marlborough House but had forgotten to pack a dark suit; he thereupon borrowed his son-in-law's, which was rather too small for him, and found the top buttons of his trousers would not fasten. A contemporary of Nielsen's described what happened next:

> 'Never mind,' he said. 'I'll just keep my hand over it and no one will notice.' With bated breath, his left hand before his midriff, he stepped towards Queen Alexandra and he expressed his deep thanks. After a while Alexandra's sister, the Empress of Dagmar of Russia, joined the company and it was announced that tea was served. Carl Nielsen was requested to lead both ladies to the table: with an empress on one arm and a queen on the other he walked across the room, hardly daring to breathe for fear his partly undone trousers should be noticed. But nobody seemed aware that the suit was too small.[5]

It is remarkable how much British literature and history has attracted foreign composers, even those who never ventured here. The inspiration provided by the plays of Shakespeare and the novels of Sir Walter Scott, for example, has resulted in several major musical works, and incidents in the Wars of the Roses and the Tudor reign seem to have been particularly attractive to composers. We can think of operas based on Shakespeare, particularly by Verdi, such as *Macbeth*, *Othello* and *Falstaff*, Mendelssohn's *A Midsummer Night's Dream* music which accompanies the play as well as Sibelius's *The Tempest*; mention must be made of that arch-Shakespeare lover, Berlioz, who set *Romeo and Juliet* to music and more recently of Cole Porter's *Kiss Me Kate*, based on *The Taming of the Shrew*. Composers, from Schubert (*Who Is Sylvia?*) to Poulenc, have set his words to song. Similarly, Sir Walter Scott's works appear as the basis of operas, ranging from Donizetti's *Lucia di Lammermoor*, Rossini's *La donna del lago* (Lady of the Lake) to Bizet's *La Jolie Fille de Perth* (The Fair Maid of Perth). Whilst mentioning Scott, it is worth noting the fondness of nineteenth-century German composers for Scottish subjects. Mendelssohn's *The Hebrides* Overture, his 'Scottish' Symphony (No. 3 in A minor), Beethoven's arrangements of Scottish folk songs, Schumann's settings of the poems of Robert Burns, and Bruch's *Scottish Fantasy* are some of the better-known examples. The earlier period of British history has provided the factual, but also much fictional, basis for operas by Donizetti, *Rosmonda d'Inghilterra*, *Elisabetta al castello di Kenilworth*, and *Maria Stuarda*, Rossini's opera *Elisabetta, Regina d'Inghilterra*, the overture of which was recycled for *The Barber of Seville*, and Mercadante's *Margaret d'Anjou*. More recently, the Spanish composer Albéniz wrote a trilogy of operas on King Arthur as well as *Henry Clifford*. The prize for the most wildly inaccurate portrayal of Britain, however, must go to Donizetti's opera *Emilia di Liverpool*, which was set in the mountains supposedly surrounding the city.

Some visitors came to Britain as escapees from political or religious intolerance. The comparatively tolerant religious climate in England in the sixteenth century enabled both Jewish refugees from Italy, Spain and Portugal, and French Huguenots to make a significant impact on English musical life. Much later, the composer–pianists Ignaz Pleyel and Jan Ladislav Dussek and the violinist composer Giovanni Battista Viotti fled from the French Revolution. In the 1690s, Johann Christoph Pepusch resolved to leave Germany after witnessing the execution without trial of a Prussian officer for insubordination, 'and put himself under the protection of a government founded on better principles'.[6] The European Revolutions of 1848 saw the flight here of many composers, if only temporarily, such as Berlioz and Chopin. In the twentieth century, a much larger influx followed the rise of Hitler in Germany when a number of Jewish composers, including Berthold Goldschmidt, Egon Wellesz and Hans Gal, left their native country for England. Roberto Gerhard, the Spanish composer, settled in Cambridge in 1939 after the Republican defeat in the Civil War. Later, Andrzej Panufnik defected from communist Poland. In a slightly different category were the seventeenth-century lutenist and composer Jacques Gaultier, who came to England from France to escape a murder charge, and Wagner, who was fleeing from his creditors. Not all visitors, moreover, were what they appeared to be. Robert Cambert, a seventeenth-century composer and harpsichordist, entered the court of Charles II as master of music to Louise de Queroualle, Duchess of Portsmouth, the king's mistress and, at the same time, seems to have been acting as a spy for Louis XIV.[7] By virtue of musicians' proximity to their royal hosts – they would often perform in the private chambers – they were ideally placed for this type of intrigue. François-André Danican Philidor, a member of the distinguished family of composers, came often to England; a superb chess player, noted for his simultaneous blindfold play, he made over twenty visits to England to display his skill between 1748 and 1792.[8] His text book *L'Analyze des échecs* was still being used into the twentieth century.

However, perhaps the greatest magnet can be summed up in a statement of the early eighteenth-century German composer Johann Mattheson: 'He who in the present time wants to make a profit out of music takes himself to England.'[9] Such was the main motive of Leopold Mozart with his child prodigies, the eight-year-old Wolfgang and his sister, Nannerl, the penurious Wagner, the dying Weber and the young Liszt, not to mention the already wealthy Rossini. The most outstanding example was Joseph Haydn, freed at last from his court duties at Esterháza and lured by substantial financial inducements. His two celebrated visits to Britain were at the behest of the German-born violinist and impresario Johann Peter Salomon, one of the great musical entrepreneurs. The dynamic concert scene in later eighteenth-century London ensured a good living for large numbers of musical visitors. Rewards, as well as losses, were potentially great if the composer himself acted as entrepreneur, as Handel sometimes did. A steadier income came from performing, for composers such as Bruckner, on the organ, or Bartók, on the piano.[10]

There were further possible rewards in the form of income from giving music lessons, common practice amongst musical visitors through the centuries. Even if they were not fortunate enough to teach the royal children, which Italian and Flemish musicians from as far back as the time of Henry VIII were to do, musicians could do very well from teaching. Until the nineteenth century, music education, and indeed the playing of music, was almost exclusively the province of the upper echelons of society, and to be involved in teaching therefore gave social respectability. From the 1760s, the piano began to dominate amateur music-making, and this was also the period when the important link between piano-makers and professional pianists was forged, to mutual advantage. This gave rise to the so-called London Pianoforte School, in effect a dynasty of composer–pianist visitors.[11] Generations of keyboard-players, from Johann Christian Bach in the 1760s to Chopin in the 1840s, were attracted both by the distinctive style of instruments and opportunities for performance in England.

From the beginning of the nineteenth century, the role of conductor began to rival and overtake that of performer. Some composer-visitors, such as Dvořák, Weber and Richard Strauss, were primarily conductors, in most cases performing their own works, though Mahler, on his only visit in 1892 conducted the *Ring* cycle.[12] The rise of music festivals, starting with the Three Choirs Festival early in the eighteenth century, produced further opportunities for visitors. An outstanding case was Birmingham, which had had a music festival sporadically since 1784. With the rise of the city as a wealthy manufacturing centre, the Festival Committee could afford to commission works from leading composers. The committee was able to persuade Mendelssohn to write his oratorio *Elijah* especially for the Festival of 1846 and this was followed by works by Gounod and Dvořák, as well as by many native composers such as Elgar. In 1842 there was a performance at the Norwich Festival of an oratorio *The Fall of Babylon* by Louis Spohr, who was then considered to be one of the greatest living composers. The work had been especially commissioned for the Festival.[13] A little later, the Leeds Festival (1858) commissioned such composers as Massenet and Humperdinck, and during the twentieth century the coming of the Edinburgh, Aldeburgh and other festivals opened up further opportunities for foreign composers.

A complementary factor was the rise of the musical entrepreneur, who from the mid eighteenth century, mounted public concerts. In 1764, Johannn Christian Bach and Karl Friedrich Abel, both composers and performers, instituted a series of subscription concerts, which continued for eighteen years. The growing demand by the public for music in the nineteenth century led to the building of concert venues such as the Exeter Hall (1831), the St James's Hall (1858), the enormous Royal Albert Hall (1871) and the Queen's Hall (1893). The last-named was particularly famous as being the home of the Promenade Concerts from their inception in 1895 until its destruction during the Second World War in 1941. These concerts attracted many foreign composers, some of whom gave the first performances of their own works. Paul Hindemith performed Walton's Viola Concerto at one of them and was pleased to make the acquaintance of 'the famous Sir Wood'. However, Hindemith strongly disapproved of one aspect of the proceedings: 'The audience stands around – SMOKING IS PERMITTED – and can do as it likes. Notices all over the place: PLEASE DON'T STRIKE MATCHES DURING THE MUSIC. One can feel really homesick for Zwickau or Biefeld.'[14] Since 1951, the South Bank Centre has witnessed the appearance of a stream of composer–conductors such as Aaron Copland and Aram Khachaturian and similarly, from 1982, at the Barbican. The Bechstein Hall (1901), renamed the Wigmore Hall during the First World War, has been a calling place for composers' chamber works. One frequent visitor to England, Gabriel Fauré, scored a great success when he appeared at the Hall in March 1908, playing some of his own pieces and accompanying a singer.[15] On 20 and 26 March 1914, a year before his death, Alexander Scriabin gave two recitals of his own works there.[16] When Janáček made his only visit to Britain in 1926, the Wigmore Hall was hired for a programme of his compositions.[17] It should also be remembered that there was an increasing number of musical venues outside London. From the eighteenth century onwards, Edinburgh was one of the cultural capitals of Europe. Dublin, too, had a rich musical life. Francesco Geminiani, the Italian composer of forty-two concerti grossi, spent several years in that city and it was also in Dublin that the first performance of Handel's *Messiah* took place in 1742. The English provinces were not ignored either. The Holywell Music Room in Oxford, the oldest purpose-built concert hall in Europe, was opened in 1748, possibly with a performance of Handel's oratorio *Esther*, directed by the composer, and the Manchester Gentlemen's Concerts, at which Chopin gave recitals some years later, were instituted in the 1770s. The first performance of *La Bohème* in Britain was given at the Comedy Theatre, Manchester in April 1897, Puccini travelling from Italy for the occasion.[18] The establishment of the Hallé Orchestra in the city provided further opportunities, whilst in neighbouring Liverpool, Max Bruch was conductor of the Philharmonic Society for three years.

Life for the celebrity has always had its drawbacks, and great composers were often not the most tolerant guests. Visiting composers frequently complained about the ritual of being fêted by well-meaning gatherings. Sibelius, who conducted many of his own works in England from the early years of the twentieth century, was a well-liked figure. He once visited The Music Club, whose members he described as comprising 'largely well off elderly gentlemen with double chins and asthmatic coughs, together with expensively bejewelled and fur-clad wives'. In 1909, the same year that Debussy, D'Indy and Schoenberg had been invited, Sibelius was the guest of honour. He was subject to the unvarying routine of these occasions: 'First the composer of the evening was seated in the middle of the stage where he was harangued by the Chairman. After this he took his place among the audience to listen to some of his own chamber and instrumental music.'[19] Sergei Rachmaninov proved to be less amenable in March 1939, when he was made an honorary member of the Savage Club. New members were expected to play 'a few pieces' in return for their hospitality, but Rachmaninov, much to their disappointment, refused to do so.[20]

The length of stay of composers varied widely, as did the number of visits. Alessandro Striggio, composer and diplomat to the Medici court, visited the court in England for just fifteen days in 1567, but in that time, a performance before Queen Elizabeth of his forty-voice motet *Ecce beatam lucem* seems to have inspired Thomas Tallis to embark on a similar project, his *Spem in alium*.[21] The German keyboardist and composer Johann Jakob Froberger was robbed by pirates between Calais and Dover on his visit in the 1650s, and beat a hasty retreat back to the Continent, where his Allemande *Plainte faite à Londres pour passer la mélancholie* laments his wretched experience of England. Among the most frequent visitors were Louis Spohr, the violinist, conductor and composer, who made six visits between 1822 and 1853, and Saint-Saëns returned several times between 1871 and 1913; Dvořák came to England six times and the lionised Mendelssohn ten.[22] Gounod stayed for three years in St John's Wood with his landlady and lover, the notorious Georgina Weldon.[23] Joseph Haydn's amorous affairs when he was in England are well known, and the fifty-one-year-old Paganini scandalised society with his infatuation with the sixteen-year-old Charlotte Watson.[24] Liszt's two visits were forty-five years apart. Johann Christian Bach spent the last eighteen years of his life in London and is buried in a mass grave in St Pancras churchyard. This was in striking contrast to Handel, resident in Britain for nearly half a century, who died wealthy and was buried in Westminster Abbey. There were those who came to this country who were nevertheless profoundly influenced by their experiences in England. Gluck left Milan for London in 1745 for the production of two of his operas at the Haymarket Theatre. During his stay, he made the acquaintance of Handel's music, thereafter declaring him to be his favourite composer, keeping a portrait of him in his bedroom.[25] The young Mozart met and was taken up by Johann Christian Bach, some twenty-one years his senior, and was greatly influenced by Bach's fresh and original style. In July and August 1905 we see Claude Debussy staying at Eastbourne, bringing with him the proofs of *La Mer*. He was impressed with the view of the sea, taking many photographs from his balcony at the Grand Hotel. It is interesting to note that the eighteen-year-old Rimsky-Korsakov, then a midshipman in the Russian Navy, spent five months in England from late 1862 to February 1863, whilst his clipper was refitted. He, along with others of his friends, visited London two or three times, going to the opera at Covent Garden, though in his autobiography he admitted that he could not remember what he had seen.[26]

One of the important features of the capital's musical life from the nineteenth century was the Philharmonic Society of London, now the Royal Philharmonic Society. Its encouragement of orchestral and instrumental concerts from its inauguration in 1813 at the Argyll Rooms attracted many foreign composers. Mendelssohn wrote for, and dedicated his First Symphony to, the Society and Saint-Saëns was commissioned by the Society to write his Third Symphony (Organ Symphony) which he conducted in 1886.[27] Dvořák's Seventh Symphony is another outstanding example. It also commissioned from Beethoven (who wished to visit England but never did) his 'Choral' Symphony, when he was in dire need of money. The Society was a showcase for composers who wished to conduct their own works:[28] Chopin was exceptional in refusing their offer. Other types of patronage which brought visitors to these shores were of a more subtle nature. The conferring of honorary degrees by Oxford and Cambridge Universities was an additional attraction for musicians. Dvořák treasured his Cambridge doctorate and was proud of the photograph of himself wearing the gown. Perhaps the most distinguished gathering of foreign visitors was at Cambridge in 1893 when Charles Villiers Stanford, the holder of the chair of music at the time, succeeded in persuading Bruch, Saint-Saëns, Boito, Tchaikovsky and Grieg to attend the ceremony. One composer who declined an earlier invitation was Brahms, who could not face the sea journey and was concerned about his lack of English.[29] There has been a history of individual patrons, loyal to their musicians, whether in the form of the thriving musical household of the Earl of Arundel during the reign of Elizabeth I or of the Duke of Chandos in that of George I, or even of a middle-ranking civil servant such as Samuel Pepys, who went to great lengths to find employment for the Italian guitarist Cesare Morelli. More recently, Mrs Samuel Courtauld, wife of the art connoisseur, commissioned Stravinsky to compose his *Capriccio* for piano and orchestra, and she persuaded him to give it its first London performance.[30]

Certainly another important reason for the increasing number of musical visitors was the improvement in means of transport from the 1830s. The most obvious was the advent of the railway, with England being the first country to adopt this mode. In Chapter 9 we see Mendelssohn's enjoyment in travelling from London to Birmingham; and Liszt's major musical tour of Britain in 1840–1 would have been impossible without a developing railway network. Chopin's journeys from London to Edinburgh and Manchester would have been tedious if attempted by coach. Continental systems were also being established: Dvořák, a railway enthusiast, made the journey from Prague to London, though admittedly at a leisurely pace. Ravel claimed that the rhythmic piccolo theme in the first movement of his Piano Concerto occurred to him in October 1928 whilst on a train from London to Oxford where he was to receive an honorary degree. The Atlantic steamships enabled musicians to cross to and from America in ever increasing numbers, and the aeroplane now regularly disgorges many individuals and orchestras from all parts of the world. A good example of this was a series given by the BBC Symphony Orchestra early in 2000 at the Royal Festival Hall where, within a few weeks, programmes of music by Stockhausen, Berio and Henze were witnessed by their respective composers. The coming of the radio in England in 1921 not only augmented the audience for live music but provided further opportunities for musical commissions. From its early days the British Broadcasting Corporation promoted new works by British and foreign composers. Bartók, for instance, who was also frequently heard playing his own piano pieces, gave the first performance of his *Cantata Profana*, specially composed for the BBC in 1931. Francis Poulenc, who was commissioned to write a *Sinfonietta* for small orchestra in 1947 fell so badly behind schedule in its completion that he insisted on accepting only £50 for the work, adding in a note of apology, 'I offer the BBC my heart and the world premiere performance of my *Sinfonietta* in exchange for a simple kiss of peace'.[31] It should be noted that there was often friction within the BBC on the policy of broadcasting modern music by foreign composers. In 1934, Adrian Boult, the BBC Symphony Orchestra's chief conductor, who had been responsible the previous year for the first British performance of Alban Berg's *Wozzeck*, clashed with the Corporation's Music Advisory Committee on this issue at a meeting at 'which I am afraid I found it impossible to conceal my irritation about foreign artists and composers and our "senseless predilection for Vienna and Berlin"'.[32]

Visitors to these shores encountered a number of problems which they readily conveyed in correspondence to friends and relatives. The most frequent one was the journey across the Channel, which could be both hazardous and slow in rough weather. Prince Pückler-Muskau, ruler of a small principality in Germany, after making the crossing from north Germany in October 1826, wrote to a friend, 'I have had a most disastrous passage. A squall, constant sea-sickness, forty hours instead of twenty, and, to crown the whole, striking on a sand bank in the Thames, where we had to lie six hours till the tide set us afloat again'.[33] English weather, too, was a constant topic of conversation. Most commented unfavourably. In 1799, the Swiss-born Henry Meister remarked, 'Do but ask our friend Montaigne whether, constantly to look up to a sky obscured with cloud and vapour, will not dispose the mind to gloomy thoughts, and melancholy ideas'.[34] Verdi, who came to London in 1847 for the premiere of his new opera *I masnadieri* which he also conducted, wrote to a friend: 'The theatres are packed out, and the English enjoy performances which – and they pay so much!! Oh, if I could stay here a couple of years, I would like to carry away a bagful of these *most holy* pounds. But there is no use my thinking about such lovely things, for I couldn't stand the climate.'[35] Both Haydn and Tchaikovsky were astonished by the dark pea-soup fog which nearly covered London in the middle of the day. An optimist wrote in 1908: 'The fog usually lifts after a certain time. We may even say that it always lifts for those who have the patience to wait.'[36]

La Rochefoucauld, on a visit to England in 1784, asked, 'Is there anything so wearisome as the English Sunday?'[37] This puritanical streak shocked many foreigners from the seventeenth century onwards. One French traveller at this time, de Muralt, noted that nothing could be bought or sold on Sundays, and even the carrying of water to the houses was prohibited. 'Nor can anyone play at bowls or any other game, or even touch a musical instrument or sing aloud in his own house without incurring the penalty of a fine.' While visitors such as Handel found a remarkably tolerant religious atmosphere in England, many others were affected by an anti-Catholic undercurrent, which lasted from the time of Elizabeth I well into the eighteenth century. Towards the end of both the sixteenth and seventeenth centuries the climate of religious upheaval meant that only a few brave – and well-connected – musical visitors, the vast majority of whom were Catholics, remained in England.

But there were also many admirable features. English food was largely appreciated. We can well imagine Mendelssohn's delight at tucking into his favourite meal, mutton chops and bread and butter pudding, Liszt eating his lamb cutlets and mushrooms in batter, and Dvořák devouring huge quantities of sandwiches in Cambridge. Not surprisingly though, it was a Frenchman, Fujas de Saint Fond, in 1784, who remarked that 'the tea is always excellent in England; but nowhere do people drink worse coffee'.[38] Another feature widely commented upon was summed up by a German professor, Christoph Lichtenberg: 'I have seen many beautiful females in my day; but since I reached England I have seen as many as in all the rest of my life together, and yet I have only been in England ten days.'[39]

Britain was well known by continental travellers for the many places there were to visit. Later composers seized the opportunity of making tours of some of the famous buildings and celebrated scenery in the British Isles. In the capital itself, of particular interest were the Tower of London, Hyde Park, Parliament (where Mendelssohn and Wagner listened to debates), and from the time of Mozart, the British Museum. Debussy spent a few days in London in September 1905 and heard the band of the Grenadier Guards parading past his hotel. He remarked sourly: 'Their marches sound to me like a drunken cross between Scottish popular songs and the Kake-Walck.'[40] The Thames with its shipping fascinated visitors, and local trips to the countryside, to villages such as Richmond and Hampstead, were popular. The seaside was particularly appreciated. Dvořák, who had never seen the sea before coming to Britain, was impressed with Brighton, and both Haydn and Richard Strauss holidayed on the Isle of Wight. In 1897, Edvard Grieg, who was recovering from a bad attack of bronchitis – 'if only someone had told me that the climate here at this time of the year is poison for people like me' – was advised by his doctor to go down to the 'coastal city of Hastings' to help his recuperation.[41] Handel enjoyed the health benefits of the spa towns of Bath, Cheltenham and Tunbridge Wells. Further afield, Mendelssohn visited Scotland as did Chopin, although Wales was a less popular destination. Apart from sightseeing, there were many composers who frequented opera houses, concert halls and theatres. It is possible for instance that Dvořák attended a performance of *The Mikado* at the Savoy, and certainly Tchaikovsky saw a ballet at the Alhambra entitled *The Sports of England* which included scenes of cricket, yachting, football and hunting. Hindemith was taken to Noel Coward's new operetta *Bitter Sweet*, in London in 1929, afterwards declaring that it 'must be one of the biggest examples of kitsch ever to have been hatched from a human brain'.[42] Anton Webern, on the other hand, on his first visit to London the same year, was taken to his first sound motion picture which he 'liked very much'.[43]

Last but not least was the admiration of visitors for the freedom enjoyed in everyday living. One wrote in 1813:

> You may live here at your fancy; nobody takes notice of whether you keep three servants or none; whether you walk or ride in a carriage, dine at six or two; on ten dishes or on a plain joint of meat; go to the play or assembly rooms; frequent fashionable company or prefer solitude; dress in the last fashion or wear your coat the whole year round, – nobody takes the trouble of observing. No police spy, dogs you hear; in public and private you may speak whatever you like, provided it does not aggrieve the rights of third parties; you may range or travel wherever you please; no tyrant's tool, ever on the watch, molests you with his examinations. You feel there is freedom here.[44]

Particularly pertinent to this book are the views of visitors on the state of musical life in Britain. Most of the early travellers were unanimous in their praise of the state of music. A Bohemian page in the service of a knight touring England in 1466 during the reign of Edward IV declared: 'Never in any place have we heard such sweet and pleasant music as here.'[45] Just over a century later, the secretary to Count Friedrich Württemberg-Mömpelgard reported, after a visit to Windsor Chapel, 'The music, especially the organ, was exquisite, for at times you could hear the sound of cornets, flutes, fifes and other instruments; and there was a little boy who sang so sweetly and amid it all trilled so cunningly with his little tongue that it was a marvel to hear.'[46] A decade later in 1602, the tutor to the visiting Duke of Stettin-Pomerania, described how on arriving early one morning at Rochester, the party were greeted by 'a fair music of viols and pandoras, for it is the custom throughout England that even in little villages the musicians wait on you for a small fee, and then take up their position before your chamber in the morning about waking time and play some hymns'.[47]

As the seventeenth century wore on, however, music itself began to be identified as something foreign, and incurred the disapproval of many English observers. The influx of French lutenists, for example, during Charles I's reign gave some English writers the opportunity to mock:

> Here is a fellow who comes into *England* with an ill *meen* and threadbare cloaths, and there presently sets up a Court of Judicature, arraigning both Musick, Instruments, and Musicians, for not being

a la mode de France . . . And if his fingers be so weak they can scarce crawle o're a Lute, then to play gently and softly is the *mode*, and if so gouty and child-blained as he rakes the strings worse than if they were grated on by a ragged staff: then *fort* and *Gallyard* is the word.[48]

With the advent of Italian opera after 1705, music was seen as a threat to the English sense of hard work, even manliness:

Musick is so generally approv'd of in *England*, that it is look'd upon as a want of Breeding not to be affected by it, insomuch that every Member of the *Beau-monde* at this Time either do, or, at least, think it necessary to appear as if they understand it; and, in order to carry on this Deceit it is requisite every one, who has the Pleasure of thinking himself a fine Gentleman, should, being first laden with a Competency of Powder and Essence, make his personal Appearance every Opera Night at the Haymarket.[49]

While the standard of instrumental playing was largely very high in England during the eighteenth century, and was in itself a reason for musicians to visit, fewer observers were impressed by the state of the arts in general. Voltaire, who was in London for three years, wrote in a preface to his drama *Merope* in 1744: 'It would seem that the same causes, which deprived the English of any great aptitude for painting or music, deprive them equally of a gift for tragedy. These islands which have produced the world's greatest philosophers are not fertile soil for fine arts.'[50] One mid-nineteenth-century visitor, Dr Carus, a physician to the King of Saxony, accounted for this situation by examining the effects of the Industrial Revolution. Given the development of manufacturing, the growth of many large towns, and the fact that 'industry absorbs all the energies of life how is it possible that, in the midst of such a tendency of public life, any time should be allotted to the artistical gratification of the finer and more intellectual wants of the human mind?'[51] Another early nineteenth-century visitor concluded that 'the climate of the country will prevent the English from ever being a musical people'.[52]

On the natives' musical tastes, foreign visitors could be even more dismissive. A professor of history at Berlin University, Frederick von Raumer, wrote to a friend in 1835: 'Of the two fundamental pillars of German musical art, the French and Italians know neither, and the English only one, – that is, Handel',[53] whereas Haydn had difficulty understanding their failure to embrace Mozart's music: 'I only regret that before his death he could not convince the English, who walk in darkness in this respect, of his greatness – a subject about which I have been sermonising to them every single day.'[54]

Orchestral concerts were often criticised for their length; scenes from operas were performed frequently between instrumental items. Raumer noted on one occasion that: 'The concert began at two and ended at half-past five, for there were no fewer than seventeen pieces.'[55] The British love for novelty in music-making was an interesting feature of the concert world. Among Haydn's competitors for the attention of the musical Londoners was a Mr Blumb, who imitated a parrot and accompanied himself on the pianoforte. Leopold Mozart advertised the spectacular talents of his son in newspapers, offering gentlemen the chance to test the boy's prowess of playing music at sight. Gluck performed a concerto for twenty-six drinking glasses – 'filled with Spring-water' – and orchestra at a London concert in 1746.[56] Liszt had to compete with other attractions on his exhaustive tours of Britain with a concert party; on more than one occasion, he accompanied a reciter of dramatic and humorous verses.

The state of opera seems to have attracted the most scorn. Johanna Schopenhauer, mother of the German philosopher Arthur, toured Europe in 1787, travelling to London on further visits. An account of an Italian opera performance she attended at the time is illuminating:

> Although the most distinguished people in the realm are its patrons, this kind of theatre is hated by the man in the street as it seems to go in every way against the national temperament. John Bull visits it but once and pokes fun at it for the rest of his life. The foreign language, the strange behaviour and, above all, the French dancers, appear to him to be sacrilegious on his own dear soil. The whole thing would have collapsed long ago were it not for its patrons' great vanity, their love of display and a preference for things foreign.[57]

Weber visited London in 1826 to perform his opera specially written for Covent Garden, *Oberon*; the work suffered from all the deficiencies of so-called English opera. Here is an account by Victoire, Count de Soligny, written three years earlier, of one such opera:

> I closed the day with the English Opera. At the end of the first act a mine falls in and buries the principal persons of the piece alive. In the last scene of the second act they reappear in the bowels of the earth, nearly starved indeed, having lain there three days, and utterly exhausted. This, however, proves no impediment to the prima donna singing a long Polonaise air, to which there is a chorus with trumpets, 'Ah, we are lost, all hope is gone!' but, oh miracle! The rocks fall asunder again, and open a wide entrance to the light of day. All distress, and with it the distressing nonsense of the piece, was at an end.[58]

The tradition of taking great liberties with operas to suit English taste, which began early in the eighteenth century, continued. In November

1826, Prince Pückler-Muskau gave an account of a performance he had attended of one of his favourite operas:

> I saw Mozart's *Figaro* announced at Drury Lane, and delighted myself with the idea of hearing once more the sweet tones of my fatherland: – what then was my astonishment at the unheard-of treatment which the master-work of the immortal composer has received at English hands. You will hardy believe me when I tell you that neither the Count, the Countess, nor Figaro sang; these parts were given to mere actors, and their principal songs, with some little alteration in the words, were sung by the other singers; to add to this, the gardener roared out some interpolated popular English songs, which suited Mozart's music just as a pitch-plaster would suit the face of the Venus de'Medici. The whole opera was moreover 'arranged' by a certain Mr. Bishop (a circumstance which I had seen noticed in the bill, but did not understand till now), – that is, adapted to English ears by means of the most tasteless and shocking alterations.[59]

Shortly after his arrival in London in April 1833, Vincenzo Bellini was startled to see a procession of men with billboards announcing performances of his opera *La Somnambula*, at the Drury Lane Theatre translated into English. After attending a performance, he wrote to a friend: 'I lack words, dear Florino, to tell you how my poor music was tortured, torn to shreds, and – wanting to express myself in the Neopolitan way – flayed [*scorticata*] by these **** of Englishmen, the more so because it was sung in the language that with reason was called, I don't remember by whom, the language of the birds, and properly of parrots.'[60]

It seems to have been the fate of English music-making, then, to have been treated severely by visitors to these shores. As late as 1914, Oscar R. H. Schmitz wrote a book *Das Land ohne Musik* which, whilst generally praising the British approach to political and social issues, was critical of its lack of musicality. He wrote: 'That the English are unmusical is known, and one will not be unduly disappointed if the performances at their concerts, save when executed by Continental talent, fall short of our requirements.'[61] But such a view has to be set against the experiences of many of the leading composers of the last five centuries who found Britain a land where music and music-making was a satisfying, and in many cases, rewarding experience.

The subject of musical visitors to Britain is an emotive one. Many who came have been subject to xenophobic attacks by those whose own livings or sense of national identity were threatened by their presence. But we hope to show in this book that these visitors have proved invaluable in enriching the artistic life and cultural heritage of Britain.

1 'Brothers in the science or art of music'

Sixteenth-century visitors

It is difficult to know how musical early visitors to Britain might have been. The Celts developed the carnyx, a tall trumpet-like instrument, usually made of bronze, whose bell often represented a fierce dragon's head with open mouth. These were used in battle, but were clearly not effective enough to scare off their Roman conquerors, who in any case appear to have been thoroughly unmusical visitors. Lyres found in excavated burial sites at Sutton Hoo, and more recently Southend, show that, by the seventh century, Saxon warrior kings would have been entertained by story-tellers who accompanied themselves with these plucked string instruments, brought with them from Germany. Soon afterwards, the harp was in evidence in England, although in 764 Cuthbert, Abbot of Jarrow, wrote to the Archbishop of Mainz, asking for a harper to be sent to him, as he had an instrument but no one to play it.

The age of the minstrel ensured a flow of musical visitors around Europe, and England was very much a part of this cultural mix. Minstrels, literally 'little ministers' or lowly servants, were paid by their noble or royal patrons to travel, telling stories or singing songs to magnify the image of their masters wherever they went. Music and poetry were not only practised by the humble minstrel: Richard I, Cœur de Lion, the troubadour king raised in Aquitaine, was himself effectively a musical visitor to England. By the thirteenth century, English kings received some of the greatest musicians of the time. Edward I played host in 1297 to Adenet le Roy, minstrel to the Count of Flanders, and in 1306 to the Frenchman Adam de la Halle, composer of the oldest surviving musical drama *Robin et Marion*. But for most minstrels, playing music was only one of their activities – tumbling, juggling, fire-eating, even impersonating animals, being amongst the others.

The first musical visitor we can name certainly had a purpose other than entertainment. Taillefer accompanied William of Normandy to England, and had the honour of leading the Norman soldiers in to the battle of Hastings with a war cry, which may have been *The Song of Roland*. This chant, in combination with dextrous sword-juggling, is said to have inspired the Norman army just as they experienced a loss of nerve when faced with the enemy positioned high on a commanding ridge. Taillefer also had the privilege of being the first to be hacked to death by the English.

Another musical visitor whose activities had a far-reaching influence on English life was Rahere, also probably from Normandy. Rahere was court jester to Henry I, and his musical skills qualified him for service as a canon at St Paul's Cathedral. While on pilgrimage to Rome, shortly after 1120, he contracted malaria, and promised that if he recovered, he would reform his life and build a hospice on his return to England. The apostle Bartholomew is said to have come to him in a vision, instructing him that he should also build a priory, at Smithfield. On his return, Rahere succeeded in persuading the king to grant a royal charter, and the land, for the building of both. Within four years, the hospital and priory of St Bartholomew the Great had been built, and both still stand today, with the church playing host to a variety of musical activities. Rahere also gained a charter for a fair on the feast of St Bartholomew, 24 August, which ran until 1855. Even after Rahere had been made prior, he could be seen performing juggling tricks at the fair.

By the time of Henry VIII's reign, performing music was becoming a more specialist activity, and it is here that our account begins in earnest.

The story of music in England in the sixteenth century, and indeed the first half of the seventeenth, is essentially that of one man's determination to modernise, organise and to raise the profile of court musical activities. This man, King Henry VIII, was Henry VII's second son, and his education was that of a prince intended for the Church: this included a thorough knowledge of music and all the arts. While he is pictured in the popular imagination as the bloated and brutal tyrant of his last years, at his accession he was regarded as the most accomplished prince of the age. Writing in 1515, Giustinian, the Venetian ambassador to Henry's court, observed, 'His Majesty is the handsomest potentate I ever set eyes on ... he speaks French, English and Latin, and a little Italian, plays well on the lute and harpsichord, sings from book at sight'.[1]

Music was one of Henry's greatest passions. He played not only the lute and keyboard but also the recorder and, to judge from his appearance in an illumination where he is portrayed as King David, the harp. He was a composer – not of *Greensleeves*, as legend would have it – but of some twenty songs which have survived, and of two 'goodly masses' of five parts, which have not; how many of these he composed himself is open to doubt, and the one piece attributed to him of unquestionable merit, a setting of the Flemish song *T'Andernaken*, was probably not written by him.

Henry valued musicians both for their company and their skill, and, especially in his earlier years, he would often make music with them. His appreciation of good music, combined with his political acumen, which dictated that great kings needed to display great art, ensured that music was made a high priority in Henry's court. This is amply demonstrated in descriptions of activities at the Field of Cloth of Gold in 1520, a summit meeting between Henry and King Charles VI of France, which was little more than an excuse for ostentatious displays of wealth, sporting prowess and sophistication. Music for the feasts and solemnities was of great importance, and for musicians the event also served as trade fair, talent contest and showcase, with royal appointments as potential prizes.

In music, as in all the arts, Henry had to look abroad to find people who could set the high standards he desired. He employed the finest tapestry-makers and glaziers from Flanders and sculptors from Italy, and later the German Hans Holbein the Younger as royal painter. From depictions of palace interiors in his psalter, which show classical designs in Italian marble, and from surviving sculptures, such as Torrigiano's magnificent tomb for Henry VII and Elizabeth of York at Westminster Abbey and the wooden screen and choir stalls at King's College, Cambridge, we can see that Henry brought not only the finest, but also the latest art to England. This was a king who would go to any lengths to bring his country into the brave new cosmopolitan world of the Renaissance.

Henry's reign was characterised by great loyalty to, and reliance on, a small number of royal servants. The story of Cardinal Wolsey's rise and fall is a well-known example, but is partly prefigured in the events surrounding the hiring and firing of the Venetian organist Dionysius Memo. Memo was a friar and a brilliant organist, who was released from his post as organist of St Mark's, Venice, and by the pope from his clerical duties, to become attached to King Henry's court in 1516. Memo's effect on king and court was extraordinary. In September of 1516, a few days after the arrival of Memo, together with a 'most excellent instrument of his, which he has brought hither with much pains and cost', he played to the king 'and a great number of lords ... not merely to the satisfaction, but to the incredible admiration and pleasure of everybody, and especially his Majesty, who is extremely skilled in music'.[2] As a result, Henry appointed him head of his instrumental musicians and, interestingly, also made him his chaplain. On another occasion in Windsor, Memo played for four hours 'to the so great admiration of all the audience, and with such marks of delight from his Majesty aforesaid, as to defy exaggeration'.[3]

Even allowing for exaggeration, and for a biased view – all these accounts come from Giustinian, the Venetian ambassador – Memo was not only a musical success in a position of power, but was also exceptionally close to the king, to a degree perhaps without parallel between musician and monarch. For example, during an outbreak of the plague in 1517, Henry was confined to his palace at Windsor 'alone with his physician and the reverend master Dionysius Memo, and three of his favourite gentlemen'. Later in the year, when the whole court was dismissed, again three gentlemen and Memo stayed with him 'who all accompany the King and Queen through every peril'.[4]

Memo also had responsibility for the musical education of the infant Princess Mary. At a court function in February 1518, the two-year-old Princess, spotting Memo, called out '"Priest!" and he was obliged to go and play for her'. The ambassador, reporting on the same event, comments, 'I perceive him to be in such favour with the King, that for the future he will prove an excellent instrument, in matters appertaining to your Highness'.[5] Memo's quasi-ambassadorial role is mentioned elsewhere: in his account of Memo's first recital, Guistinian does not doubt 'but that he will obtain everything he can desire',[6] and Memo is later called upon to 'investigate thoroughly' some incident relating to the sudden dismissal of several of Henry's servants, an example of how his role in England extended far beyond his musical activities.

Little is known of the circumstances of Memo's departure. It seems likely that he was acting as agent for the Venetians, and was said to have left London in fear of his life some time around 1525, travelling via Portugal to Spain, where he was organist at Santiago de Compostella by 1539.[7]

At Henry's accession, the structure of the musical household was little changed from medieval times, with most musicians performing solo, and employed on a casual basis, musical performance being only one of their court duties. Often, as in previous centuries, they came from abroad, and the international trade in individual musician–entertainers remained strong. But musical practice abroad was changing. As the sixteenth century progressed, musicians began to be more often employed at the English court to play in ensembles, either for dancing or as background music.

The expanding body of court musicians required a good leader, and Henry was fortunate to find such a capable and loyal servant as the Flemish-born Philip van Wilder, who arrived in England about 1520, or shortly thereafter. Van Wilder's rise through the ranks of the court was speedy, and his administrative skills served Henry's ambitions perfectly. Listed as minstrel in 1526, by 1529 he was one of the king's 'lewters' and he commanded a monthly salary of 66s. 8d., the highest of any court musician. Beyond his lute-playing duties, van Wilder had responsibilities for composing music for a variety of situations, for the purchase of musical instruments, for the musical education of the royal children, and for running the music of the Privy Chamber, a role which was later given the title of 'Master of the King's Music'.

In all these tasks, van Wilder was notably successful. As composer, his works were extremely popular both during his life and after his death, and include French chansons, Latin motets and instrumental fantasies. More than forty of his works survive, most of them in manuscript, but some of them published on the Continent in collections by Susato among others. It has been suggested that the painting *Man with a Lute*, by

Hans Holbein the Younger, of a gentleman dressed in the French style, is of Philip van Wilder,[8] and it is interesting to observe the comparisons between van Wilder and Holbein, who were almost exact contemporaries. While van Wilder did not dominate the court musical scene in the same way that Holbein reigned supreme in the visual arts – the Chapel Royal, the real musical élite, was filled exclusively with English musicians – they both were responsible for modernising attitudes within their respective fields. Like Holbein, van Wilder probably spent time in Italy before coming to England and both artists were able to combine the sophistication of northern European Renaissance techniques with the vivacity and clarity of recent Italian developments to form an attractive style accessible to English taste.

As royal educator, he was responsible for teaching both Princess Mary and Prince Edward the lute. In a letter from 1546, Edward thanks his father for 'sending him Philip, who is both a prominent musician and a gentleman, for his improvement in playing the lute'.[9] He continued to serve Edward after his accession to the throne, just predeceasing him. Mary, whose first music master was Dionysius Memo, evidently continued to thrive under van Wilder's tutelage, as we can see from a report in 1557, written about her when she was Queen of England, by the Venetian ambassador of the time:

> she is very greatly proficient in music, playing especially on the harpsi-chord and lute so excellently, that when she attended to this (which she does now but little) she surprised good performers, both by the rapidity of her execution and method of playing.[10]

Van Wilder's time in charge of the royal instruments represents a golden age in the history of instrument-making in England. By 1530, he was responsible for purchasing instruments for the royal musical establishment, and at the time of Henry's death in 1547, van Wilder was required to draw up an inventory of the royal collection.[11]

Instruments, of course, require musicians to play them, and it was the newly created King's Musick that remains Henry's and van Wilder's greatest legacy to music at the English court. Only five musicians were regularly employed at Edward IV's court; this number had risen to fifteen in Henry VII's reign, but by Henry VIII's death, there were no fewer than fifty-eight. With only minor changes, the structure of the King's Musick remained intact until the accession of James II in 1685.

Van Wilder's prosperity was reflected in material wealth and, unlike many other successful musicians, he managed to hold on to the gains he made, acquiring property in London and Dorset. By 1540, he had become a Gentleman of the Privy Chamber, and in 1550 he received a coat of arms and crest. Such a position of eminence attracted the interest of those seeking favours from the king, and we can get a glimpse of how skilled a political operator van Wilder was from the evidence of the legal action brought against him by a London grocer, Thomas Norton, in October 1540. It seems that Norton had given the huge sum of £100 to van Wilder in the hope of acquiring the rights to some property. Norton lost the action, and was effectively accused of bribery, but van Wilder was allowed to keep the money, since he apparently did not know of Norton's motives.

Politician, composer, administrator and bureaucrat, van Wilder, like many composers before and after him, was best known during his life as a performer: this moving extract from the anonymous elegy 'On the Death of Philips', published in 1557, gives us a valuable insight into how he was seen and respected:

> The stringe is broke, the lute is dispossest,
> The hand is cold, the bodye in the ground.
> The lowring lute lamenteth now therefore,
> Phillips her frende that can touche no more.[12]

Around 1520, there was a sea change in the style of dance music in England, reflecting an earlier change abroad. Before this time, most dance music was performed in the *basse danse* tradition, whereby typically a shawm or slide-trumpet would play the slow-moving notes of the melody, which dictated the rhythm of the dance steps, while two or more wind instruments would improvise faster notes around this melody, often with great virtuosity and according to rules and conventions now lost. This form of music, which belongs to the late medieval tradition, would not have sounded anything like what we now consider to be dance music, except perhaps for the presence of a drum.

But from the early 1520s, possibly as a result of the Field of Cloth of Gold, a new type of dance, the Italian *ballo*, was introduced to England, which used a quite different – and, to us, more familiar – type of music. This was the birth of the pavan and galliard, which were danced to music which had much shorter phrases and simpler rhythms and textures, with the melody in the highest part and a bass line which supported straightforward harmonies: the dance music we associate with Renaissance England. When the Emperor Charles V danced a pavan at a ball held in Windsor in 1522, Henry was obliged to sit it out, presumably because he did not know the steps of the dance. A piece of music entitled 'The emporose pavyn' survives from that period, and would most probably have been brought over to England by the emperor's musicians.[13]

This new type of music had a profound effect on ensemble playing at Henry's court. It was now possible, and desirable, to have larger ensembles playing for dances, as the simplified textures allowed five or six musicians to play at once, by simply adding more middle parts to the music. In addition, this new style of music, which was developed in northern Italy, demanded that the finest practitioners of this music, and their new instruments, be imported from Italy; not for the last time, the popularity of Franco-Flemish music would be eclipsed in England by that of the Italian school.

It was in preparation for Henry's doomed fourth marriage, to Anne of Cleves, in January 1540, that his Lord Great Chamberlain Thomas Cromwell ordered his agent in Venice to look for musicians who could be enticed to England. The result was the establishment in England of two six-part consorts: a string band and a recorder consort. The establishment of these two consorts dominated the court musical scene, and helped shape the future of English instrumental music for the next century.

The string consort, or the 'new viols' as they were called, would have been new in every sense – an established consort, bringing with them the latest music and sets of matched instruments from Italy and, possibly for the first time in England, the violin.[14] While their music undoubtedly made an impact, almost everything else about them – their origins, their familial relationships, even their names – is surrounded by uncertainty. Indeed, they got off to an unpromising start in England, and within two years of their initial engagement at court, those who survived had returned to Italy.

Recent research has shed some light on the origins of the string consort.[15] For although they arrived in England from Venice in November 1540, it seems that none of them originated from Venice. Ambrose Lupo, often known simply as 'of Milan', on one occasion signed himself 'deolmaleyex', which has been identified as a variant of Elmaleh, a more common version of the name of this prominent Iberian Jewish family. Lupo, his adopted name, the Italian for 'wolf', is probably a pun on the fact that Jews were often compared, as outsiders, with the wolf. Innocent and George Comey (also known as Comy and de Combe) of Cremona, are elsewhere referred to as 'de Coimbre', showing that their family was from the city of Coimbra, an artistic centre in Portugal and home to many Jews. Francis of Venice, who joined the group in 1543, is elsewhere listed as Francis Kellim, and would have acquired his name from the Hebrew word 'kelim', meaning 'instruments' or the voice of the cantor of the synagogue. It is safe, then, to conclude that all were of Jewish origin, and had been forced to flee Spain and Portugal in the 1490s, during the expulsion of the Jews from the Spanish Empire. As nominal Christians, they were further hounded from the Duchy of Milan by the Inquisition in 1535, and sought the relative security of the Venice. Further persecution necessitated the journeys to and from England – where they could not entirely escape the clutches of the Inquisition – before they finally settled in London in 1543, to earn good and ultimately secure livings as court musicians.

These Jewish immigrants suited Henry's purposes perfectly. They were fine musicians who gave long and loyal service to the court, more than fulfilling their desired function of improving standards of performance at court. Indeed, their arrival precipitated a sudden growth in popularity of the viol in England. The Italian-influenced viol fantasies by composers such as Thomas Lupo, Ambrose's grandson, encouraged the viol consort to flourish until the time of Henry Purcell, long after the form had been abandoned by other musical nations. These musicians also brought the latest and finest instruments with them, and they succeeded in popularising the violin as the instrument of choice for accompanying dancing. Effectively illegal immigrants, their safety and living depended entirely on Henry, ensuring their total loyalty to him. And as Jews they were free of any ties in the religious disputes raging at the time, having allegiances to neither of Henry's religious adversaries: the pope and the Lutherans.

The circumstances of the arrival of the recorder consort, who were all named Bassano, are rather different. Nine years before their court appointment, four Bassano brothers, Alvise, Anthony, Jasper and John, came to England in 1531.[16] The Bassanos too were of Jewish origin; Henry was very interested in the Jews of Venice at this time, since he was desperately trying to find a way out of his marriage with Catherine of Aragon. In Jewish law, marriage to one's brother's widow is invalid, and since Catherine had been married to Henry's older brother Arthur before him, Henry sought the authority of Jewish scripture to annul the marriage. His agent in Venice happened upon Mark Raphael, an apostate, who was invited to England to counsel the king. There is evidence to link the Bassanos with Raphael, and they might even have travelled in his entourage, and by April 1540, five of the Bassanos, 'brothers in the science or art of music', were granted places at court.

Their father, Jeronimo, seems to have been an instrument-maker, and was sackbut-player to the Doge of Venice. However the Bassanos were not originally from Venice, but by 1515 had moved there from the nearby town of Bassano del Grappa. They were from a family of silk farmers, and their coat of arms, one version of which can still be seen on a shield in the cathedral at Lichfield in Staffordshire, features silk moths and a mulberry tree. Before they lived in Bassano, they may have lived in the Sicilian town of Cantanzaro, famous for its community of Jewish silk farmers. So migration was part of life for the Bassanos, and helps to explain their success, once they were finally settled in England. Alvise, the eldest of the five brothers who remained in England, was paid £50 per annum, the highest salary of any court musician. They were given excellent accommodation in the recently dissolved Charterhouse monastery in London, later acquired large properties, notably in Hoxton, Walthamstow, Waltham Forest and Bletchingley, and many of the family became gentlemen.

The Bassanos were employed at court and are often identified as 'musicians for the recorders'. The recorder was not new to England: Henry VII paid the sackbut-player Guillam van de Burgh in 1501 for some new recorders, and there are reports of Henry VIII playing the instrument as a young man. However, nothing in England would have compared with the skill and panache of this slick six-part team of musicians, who were described as the best in Venice, and who would have brought with them the finest Italian dance and vocal music, and the latest instruments. At this time the basic recorder consort consisted of treble in G, tenor and bass, but the Bassanos would have introduced the descant in D, newly developed in Italy, and later might have added the great bass in B flat. Therefore, their recorders were tuned a fifth apart, not in alternating fourths and fifths, as later.

In addition to their many duties playing and composing for a range of court functions, they were employed by the court to make and repair instruments. Their skill in this department was a crucial part of the Bassano package, and they were among the most important instrument-makers of the sixteenth century. Their maker's mark, often described as 'rabbit's feet', but which might instead be a silk-moth, is found on over a hundred surviving wind instruments. They came to England 'with all their instruments' which suggests not only the ones they played but also their current stock and many of the seventy-six recorders listed in van Wilder's 1547 inventory of instruments would have been made by the Bassanos, or brought with them.

They made not only recorders, but also other wind instruments, and even string instruments, and may have helped to develop a characteristically 'English' style of viol-making. They also probably made the 'fair cittern' that they gave to Queen Mary in 1556, and received orders for wind instruments from other noble and royal patrons in Spain, Germany, Belgium and England. For this purpose, Alvise had his own workshop at the Charterhouse, in a separate building, and he and John were paid higher rates than the other brothers, probably indicating that they were instrument-makers to the king.

Not everything ran smoothly for the Bassanos, however. Their landlord, Edward North, who had bought the Charterhouse from the Crown in 1545 after the dissolution of the monasteries, began to make conversions to the property whilst the Bassanos were living in it, destroying most of the cloister and using the church as his dining-hall. His offer to rehouse the Bassanos was either refused or not genuine and he began to dig under of the foundations of their premises, destroying walls and the water supply. The Bassanos, harassed and virtually homeless, brought a legal action, in which North described them as 'men past all shame'.[17] They evidently lost and were quickly evicted, around 1552. Alvise's death two years later precipitated a twenty-year battle with the Crown in an attempt to have his court place filled by his son Lodovico, and for arrears of payment. In the burial record, Lodovico's death is attributed to 'a thought', an Elizabethan term which roughly equates to 'depression'.

This dark streak in the Bassano family shows itself in the life of the youngest brother, Baptista, who survived a plot to kill him, and died in poverty, and in particular in his daughter Emilia, the first notable English Renaissance woman poet. Another of the Bassanos to marry into a family of musical visitors – Alphonso Lanier, son of the Huguenot flautist and cornettist Nicholas[18] – Emilia was a troubled spirit and notorious courtesan at the court of the 1590s. She was mistress to Henry Carey, Lord Hunsdon, who was Lord Chamberlain, and had a son by him. Interestingly, Hunsdon was patron of the company of actors to which William Shakespeare belonged, and it is virtually certain that Emilia would have known Shakespeare. Sonnet 128 makes great play of the Dark Lady's musical heritage. It is surely no coincidence, either, that there is a Bassanio in Shakespeare's *The Merchant of Venice*, and a Bassianus in *Titus Andronicus*; perhaps Shakespeare's 'Italian phase', which from 1592 included *Two Gentlemen of Verona, The Taming of the Shrew, A Midsummer Night's Dream* and *Romeo and Juliet*, was the result of his infatuation with her.

Few descriptions of members of the Bassano family survive, but two incidents give a small insight into the characters of the Bassanos, and illustrate the perils of being a foreigner in sixteenth-century England. The first relates to the wrongful arrest of three of the second generation of Bassano brothers, all of them court musicians, in 1584. John Spencer, a former Sheriff of London, thought the three were acting suspiciously and told them to move on. When they refused to do so, citing immunity from arrest for members of the royal household, Spencer threatened to send them to ward (prison), to which one of them, 'a little black [i.e. black-haired] man who was booted – answered in very despiteful manner, saying "Send us to ward? Thou wert as good kiss our etc"'. It was recorded that subsequent 'resistance and offer of force on their part was so violent and outrageous that, if their power had been agreeable with their wills, they would have done much mischief'.[19]

In case this incident gives the impression that the Bassanos were violent and foul-mouthed, an incident during the following year, when England was at war with Spain, concerning the sackbut-player Mark Anthony, son of Anthony Bassano, paints a different picture. Mark Anthony was heard to 'speak in Italian to the strangers [i.e. foreigners] then in his company'. A passer-by went to some soldiers standing near by, claiming Bassano had spoken ill of them. One of the soldiers walked over to Bassano, and said: '"Sir, what say you of soldiers?" To whom . . . Bassano answered . . . "Why, nothing; but God bless you".' One of the soldiers then struck him on the ear, to which Bassano said 'I thank you; I must take it in good worth'. On being further harassed, Bassano was forced to take refuge in the house of one of the queen's drummers, 'or else . . . to have been slain, for that the soldiers thought him to be a Spaniard'.[20]

Despite such setbacks, the Bassanos can lay claim to have been the most successful family of musical visitors ever. Three generations of the family were employed at court, totalling seventeen musicians in royal service.

Henry Bassano, the last survivor of the third generation of musicians in the family, served Charles II as recorder-player until 1665. Even today, a descendant of the Bassanos, Peter Goodwin, is a professional musician.[21]

The best known, and certainly the most controversial, musical visitor of the sixteenth century was Alfonso Ferrabosco, singer, lutenist and composer. The Ferrabosco family was a well-connected dynasty, highly regarded in the ruling Bentivoglio court in Bologna since the middle of the fifteenth century. Domenico Maria, Alfonso's father, moved with his family from Bologna to Rome to France, to take up various musical appointments. In Rome, he sang in the Sistine Chapel choir with Palestrina. While in Paris, he acted as agent for the Cardinal of Bologna. At the French court, Alfonso was a teenage sensation as singer to the lute and, with his two younger brothers, sang and played at various royal weddings during the late 1550s, probably including that of Mary Queen of Scots to the dauphin.

Alfonso came to England in 1562, aged nineteen, against the will of his father, to serve Queen Elizabeth I, and lived in England intermittently until 1578. Immediately accepted into the Queen's Musick, he was said to enjoy 'extreme favour' with the queen on account of his skill as a musician. At a time of comparative miserliness with regard to musicians, and at a time when there were far fewer foreign musicians at the court than under her father, Alfonso was paid the handsome annuity of £66 13s. 4d.

Ferrabosco was a member of a distinguished and exclusive circle of Italian poets, historians and scholars living in London, and he was seen as the representative of the latest style of Italian music. He became the first major composer for the lute in England, and his vocal works introduced the lively and sophisticated style of Italian madrigals and motets. He quickly became the focus of interest for many of the best young composers in England. In particular, he worked closely with his exact contemporary William Byrd, whose settings of the *In Nomine* for viol consort appeared at about the same time as Alfonso's, and show many similarities thereto. Later, the two composers engaged in what the composer Thomas Morley described as a 'vertuous contention in love',[22] setting eighty canons – forty each – on the *Miserere* plainchant, now sadly lost. Indeed, careful analysis of Byrd's works not only shows the profound influence of Ferrabosco on Byrd, but also that Byrd's recusant – that is, more assertively Catholic – works are the ones owing most to the Italian composer.

But Ferrabosco was not simply a musician. He took a leading part in a masque in 1572 and even acted in an Italian comedy at Whitehall in 1576. He was promoted to groom of the Privy Chamber, and his duties included liaising with visiting Italian diplomats. Most interesting of all, his stay in England was punctuated by frequent visits to Italy and France, and during these visits he often found himself in trouble. Within a year or so of his arrival in England, he was back in Rome, in the service of Cardinal Farnese, apparently on the recommendation of his father. Ferrabosco, wishing to return to England, needed permission from the cardinal to travel in a country prohibited by the Inquisition; when this was refused, he left in secret. From this time on, Rome had Ferrabosco within its sights. Meanwhile in England, his annuity was increased to £100 from 1567, more than that of any other royal musician, but on condition that he remain in England except when given royal permission to travel. It is not clear whether Ferrabosco was acting as a spy for Elizabeth in Italy, as the high salary might suggest, or indeed if he was working as a double agent, but his devious behaviour aroused the suspicions of both the English and the papal courts.

He associated with many of the most powerful nobleman of the time, including the Earl of Leicester, Elizabeth's first favourite, and patron to most of the Italian artists in London, the Earl of Sussex, Leicester's rival, and William Cecil, Lord Burghley, who definitely did employ Ferrabosco as an agent abroad. He was also well known to the great patrons of the arts, Sir Philip Sidney and Henry Fitzalan, twelfth Earl of Arundel, Lord High Steward to Elizabeth. Arundel was one the leading Roman Catholics in England and his palace at Nonsuch was the most significant arena for foreign musicians in England. Seemingly happy to address any of these men as 'my patron and protector', Ferrabosco was playing a dangerous game in the potentially treacherous environment of the Elizabethan court. Indeed, by late 1570s, when things were getting uncomfortable for foreigners, and especially Catholics, in England, his annuity was inexplicably halved. He was then accused of the robbery and murder of one of Sir Philip Sidney's servants, a charge that was certainly fabricated and, worst of all, for one who affected to be a Protestant, he was accused of attending Mass with the French ambassador, and was virtually excluded from court. Clearly the knives were being sharpened.

Despondent and protesting his innocence, and despite being assured of his eventual reinstatement at court, Ferrabosco left England for the last time in 1578 with his new wife and went to Paris, where he was employed as musician by the Cardinal of Lorraine. A letter of 23 June 1578 from Anselmo Dandino, the papal nuncio in France, to Cardinal Gilli in Rome, reveals the extent of suspicion over Ferrabosco's behaviour:

> I understand that this is a most evil-spirited, evil-minded man, and very knowing, and excellently informed of the affairs of those countries; that the queen of England makes much use of him as a spy and complotter, in which character he might now be employed, so that if one had him in one's power, one might learn many things; that it is in order that he may better play his game that he affects to have a grudge against the queen of England ... I know not what of good to believe, as here he has gone to dine with the ambassador of England on Friday, and has eaten meat, and is constantly busy there.[23]

Dandino had Ferrabosco watched and discovered that on his departure from England he was in receipt of the sum of 8,000 crowns from Elizabeth, as well as two jewels for 'two persons of quality'. Later in the year, Ferrabosco was found to be a companion of the infamous Egremont Ratcliffe, brother of the Earl of Sussex. Ratcliffe had been captured in Flanders, accused of intending to kill Don John, an Italian prince, and executed. Things were not looking good for Ferrabosco. Some time after his departure for Italy in September 1578, he was imprisoned, probably in Rome, on the orders of the pope, on the grounds of apostasy and defection.

Elizabeth asked Catherine of Medici to intercede with the pope on Ferrabosco's behalf, thus extraordinarily involving the three most powerful figures in Europe of the time over the fate of an ostensibly humble lutenist. Catherine's motivation in agreeing to do so was probably that she wanted one of her sons to marry Elizabeth. Elizabeth's reasons for interceding on Ferrabosco's behalf can only be guessed at. Alfonso was eventually released in February 1580 and regained employment, and a restored reputation, at the court of the Duke of Savoy, where he was to remain until his death in 1588.

In England he had left his infant son, Alfonso II, and a daughter, who were effectively held hostage against his return. Ferrabosco made repeated attempts to have the children brought to him in Italy, but despite continuing good relations with the queen, and despite his sending money to their guardian, the Flemish court flautist, Gomer van Awsterwyke, the children remained in England to be raised at Elizabeth's expense.

Posthumously, Alfonso's reputation as madrigalist was enhanced, first by the inclusion of his works in the publication *Musica Transalpina* (1588), translations of Italian works which inspired the rise of the English madrigal, and subsequently by the championing of his work by his son, Alfonso II. In 1597, Thomas Morley, in his list of compositional masters, recommends imitating Alfonso's madrigals 'for deepe skill', and Morley himself, and the great song composer John Dowland, both quote from Alfonso in their own madrigals.

Perhaps an even greater influence on the course of English musical history was the fact that the younger Alfonso remained in England. For Alfonso II was a composer of greater stature than his father, helping to develop the declamatory style of song characteristic of the new baroque era, and arguably the most innovative composer of viol music of his generation, influencing English composers as late as Purcell. Under James I, he extraordinarily held four court places at once, and his works, such as the *Four Note Pavan*, are still familiar to us today. Seen in the strongly dynastic context of the Ferrabosco family, fathering such an influential son was perhaps the elder Alfonso's most significant achievement. Yet Alfonso II had much good publicity to gain both from the circulation of his father's music, and from enhancing the reputation of this remarkable and troubled foreigner in England. Thomas Campion praised the younger Alfonso as

> *Musicks* maister, and the offspring
> Of rich *Musicks* Father
> Old *Alfonso's* Image living.[24]

2 The Restoration

New music, new faces

With the accession of James I in 1603, the Stuart monarchy gave English life a more cosmopolitan outlook once again. In 1611, King Christian IV of Denmark sent four of his musicians to his sister Anne, James's queen, as he was at war and had no use for them. They remained in England for three years, and the most talented of them, Mogens Pedersøn, whose madrigals bear comparison with those of Marenzio and Monteverdi, may have helped to spread the new expressive 'baroque' style of singing to England. Charles I's marriage to Queen Henrietta Maria sparked a fashion for French music. In 1617, the lutenist and composer Jacques Gaultier fled from France, suspected of involvement in the murder of a young nobleman. He was imprisoned in the Tower of London pending extradition but was eventually freed, and he stayed in England, serving and outliving Charles I. Controversy continued to surround this volatile and rakish character, who was often either in debt or being accused of improper affairs. But he profoundly influenced lute-playing in England, was lutenist to the queen – even rumoured to be having an affair with her – and popularised the double-headed lute, which continued to be played for the rest of the century.

The restoration of Charles II to the throne in 1660 brought foreign influences to the fore. Charles had spent much of the Interregnum in France, and may have seen the young composer Jean-Baptiste Lully and the even younger King Louis XIV dance together during his stay at the French court. His preference was for French dance music, and the music historian Roger North claimed that 'he could not bear any musick to which he could not keep the time'.[1] Taste in foreign music was only one of the exotic and ostentatious aspects of court life. The theatre was the playground of the royal family and their clique, and both Charles and his brother James, Duke of York, had their own theatres. After the austerity of the Commonwealth, the court assumed French fashions; in 1666 dressing in the Persian style became all the rage.

Like some other European monarchs of the time, Charles II formed a violin band, called the Twenty-Four Violins, in imitation of Louis XIV's *Vingt-quatre violons*. Though the Twenty-Four Violins consisted exclusively of English musicians in 1660, there is no doubt that Charles preferred the French style of playing. During a performance at Whitehall, which the diarist Samuel Pepys attended that year, the king made them stop and 'bade the French musique play'.[2] In an attempt to raise the standard of the Twenty-Four Violins, its director, John Banister, was sent to France, possibly more than once, to study Lully's methods and to learn the French style of composition. He copied Lully's discipline and methods by synchronising bowings and by beginning a piece exactly together from silence.

The next logical step in Charles's Frenchifying process was to appoint Luis Grabu as Master of his Majesty's Musick in 1666. Though originally from Catalonia, he had spent time in Paris, and was thought of in England as a musician in the French mould. Grabu immediately assumed authority over the Twenty-Four Violins, an appointment that was deeply unpopular among some of the leading English musicians: 'the king's viallin, Bannister, is mad that the King hath a Frenchman come to be chief of some part of the King's music'.[3] Although Grabu succeeded in improving the standard of playing, he lost the mastership of the King's Music in 1674, probably as a result of the passing of the Test Act, which debarred Catholics from holding court appointments, but he stayed on in England.

As well as arousing the jealousy of English musicians, Grabu also suffered bad luck. He was part of the project to establish a Royal Academy of Music, a company modelled on French lines to perform French operas. The project failed, and by 1677 he was petitioning the king for arrears of salary, eventually being paid £627. 9s. 6d. Forced to leave England at the height of the Popish Plot in 1679, he returned to England to embark on another operatic enterprise suggested by Charles II. This was the allegorical *Albion and Albanius*, with text by Dryden, 'to represent something at least like an Opera in England for his Majestyes diversion'[4] which was intended to glorify the king and his brother. Rehearsals were abandoned when the king died on 6 February 1685, and when it was finally staged on 3 June of the same year, it ran for six nights before being interrupted by news of the Duke of Monmouth's rebellion reaching London. Grabu left England for good in December 1694.

Grabu may also have been partly responsible for the arrival of perhaps the most distinguished musical visitor of the period, Robert Cambert. Reputed to be the composer of the first French opera *Pomone*, which was first performed in Paris in 1671, Cambert is little known now, partly because the bulk of his music has been lost. *Pomone* was in fact extremely successful, running for eight months. However, the privilege to stage operas in Paris, at this time owned by Pierre Perrin, Cambert's librettist and business partner, was shrouded in politics. With Perrin in gaol for debt, Lully managed to obtain the privilege in April 1672, and set up an 'Académie Royale de Musique', producing a whole host of hugely successful operas, now considered the master works of seventeenth-century French music.

IACOBO GOVTERO INTER REGIOS MAGNÆ BRITANNIÆ ORPHEOS ET AMPHIONES
LYDIÆ DORIÆ PHRYGIÆ TESTVDINIS FIDICINI ET MODVLATORVM PRINCIPI
HANC E PENICILLI SVI TABVLA IN ÆS TRANSSCRIPTAM EFFIGIEM IOANNES LÆVINI
FIDÆ AMICITIÆ MONIMENTVM.L.M.CONSECRAVIT.

2 Jacques Gaultier, lutenist, by Jan Lievens, *c.* 1632

Cambert came to London in 1673 to join Grabu, who had been his pupil in Paris, and his arrival coincided with, or possibly caused, a whole flurry of theatrical activity over the next two years. He provided the music for the *Ballet et musique pour le divertissement du roy de la Grande Bretagne*, which was performed at court early in 1674 to celebrate the marriage of James, Duke of York to Mary of Modena. Cambert brought

with him singers and instrumentalists to perform his music, which were
to form the nucleus of the intended Royal Academy of Music. Unfortunately for Cambert, there was only a single performance of the work, for
on the opening night one of the singers insulted the librettist and was killed
in a sword-fight the next day. Cambert's next project, the opera *Ariane*,
was also cut short, when

> the leader of the French troupe, who had been made prisoner for debt,
> was forcibly liberated by his fellows from the hands of the justice, two
> of whose officers were wounded. This is so great a crime in the realm
> that those from the said troupe who are taken cannot escape the
> gallows unless they obtain a special pardon from his Majesty.[5]

Thus, the Royal Academy of Music lasted only a month. But it seems
Cambert may have had other activities to keep him occupied, for it is likely
that Louis XIV had despatched him to England in 1673 both to provide
musical services to, and to keep a watch over, Louise de Queroualle, Duchess
of Portsmouth, Charles's *maîtresse en titre*. Louise, whom Louis had sent
over to Charles in 1671, was a powerful figure, having been given twenty-
four rooms and sixteen garrets in the Palace of Whitehall, which were
redecorated three times during her time there, and according to Evelyn,
living in 'ten times the richnesse & the glory beyond the *Queenes*'.[6] She also
wielded political power over the king, and acted as an unofficial French
ambassador at the court. It is not hard to see why Louis was at pains to
ensure her continued presence in England.

A group of Louis's enemies, attempting to topple Louise from her
position of influence, chose Hortense, Duchess of Mazarin, a beautiful and
passionate French lady and a former lover of Charles during his exile in
France, to rival Louise as Charles's mistress. This had the desired effect
on Louise, who, through ill health caused by her anxiety, lost the king's
baby she was carrying. From reports of the French ambassador from the
summer of 1676, Louis sent over three singers to perform with Louise's
private musicians, under Cambert's directorship, and they were often to be
seen in Louise's apartments at this time, singing many of Charles's favourite
songs. These included the Sleep Scene from Lully's *Atys*, which Charles
heard four times in just a few days, surely an attempt to entice the king
back to Louise's bedroom. It seems that Louis was using the singers as
spies, well placed as they were in ladies' apartments, to report on Charles's
activities *vis-à-vis* both women. Thus a musical visitation helped Louis XIV
to ensure that Louise won back her position as Charles's favoured mistress, and also that Anglo-French relations remained on course. Cambert
died in 1677, but thanks to him, and his work in the service of Louise de
Queroualle, Lully's music was heard and seen by many of Charles's musicians: the keyboard works known at *The Cibell* come from the 'Descent

of Cybèle' from Lully's *Atys*; Purcell was one of many to have written a *Cibell* tune.

Also through the visit of Cambert, the latest wind instruments – the newly modelled oboe and recorder – made their way over from France. Four oboists, or 'hautboys' as they were often called, came to England with Cambert in 1673, and were quickly established at court and caused a sensation at the London theatres. A prologue added to a revival of Ben Jonson's *Volpone* for the 1674 season, upbraids theatre audiences for being distracted by this new sound:

> Did Ben now live, how would he fret and rage,
> To see the Musick-room outvye the stage?
> To see French Haut-boyes charm the listning Pitt
> More than the Raptures of his God-like wit!
> Yet 'tis true that most who now are here,
> Come not to feast their Judgement, but their Ear.
> Musick, which was by Intervals design'd
> To ease the weary'd Actors voice and mind,
> You to the Play judiciously prefer,
> 'Tis now the bus'ness of the Theatre . . .[7]

Two years later, in George Etherege's play *The Man of Mode; or, Sir Fopling Flutter*, the character of Emilia is asked, 'What, are you of the number of the Ladies whose Ears are grown so delicate since our Operas, you can be charm'd with nothing but Flute doux and French Hoboys?'[8] Composers were likewise charmed, and Matthew Locke, whose incidental music for *The Tempest* from 1674 is for strings alone, only a year later, in *Psyche*, includes flageolets, recorders, flutes, pipes and 'hoboys' in the list of instruments used.

Of the four French hoboys, Jacques Paisible, often called James Peasable, had the most notable success, and the longest career; with only a short break, he was in England until his death in 1721. Paisible's meteoric rise in court circles was due not just to his prodigious talent, but also, to quote the rakish Earl of Rochester, because 'the greatest and gravest of this Court of both sexes have tasted his beauties'.[9] Paisible was associated with the circle of the Duchess of Mazarin, who was also a patroness of the arts; Paisible wrote music for several plays written for her by the French *philosophe* Saint-Evremond, who loved to make puns on the name 'Paisible'. Later, Paisible married the singer and actress Moll Davis, Charles II's former mistress, and was even shipwrecked whilst in the service of James, Duke of York, the future James II of England.

There are reports of Paisible's laziness: the viol-player Ernst Chrisitan Hesse, writes of him, in a letter of 1711: 'I should have thought, however, that Paisible would have carried out the commission which he undertook, were it not that I have known him for a long time, so that I am afraid that he is likely to forget in the morning what he promised the day before, that being the sort of person he really is.'[10] Despite this, Paisible was a virtual fixture at the London theatres and also at the public concerts that had started to flourish during Charles II's reign. He played not only the oboe, but also the cello and bass violin – a low cello in B flat – in the band and, most especially, recorder in the interval entertainments at the theatre. His virtuosity in this instrument can be judged from his surviving recorder sonatas, which still tax players today. Above all, he is associated with theatre and dancing: for over twenty years he wrote an annual birthday dance for Princess, later Queen, Anne. His greatest legacy, however, is his output of music for oboe band, and his most famous piece, *The Queene's Farewell* is a slow march written for the funeral of Queen Mary in 1695.

The success of Paisible and of the new wind instruments notwithstanding, the influence of French music was now on the wane, and, after Cambert's death there were virtually no further French composers or instrumentalists visiting England for the rest of the seventeenth century. This may have reflected a wider turn of opinion against the French: the Treaty of Dover which Charles had signed in secret with Louis XIV in 1670 resulted in an Anglo-French attack on Holland in 1672, a war which was deeply unpopular in England. Charles was seen by many as Louis's puppet, his equally unpopular Catholic tendencies had a distinctly French flavour and, as the dominant political and military force in Europe, France and her expansionist policies were viewed with fear and suspicion.

There were other reasons for changes in taste. The arrival of the violinist Nicola Matteis caused something of a sensation and 'left with them [the English] a generall favour for the Italian manner of harmony, and after him the French was wholly layd aside'.[11] This shift in taste is nicely captured in reports of a violin-playing contest with the Frenchman Michel Farinel, who was so impressed by Matteis that he could only 'stand and stare at him'.[12]

Matteis is perhaps the most colourful figure to enter the London scene from abroad during this period. Born in Naples, he arrived some time around 1670, and was said to have travelled through Germany on foot with his violin on his back. Accounts of his virtuosity abound, and according to Evelyn: 'that stupendious Violin Signor *Nicholao* ... had a stroak so sweete, & made it speake like the Voice of a man; & when he pleased, like a Consort of severall Instruments: he did wonder upon a note.'[13] His progress was impeded at first by being what was described as 'inexpugnably proud'[14] – an accusation often levelled at Italian musical visitors – and his insistence on silence while he played was not well received. Perhaps because of this, and because the king preferred French dance music, Matteis never received a royal appointment, and although he is now the best-known and most performed composer of all the musical visitors to England of the period, he was always a marginal figure at court.

With the advice of friends, however, he was persuaded to be 'easy, free, and familiar, and to let Gentlemen, Not the best hands, have his company in consorts', and he became 'a Most complaisant master ... loved and courted as much as any fureiner ever was'.[15] His playing attracted attention not only for its spontaneity and passion, which displaced the more prosaic style of variation or division form of the English violinists, but also because of Matteis's technical innovations.

> He was a very robust and tall man, and having long armes, held his Instrument almost against his Girdle, and his bow was long as for a Base violl, and he touched his devision with the very point [i.e. played with the tip of his bow] ... He first shew'd us the Holding the bow, without touching the hair, which before him was not done in England: but from the first hint, it was immediately taken up by the best hands in a few years and became the universall practise.[16]

His variety of bowings, *cantabile* sound and use of double-stops all contributed to the ascendancy of the violin over the hitherto popular treble viol.

Matteis is said to have played only his own compositions, many of which were included in the four books of *Diverse Ayres* for violin and bass, which were first published in 1676. The old English master violinist, John Jenkins, is reported to have played through a suite from the second book, and 'pulling off his spectacles, clapt his hand on the book and declared he had never heard so good a peice of musick, in all his life'.[17] Conscious of his role in developing violin-playing in England, Matteis organised the third and fourth books like tutor books, with the pieces becoming successively more difficult. In his preface he characteristically issues a challenge to his public: 'If you find these at all to your taste, I shall be both contented and rewarded for my pains. If not, you will have the goodness to compose something better, and then I shall have the means of studying to greater advantage, so as to be ready to serve you on a more excellent occasion and opportunity'.[18]

At least as important as his compositions, from our point of view, Matteis's lifestyle made him something of a role model for the next generations of visitors, for he demonstrated that it was possible to prosper as a freelance foreign musician in England. Like other successful musical visitors before and since, Matteis was able to strike a balance between the exoticness of his foreign origins and the need to cater for, and to some extent adapt to, English taste. Matteis set several English texts to music, wrote sonatas for, and in imitation of, the trumpet, a very popular idiom in English music of the time, and included 'A pretty hard ground after the Scotch humour'. In the preface to the first books of his *Diverse Ayres*, Matteis neatly summarises the situation facing all musical visitors:

It is an honourable and proper thing to adjust oneself to the mood of those with whom one resides. Having lived myself for some years under the northern sky, I have tried to adopt the musical tastes of the people of this country, although not to so great an extent as to separate myself too much from the Italian school.[19]

Although the success of his publications enabled him to buy a large house in Norfolk, where he 'had a thing called a wife . . . Excess of pleasure threw him into a dropsie, and he became very poor . . . He came at last to loos both his Invention, and hand and in a miserable state of body purs and mind, dyed'.[20]

Thanks to Matteis, the Italian school of violin-playing was now in the ascendancy, and was here to stay. Whereas Banister, Grabu's predecessor as director of the Twenty-Four Violins, had been sent to France, Nicholas Staggins, his successor, was ordered to go and study in Italy. The presence of other Italian musicians also influenced English musical life. Italian singers were famed across Europe, and under Giacomo Carissimi's direction, held sway in Paris. Charles himself spoke the language and sang well enough to hold a bass part in Italian songs, and tried to establish Italian opera in London, without success. Even so, famous singers such as the Modenese castrato Giovanni Francesco Grossi, known as Siface, was sent to London for the first half of 1687, to entertain the queen, and perhaps to cure her of homesickness.[21] Thanks to the influx of Italian harpsichord masters, that instrument began to replace the lute as the instrument of choice for accompaniment of singers.

The craze for the guitar was another fashion borrowed from Italy. Both Charles and his brother played the five-course guitar, referred to as the 'Spanish guitar', or what we now call the baroque guitar, and owned several instruments. Early in his reign, Charles brought over the virtuoso guitarist sensation, Francesco Corbetta, an Italian whose exceptional gifts had already established him in a number of European courts. Louis XIV shared Charles's passion for the guitar, and Corbetta wrote two volumes of guitar music entitled 'La guitarre royalle', the first dedicated to Charles in 1671, the second to Louis in 1674. Containing a good deal of technically demanding music, the English 'guitarre royalle' also contains titles reflecting events of the day, such as a suite 'sur la mort du Duc de Glocester' commemorating the death of the king's youngest brother in autumn 1660, and the 'Tombeau sur la mort de Madame d'Orléans' that of Charles's sister ten years later.[22] It is likely that he also taught James's other daughter, Mary. Matteis was also an excellent guitarist and his guitar tutor book 'The False Consonances of Musick' is one of the best treatises on the art of guitar continuo playing.

There was some opposition from those who favoured the lute. Pepys heard Corbetta play, 'which he did most admirably – so well that I was mightily troubled that all that pains should have been taken upon so bad an instrument',[23] but Pepys himself was eventually won over. He employed a singer, lutenist and composer named Cesare Morelli as his household musician from 1674 at £30 per annum, and chief among his tasks was to provide guitar parts for Pepys to play. During the time of Popish Plot, because of his employment of Morelli, Pepys was hounded for harbouring a suspected priest, and was even briefly imprisoned in the Tower.

Seemingly immune to the vicissitudes of religious politics of the period, Giovanni Battista Draghi enjoyed a career of approximately forty years' royal service. Unlike those other long-servers, Paisible and Matteis, Draghi's is not a name much known to musicians today,[24] and unlike those more colourful characters, Draghi was simply described as 'learned and Civill; Civility being no vere ordinarye quality of a Musicien'.[25]

Draghi was appointed organist of the queen's Catholic chapel in Somerset House over the highly esteemed Matthew Locke. He contributed instrumental dance music to Locke's scores for both *The Tempest* and *Psyche*. On 18 November 1679, the day after an effigy of the pope was carried past the queen's window and burned, a petition from four Italians, including Draghi, was referred to the Treasury, in which they protested that their salaries were four years in arrears. However, Draghi's service continued uninterrupted; he was appointed organist at James II's Catholic chapel in 1687, and he was responsible for the musical education of Princess Anne and probably also her sister Mary, and was generally much in demand as a music teacher.

But from an historical point of view, Draghi was a significant influence on English composers of the period, especially on the prevailing genius of English music, Henry Purcell. As a chorister at the Chapel Royal, Purcell was in the circle of Humfrey and Banister who, as we have seen, were thoroughly versed in the French style. Cambert's overtures, which Purcell would have heard, with their dotted rhythms, were immediately imitated by English composers, and some of Grabu's theatre suites have been misattributed to Purcell; while the characteristic rushing scales to indicate demons and furies were also famously adopted by Purcell in his theatrical music. As we have seen, Lully's *Cybèle*, through the agency of Cambert's musicians, inspired Purcell's *Cibell*. The French connection was everywhere.

So it was with the Italian style. Well before Purcell began as chorister, in 1663, Pepys records seeing the boys of the Chapel Royal rehearsing an anthem: 'And after that was done, Captain Cooke and his two boys did sing some Italian songs, which I must in a word say I think was fully the best Musique that I ever yet heard in all my life – and it was to me a very great pleasure to hear them.'[26] There is no evidence that Purcell met Matteis but, by the later 1670s, the latter's school of violin-playing was established in London, and in the preface to his *Sonnatas of III Parts*, published in 1683, Purcell claims these works demonstrate a faithful imitation of famous Italian masters. While their identity remains a source of conjecture, the Italophile Roger North wrote that, in imitating them, he outdid them, and that this set of sonatas 'which however clog'd with somewhat of an English vein, for which they are unworthily despised, are very artificiall and good musick'.[27]

The ground bass, a repeating sequence of a few bars, is especially associated with Purcell, and he often reserved the use of it for his most tragic sung works such as Dido's lament 'When I am laid in earth'. Whilst the ground bass was an import from Italy and was already much used in English dance music, this new affective vocal form, very often in the minor key, was derived from composers such as the Italian Pietro Reggio, resident in London since the 1660s, some of whose songs Purcell imitated.[28]

Above all, it was Purcell's association and his affinity with Draghi that was perhaps most influential. The harpsichord works of the two composers show many similarities, and the discovery in 1994 of a manuscript note-book containing works by both composers, demonstrates, if not necessarily a collaboration, then at least the equally high regard in which the two harpsichord masters were held. Proposals put forward by various noble-men to set up a Royal Academy in 1695 list both Purcell and Draghi as harpsichord tutors.[29] Students were to be chosen by a lottery, but the plans for the academy were never realised.

Draghi's parity with Purcell as organist is well documented in the famous 'Battle of the Organs' of 1684. In this bizarre episode, rival organ-builders Renatus Harris and Bernhard Schmidt (known as Father Smith), were called upon each to build a new organ for the Temple church. John Blow and his student Purcell demonstrated Smith's organ 'on appointed days to a numerous audience',[30] and Draghi played Harris's. This contest lasted nearly a year, during which time Harris and Smith challenged one another to develop additional organ-stops. The competition was fierce, and 'in the night preceding the last trial of the reed stops, the friends of Harris cut the bellows of Smith's organ in such a manner that when the time came for playing upon it no wind could be conveyed into the wind-chest'.[31] Finally Lord Chief Justice Jeffreys, only a year before his notorious judgements at the Bloody Assizes following Monmouth's Rebellion, chose Father Smith's organ; Harris's instrument 'was taken away without loss of reputation'[32] and no doubt the organists suffered no loss of reputation either.

Draghi's crowning achievement, and his major contribution to the development of English music was his setting of Dryden's ode 'From harmony, from heavenly harmony' for St Cecilia's Day, 1687. With its flamboyant vocal style, contrapuntal choral writing and ambitious scale, this work deeply influenced Purcell's odes, and helped establish a choral style which, through Purcell, we tend to regard as typically English.

Finally, if we appear to overemphasise the role of foreigners in the musical life of England in the late seventeenth century, it is worth considering Evelyn's diaries, which cover the whole of the Restoration period, and more besides. Henry Purcell – whom he refers to as 'Dr Purcell' – only gains one mention, and that is after the composer's death. For Evelyn, a highly cultured and musically aware man of his time, Reggio, Draghi, Bartolomeo, Siface, Matieis, even Grabu, were more significant than Purcell in the rough and tumble of musical life in London.

3 Handel (1)

First among visitors

The decade after the death of Purcell in 1695 was a relatively fallow one for music in London. Native composers such as John Blow, William Croft and Jeremiah Clarke were amongst the most active, and masques and semi-operas, in the mould of Purcell's *Dido and Aeneas*, dominated musical theatre. As the first decade of the eighteenth century wore on, the fashion for Italian music began to take hold. According to the historian Roger North, the publication of Corelli's sonatas 'cleared the ground of all other sorts of musick whatsoever'.[1] In 1714, when the sheet music for Corelli's twelve *Concerti Grossi* Op. 6 arrived in London soon after publication, the amateur violinist Henry Needler and his fellow musicians were so taken by them that they played all twelve at a single sitting.[2]

In 1705, Thomas Clayton's *Arsinoe, Queen of Cyprus*, the first all-sung work ('in the Italian manner') to be publicly staged in London, was produced at Drury Lane Theatre. Although the work was second-rate, it was a commercial success and ran for twenty-four nights. It was followed by a series of similar works, many of them adapted from Italian operas; these spectacles were as often comic as dramatic. William Chetwood, the prompter at Drury Lane, described the production of Giovanni Bononcini's *Camilla* as 'an odd Medley – Mrs *Tofts*, a mere *Englishwoman*, in the part of *Camilla*, courted by *Nicolini* in *Italian*, without understanding one single Syllable each other *said* or *sung*'.[3] In particular, the declamatory nature of sung recitative, whereby the story-line of Italian opera is advanced, transferred with great difficulty into English. By now, with the influx of Italian singers, there was an increasing need for works performed in Italian. Despite the efforts of the London-based German Johann Christoph Pepusch, and performances of imported works by leading Italian composers such as Giovanni Bononcini and Alesssandro Scarlatti, something more was required. London's theatres needed a composer who was experienced in Italian opera, who could provide the vehicle for the star singers to express themselves.

Georg Friedrich Händel (to give him his German name) was born on 23 February 1685, the son of Georg Händel, a barber-surgeon, who held a court appointment at the ducal residence in Weissenfels, and his second wife Dorothea. Handel's talent for music was apparent at a young age, although the familiar story recounted by his first biographer, John Mainwaring, of Handel as a child having to smuggle a clavichord into the attic because of his father's ban on musical instruments, and of playing it when the family was asleep, is probably spurious.[4] On hearing the boy playing the postlude to a service, the duke recommended to Handel's father that he be given a musical education with one of the most learned musicians in Germany at the time, Friedrick Wilhelm Zachow.

In 1702, whilst enrolled at University of Halle to study law, Handel was appointed probationary organist at Halle Cathedral. Around this time, Georg Philipp Telemann was on his way to Leipzig and, like Handel, about to embark on a career in law. On the way, he stopped at Halle, where he met Handel, whereupon in his own words he 'imbibed again the poison of music'.[5] The two composers remained lifelong friends, Handel subscribing to Telemann's *Musique de table* (1733), and borrowing sixteen movements in his own works. Later, they exchanged crates of exotic plants.

Impatient for a more colourful and varied musical career than the post of organist could offer, however, Handel resigned within a year to set off for Hamburg, the start of more than ten years of nomadic existence. Hamburg was then a 'free' city, not bound by the strictures of class-ridden provincial Saxony, and offered Handel the life of culture he craved. Soon after his arrival in Hamburg, Handel met the composer, performer, and later musical theorist, Johann Mattheson, and the two became inseparable. Within a month, they had travelled together to Lübeck, to apply for the post of organist there, in succession to the famed composer Dietrich Buxtehude. On their arrival, however, it transpired that the old organist's daughter's hand in marriage was one of the conditions of employment, and the two young composers refused to apply, as J. S. Bach was later to do.

Mattheson and Handel learnt a great deal from one another, Handel being especially receptive to Mattheson's thorough knowledge of opera. Mattheson was also a canny businessman, a diplomat, and well versed in English ways – he married an Englishwoman in 1709 – and is likely to have influenced Handel in his final decision to go to England. Handel soon generated an income from teaching the harpsichord to the son of John Wyche, the English consul in Hamburg, but he had opera in his sights, and also held a place in the violin section of the orchestra. His first opera *Almira* (1705) was a resounding success.

Handel and Mattheson were not just friends but rivals, and it was at about this time that their well-documented altercation took place. Mattheson's opera *Cleopatra* was very successful, and Mattheson himself starred in the role of Antonius. In one performance, with half an act remaining, Mattheson, his singing duties having finished, attempted to take over the harpsichord chair from Handel, who was by this time directing the orchestra from the harpsichord. Handel refused, and the two fought a duel with swords, Handel's life being spared by the lucky intervention of a metal button on his coat. As Mattheson later wrote: 'It was the result of a misunderstanding such as with young and ambitious people is nothing new ... we became better friends than ever',[6] and the two continued to correspond for the rest of their lives.

The craze for Italian music was felt not just in England. Whilst in Hamburg, Handel met the Grand Prince of Tuscany, Ferdinando de Medici who, according to Mainwaring, encouraged him to travel to Italy to continue his musical education. The Medici court is likely to have been his first stop on his arrival in Italy in 1706, and in the next three-and-a-half years, Handel was the honoured guest, not only of the Medicis, but also of Prince Ruspoli and Cardinals Pamphili and Ottoboni in Rome, amongst the richest and most powerful figures in Italy, and great patrons of music and the arts.[7] Mainwaring claims that, wherever Handel went, he 'had a palazzo at command, and was provided with table, coach, and all other accommodations'.[8]

Handel proved to be a musical sensation. In Rome, where he spent most of his time, he composed the masterly sacred choral work *Dixit Dominus* and the dramatic oratorio *La Resurrezione*, among others, and for several of Handel's works, the leader of his orchestra, which Handel led from the harpsichord, was Arcangelo Corelli himself. Rome was where Handel also met the brilliant keyboardist, and his exact contemporary, Domenico Scarlatti. In a trial of skill, which musicians of this period seemed so often to have to undergo, the two men performed on harpsichord and organ. There was no decision as to who was the finer harpsichordist, but even Scarlatti was happy to admit Handel's superiority at the organ. After this meeting, the two became close friends, and Scarlatti followed Handel all over Italy.[9]

Productions of the operas *Rodrigo* in 1707 in Florence, and especially *Agrippina* at the winter carnival of 1709–10 in Venice, demonstrated Handel's success in adopting the Italian style. *Agrippina*, which received twenty-seven successive performances, was hailed with cries of 'long live the beloved Saxon'.[10] Handel now had the opera houses of Europe at his feet.

During his stay in Italy, Handel met Baron Kielmansegg, then the Hanoverian ambassador and the Earl, later Duke, of Manchester, the British ambassador, and it is likely that both these men invited Handel to their respective courts. Handel did indeed travel to Hanover from Italy, and soon after his arrival, was appointed *Kapellmeister* to the Elector, later George I of England, in June 1710. Handel was at first unwilling to accept the 1,500-crown pension which he was offered, but when it was agreed that he had leave of absence for a year, or more if he wished, Handel accepted. After a brief stay with the Elector Palatine in Düsseldorf, he arrived in London in November 1710.

Why did Handel abandon Italy, where he had just become the jewel in the operatic crown, for Hanover, where the opera house had just been closed, and why did he then leave Hanover, having landed a prime court post?

There are many possible answers, and because so little is known of Handel's thinking – he never kept a diary, or expressed intimate thoughts in letters – they are all speculative. But Handel was always noted for his independence, had a keen eye for business, and was a spotter of trends. London was noted as a commercial centre, and the new taste for Italian opera was backed up by large sums of money, such as the salary paid to the singer Nicolini. Handel would have seen the potential for realising his own operatic ambitions in London. Perhaps he also saw that the elevated style of serious opera had reached its zenith in Italy and that the tradition was beginning to decline in favour of a more popular and comic type of opera. As a composer of intensely dramatic music, with a need to portray psychologically realistic characters, this trend towards the superficial held no interest for Handel. In Hanover, Handel was able to acquaint himself with the future king of England, to receive a generous salary, and to have a secure base from which to test the waters in England with a minimum of risk. And in London he was able to combine the advantages of the old way, patronage, with the new, commercial enterprise.

One other advantage of England over Italy was the question of religious affiliation, and makes a general point about the attractiveness of England for musical visitors. Later in life, Handel said that one of the things he liked about England was that religion was a man's private affair.[11] Although as a musician, Handel had fitted in well in Italy, the elaborate ritual associated with Catholicism never tempted him. And even in England, although he was a regular churchgoer, especially towards the end of his life, he never affiliated himself with the Anglican Church.[12]

Within weeks of his arrival in London, Handel, never far away from the corridors of power, was received by Queen Anne, and performed privately for her. Shortly afterwards, in February 1711, the music for the traditional birthday celebrations – an event which was established during the reign of James II and continued until the death of George III – was provided by Handel, who wrote an Italian cantata in which Nicolini sang. The task of writing this music had traditionally fallen to the Master of the Queen's Musick, who at this time was John Eccles; the choice of Handel for the task, and the large presents he received from her before his subsequent departure for Hanover in June, demonstrate the high regard the queen had for him.

Neither was Handel slow to make his mark on the London opera scene. Perhaps through acquaintance with the German composer and oboist Johann Ernst Galliard, who was heavily involved with the London theatre, Handel met Aaron Hill, manager of the Queen's Theatre's all-Italian opera company. Hill commissioned an opera from Handel, *Rinaldo*, based on a scenario by Hill himself, translated and adapted by the Italian Giacomo Rossi. Even with significant borrowings from his works, the opera was written in only a fortnight, outpacing the librettist. On 24 February 1711, *Rinaldo* opened, and was to put Handel permanently on London's musical map.

Rinaldo was a huge success with the London public and ran for fifteen sold-out performances, with frequent revivals in subsequent seasons. It was the first Italian opera to be staged in London with the composer present; Handel was directing from the harpsichord, and drew a great deal of praise for his virtuosic accompaniments on the instrument. Nicolini, who created the title role, was greatly acclaimed, and arias such as 'Lascia ch'io pianga' began to permeate the popular consciousness, where they reside once again. Hill's 'magic' scenic effects and use of real singing birds delighted the audience, and cleverly maintained the English theatrical traditions associated with Purcell performances.[13]

Rinaldo had, at a stroke, put an end to 'the reign of nonsense' in the London opera houses,[14] and Handel's success threatened vested interests in the theatre, such as those putting on plays and operas in English. The critics were quick to sharpen their pens. Joseph Addison, now firmly opposed to Italian opera, observed with heavy irony in the recently inaugurated journal *The Spectator* of 21 March 1711,

> I cannot forbear thinking how naturally an Historian who writes two or three hundred Years hence . . . will make the following Reflection, *In the Beginning of the Eighteenth Century the* Italian *Tongue was so well understood in* England, *that Operas were acted on the publick stage in that Language.*[15]

Handel left London for Hanover at the end of the run of performances in June but, as his studying of English whilst there shows, he intended to return. The fifteen months he spent away from London represents the last time Handel was away from Britain for any significant period.

On his return in the autumn of 1712, Handel was quick to re-establish himself in London life. After a brief period staying in Barn-Elms, now Barnes, he became the honoured guest of the young Richard Boyle, third Earl of Burlington, at Burlington House, which was then undergoing a transformation into the Palladian mansion which now houses the Royal Academy of Arts in Piccadilly. Burlington was a great patron of the arts, and of music and architecture in particular. An architect himself, Burlington, together with William Kent and Colen Campbell, whom he also

patronised, helped to establish the Palladian style in England. Handel also
met the brightest literary stars of the period whilst there: Alexander Pope,
John Gay and John Arbuthnot.

It was possibly Arbuthnot, who was also royal physician to the queen,
who advanced Handel's cause in royal circles. Handel wrote the Queen's
Birthday Ode in 1713, his first major attempt at setting English words and
at the end of the year was awarded an annual pension of £200. Remarkably
the queen also consented to the use of his *Te Deum* and *Jubilate* for the

3 George Frederick Handel by Thomas Hudson, 1749

celebration of the Treaty of Utrecht, signed by Britain and France on 31 March 1713, to bring an end to the War of the Spanish Succession. That Handel, a foreigner, should have been allowed to provide the music for this patriotic event, ahead of the Chapel Royal's own William Croft, who had written his own *Te Deum* setting in 1709, was not universally well received.

The newly rebuilt St Paul's Cathedral, where the thanksgiving service took place, also contained an organ by Father Smith, of which Handel was very fond. According to Hawkins:

> When Handel had no particular engagements, he frequently went . . . to St. Paul's church . . . a little intreaty was at any time sufficient to prevail on him to touch it, but after he had ascended the organ-loft, it was with reluctance that he left it; and he has been known, after evening service, to play to an audience as great as ever filled the choir.[16]

Afterwards he would repair to the Queen's Arms tavern in St Paul's churchyard with 'principal persons of the choir'. It is interesting to note that, apart from an occasional presence at the informal concerts of the musical 'small coal-man', Thomas Britton, Handel did not appear at any of the public concerts at Mr Hickford's Great Room in Panton Street, or the York Buildings, which were the haunts of many other musical visitors. Handel was clearly more interested in cultivating the image of the gentleman composer, royally connected and a guest of the nobility, than of the professional musician.

Opera remained a priority however, and Handel produced four more in the next three seasons. *Il Pastor Fido*, a gentle pastoral drama, was not a success, but was followed by the more heroic *Teseo*, which was notable not least for the manager, an Irishman named Owen Swiney, running off to Italy with the entire takings of the opera. *Silla* was not staged publicly, but might have been performed at Burlington House. By 1713, the Swiss impresario John Jacob Heidegger, with whom Handel was to work for more than twenty years, had taken over as manager at the Haymarket Theatre. The 'Swiss Count' as he was known, whom Handel's friend Mary Granville (later Mrs Delany) described as the ugliest man she had ever seen, mounted a production of Handel's next opera *Amadigi* in May 1715. Another of the 'magic' operas and another to feature the *castrato* Nicolini, *Amadigi* was a huge success, and was revived in both the next two seasons. Thereafter, Italian opera, burdened with unpopular Catholic associations after the Jacobite rebellion of 1715, and disrupted by a rift between the king and the Prince of Wales, disappeared from the London stage by the summer of 1717.

On 1 August 1714, Queen Anne died after many years of ill health and the Elector of Hanover claimed the British crown as George I. The previous year, Handel had been dismissed from his post as *Kapellmeister* in Hanover, not – as is often assumed – because of his continuing absence in London, but more likely because the support Handel demonstrated for the Utrecht peace treaty ran counter to Hanoverian interests, George being a fierce opponent of the *rapprochement* between England and France. Correspondence on the issue of Handel's dismissal reveals that the Hanoverian court had been interested to use Handel in a diplomatic capacity, by sending information about the queen's health. In any case, the Hanoverian consul in London writes in July 1713 of 'dropping a few words to the effect that he will be quite all right when the elector comes here'.[17]

Indeed, in financial terms, Handel was 'quite all right', as George had little hesitation in awarding Handel a pension of £200, as well as allowing payment of the pension granted to Handel from Queen Anne's reign to continue. Later on, when Handel was tutor to the royal children, he was paid a third pension of the same amount, and the annual salary of £600 made Handel a wealthy man.[18]

Although Handel was overlooked as the supplier of the coronation music for George I – the choice of William Croft for the task helped allay public fears of a monarchy biased towards Germans – he was chosen to write the music for the king's summer party on the Thames in July 1717, the famous *Water Music*. There is some controversy over the reasons for Handel being commissioned for this event. Mainwaring states that the *Water Music* was the occasion of a reconciliation between the king and Handel, presumably over his absence from his post in Hanover. A rift had also developed between George I and his son, the Prince of Wales (later George II), and this was the opportunity for Handel, a favourite of the younger George, to demonstrate that his first loyalty was to the king.

The circumstances of the performance of the *Water Music* are well known. The king, accompanied mainly by noble ladies of his acquaintance, took a barge from Whitehall to Chelsea, accompanied by many other barges with Persons of Quality. In a separate barge was an orchestra of fifty musicians, who played the specially composed collection of dance movements Handel had composed for the occasion. The music makes significant use – almost for the first time in England – of French horns, most especially in the famous *Hornpipe*. The king enjoyed the music so much that he ordered it to be played three times through on the outward and return journeys.

Handel was the dominant figure in musical London almost from the moment of his arrival, but he was by no means the only early eighteenth-century musical visitor of note. The demand for Italian instrumental music, in particular that of Corelli, paved the way for a generation of Italian composers and performers to make their careers in London.

The Florentine composer and violinist Francesco Maria Veracini came to London in 1714 and appeared in benefit concerts and between the acts at the opera. His virtuosic sonatas, and the manner of their execution was, in the words of Charles Burney, 'too wild and flighty for the taste of the English at this time', and he, along with Vivaldi, 'happening to be gifted with more fancy and more hand than their neighbours, were thought insane'.[19] Before the end of the year, he had left London, but was to return in the 1730s.

1714 also saw the arrival of the Neapolitan violinist and composer Francesco Geminiani, whose career in Britain rivalled that of Handel for longevity. A pupil of Corelli, he came to England with the reputation of being the greatest living violinist, Corelli having died the year before. His style of playing was much more to English tastes: 'he had none of the fire and spirit of the modern violinists, but . . . all the graces and elegancies of melody, all the powers that can engage attention'.[20]

Soon after Geminiani's arrival, Baron Kielmansegg arranged for him to play before the king, to which Geminiani assented only on condition that he be accompanied on the harpsichord by Handel. Geminiani's chief works were, like those of Corelli before him, violin sonatas and concerti grossi, but he wrote no operas, possibly due to a lack of compositional fluency. From reports of his ability as director, neither did he have the personal qualities to draw good performances from orchestras or singers.[21]

Like Handel, Geminiani was a fiercely independent character, who avoided all patronage during his lifetime, preferring to draw an income from performing, teaching and publishing. He was also involved in managing concert series; these included the direction of a masonic society with the improbable title of the Philo-Musicae et Architecturae Societas, from 1725 to 1727. As well as the highly acclaimed violin sonatas, Op. 1, dedicated to Kielmansegg, the concerti grossi, Opp. 2 and 3 and his arrangements for string orchestra of Corelli's Op. 5 violin sonatas, Geminiani published a good number of treatises on violin-playing and music in general. In one of these, he gives a fascinating insight into what he regarded as a change in English taste:

> When I came first to *London*, which was Thirty-four Years ago, I found Musick in so thriving a State, that I had all the Reason imaginable to suppose the Growth would be suitable to the Excellency of the Soil.
>
> But I have lived to be most miserably disappointed . . . The Hand was more considered than the Head; the Performance than the Composition; and hence it followed, that instead of labouring to cultivate a Taste, which seem'd to be all that was wanting, the Publick was content to nourish Insipidity.[22]

Another source of Geminiani's income was from dealing in Old Masters, a hobby shared by Handel, and in his later years, his passion for them seemed to eclipse his interest in music. According to a contemporary music historian:

A person who had the curiosity to see him, and went thither to purchase the book, gives this account of him: 'I found him in a room at the top of the house half filled with pictures, and in his waist-coat. Upon my telling him that I wanted the score and parts of both operas of his concertos, he asked me if I loved pictures; and upon my answering in the affirmative, he said that he loved painting better than music, and with great labour drew from among the many that stood upon the floor round the room, two, the one the story of Tobit cured of his blindness, by Michael Angelo Caravaggio; the other a Venus, by Correggio . . .' After some farther conversation, in which it was very difficult to get him to say any thing on the subject of music, the visitor withdrew, leaving Geminiani to enjoy that pleasure which seemed to be the result of frenzy.[23]

In common with his friend, the Italian oboist and composer Francesco Barsanti, Geminiani developed a keen interest in Scottish folk tunes, and both composers made frequent use of these tunes in their compositions. Indeed, such was Geminiani's interest in Celtic music that when he was in Dublin, where he spent much of the last thirty years of his life, he was interested to test the skills of the famous blind harpist, Turlough O'Carolan. Geminiani took an Irish tune and 'here and there he either altered or mutilated the piece, but in such a manner, as that no one but a real judge could make a discovery'. The piece was sent to O'Carolan, who when he heard it 'declared it was an admirable piece of musick; but, to the astonishment of all present, said, very humorously, in his own language, *tá sé air chois air bacaighe*, that is, here and there it limps and stumbles'. Asked to correct the errors, he did; the piece was sent back to Geminiani in Dublin who pronounced Carolan to be a true musical genius.[24]

Geminiani continued to perform and to publish treatises on music well into his old age, including one on harpsichord accompaniment and another on guitar-playing. It is possible that the theft of the manuscript of his last treatise, by a servant, hastened his death in Dublin at the age of seventy-four. He remains an enigmatic figure, at once eminent and virtually unknown.

Italian musicians were not the only long-lived and long-standing visitors: the German composer Johann Christoph Pepusch had a distinguished career of almost fifty-five years in England. By the time Handel arrived, Pepusch was probably the most active figure on the London musical scene, as harpsichordist at the Drury Lane Theatre, and then chief musical arranger at Vanbrugh's opera house. A regular performer on the harpsi-chord and violin in London's concert scene, he may have encountered Handel at Thomas Britton's concerts. Pepusch was also respected as a teacher and scholar of music, and in 1713 received a Doctorate of Music from Oxford University, becoming a Fellow of the Royal Society in 1745. He is credited with being England's first musicologist – and one of the first anywhere – and his pupils included the composer William Boyce. He also married Margherita de l'Epine, one of the leading singers in Handel's first London operas.

Sometime around 1717, Pepusch was appointed director of the musical establishment at Cannons, in Edgware, Middlesex, the country home of James Brydges, Earl of Carnarvon, later Duke of Chandos. Brydges had made his fortune as paymaster-general of the Duke of Marlborough's forces, and estimates of his profit from the War of the Spanish Succession run into millions of pounds. He spent it on the creating the most lavish home in the land, entirely remodelling the existing house, under the supervision of the architect James Gibbs, with decoration by Sir James Thornhill and a host of Italian sculptors and painters. The eighty-three-acre garden included a wilderness, and exotic birds, including eagles, flamingos and macaws.[25]

Brydges also spent extravagantly on his musical household, which was the largest outside the court. Over twenty musicians were employed in the orchestra, and in addition to a musical director, Brydges asked Handel to be his composer-in-residence, a post Handel probably held until 1719. Although the two composers were to some extent in competition, there does not appear to have been any animosity between them, and Pepusch's contrapuntal skill probably influenced the younger composer in what became a characteristically 'English' period of music for Handel. The eleven Chandos (or Cannons) anthems were composed during this period, as well as the masque *Acis and Galatea* – with words by John Gay and Alexander Pope – and the oratorio *Esther*. Handel also prepared for publication the scores of his eight harpsichord suites, of which the fifth in E major includes the famous variations on the melody now known as the *Harmonious Blacksmith*. Unfortunately, for romantics, the story of Handel being inspired by hearing the whistling of the local blacksmith is nothing more than that – a story, concocted in the nineteenth century.

Away from the Augustan idyll of Cannons, in the cut and thrust of the world of the theatre, Pepusch understood Handel's superior skill in the field of Italian opera, and quietly pursued his own path. Pepusch's moment of triumph did come, however, in 1728, with his involvement in the music for John Gay's hugely successful *The Beggar's Opera*, for which he wrote the overture and arranged the songs, some of which were appropriated from Handel.

The setting up of the Royal Academy in 1719 was a fascinating enterprise, with the specific intention of mounting Italian opera on a sound financial footing. Shortly after the South Sea Company had been formed – and shortly before the bubble burst – this was a time when playing the market was all the rage, and the academy was set up as a joint stock company. Each of the sixty-three subscribers guaranteed at least £200 of the company's stock, and George I, dignifying the project with his title, gave an annual subsidy of £1,000. The aim of the directors was to bring together the finest composers, singers, librettists and designers of Italian opera, and as such it brought Handel into close contact, and often rivalry, with some of the finest practitioners in each field – all of them visitors.

At the inception of the academy, Handel was given the role of 'Master of the Orchester with a Sallary', and was instructed to find singers good enough to perform on the London stage. For this purpose he went to Dresden, where he procured the services of the great castrato Senesino. Handel's first opera for the academy was *Radamisto*, premiered in April 1720, the libretto of which was dedicated to George I. But the 'free market' principles of the academy applied not only to financial, but also to artistic matters, and for the 1720–1 season Giovanni Bononcini was brought to England.[26] The first production of the season was of Bononcini's perhaps conveniently titled *Astarto*, which ran for twenty-three nights, and in his first two seasons, Bononcini's operas proved at least as popular as those of Handel. Handel, motivated by Bononcini's presence in London, is likely to have instigated the unique idea of the two of them, together with a third composer, Filippo Amadei, each setting one of the acts of the opera *Muzio Scevola*. Handel's setting of Act III, which seems to have been calculated to impress the audience, was unsurprisingly the most acclaimed.

Much was made of the comparisons between the music of Handel and Bononcini, and notoriety was achieved by the 'Epigram on the Feuds between Handel and Bononcini' written by one John Byrom:

> Some say, compar'd to Bononcini,
> That Mynheer Handel's but a Ninny;
> Others aver, that he to Handel
> Is scarcely fit to hold a Candle:
> Strange all this Difference should be
> 'Twixt Tweedle-dum and Tweedle-dee![27]

Handel was also the more accomplished politician, mixing happily with Whigs and Tories alike. At a time when the country was deeply divided, opera provided one of the most significant arenas where supporters of both parties mingled freely. As such, it had the potential to be a force for political and social change, and was a constant focus for pamphleteers and essayists. Handel was even eulogised by one anonymous poet as a figure who could heal political division with his music, which

> Our Souls so tun'd, that *Discord* grieves to find
> A whole fantastick Audience of a Mind.[28]

Neither Tweedle-dum nor Tweedle-dee was the easiest of characters, but Handel's eccentricity – sometimes described as madness – was preferred to what was seen as Bononcini's pride and arrogance. Bononcini also had the disadvantage of being a Roman Catholic, and was caught in a wave of anti-Catholic feeling in 1722. He was not re-engaged for the following season, instead becoming the protégé of the Duchess of Marlborough.[29] The way was now clear for Handel to excel himself and between January 1724 and January 1725, he wrote three contrasting masterpieces, the operas *Giulio Cesare*, *Tamerlano* and *Rodelinda*.

Another factor in the success of an opera is of course the quality of the libretto, and the relationship between composer and librettist, and in these three great operas, Handel was working with Nicola Haym. Probably of German Jewish ancestry, Haym was born in 1678 in Rome, where he made his name as a cellist. He is credited with popularising the cello in England, and his arrival in London in 1701 might have seen the instrument's first appearance in the country.[30] A composer in his own right, he also worked as librettist, and was responsible for the extremely successful adaptation of Bononcini's *Camilla* in 1706. Haym, like Handel, understood the need to accommodate English taste, which in the case of Italian opera demanded that he cut two-thirds of the existing recitative from the original libretto, and rewrite most of the remaining one third.[31]

No doubt Haym's 'uncommon Modesty, Candour, Affability'[32] and amiable qualities made for an easier relationship than the one Handel had with Paolo Rolli. Rolli, who maintained serious poetic aspirations, adapted librettos only under sufferance: 'I knock up old dramas in a new style and tack on dedications … A good drama or a bad one, what does it matter so long as it's cheap.'[33] The official librettist and Italian secretary to the academy at its foundation, Rolli was replaced, after a disagreement with the directors, by Haym in 1722. He emerges from copious letters as scheming and embittered, if perceptive, and he and Handel barely tolerated one another. In general, Handel's collaborations with Rolli produced less successful results.

If Handel's relations with Rolli were strained, those with his leading singers could be positively explosive. The *castrato* Francesco Bernardi, known as Senesino, was a turbulent character, and he and Handel had constant disagreements throughout their working relationship.[34] However, he appeared in all thirty-two of the academy's operas, including the fourteen of Handel's. The quality of the singing was the single most important factor in the success of an opera, and was reflected in the exorbitant sums the stars commanded: there are reports of Senesino being paid 2,000 guineas for the 1720–1 academy season.[35] Acting was less of a priority, with no stage director, and no extended rehearsals, and a report of Senesino's stage presence notes that 'he stands like a statue, and when occasionally he does make a gesture, he makes one directly the opposite of what is wanted'.[36]

Most famous of all was the rivalry between the leading sopranos, Francesca Cuzzoni and Faustina Bordoni. Cuzzoni arrived late in the 1722 season, after prolonged contractual wrangling, and in rehearsals for her début opera, *Ottone*, Handel had to threaten to fling her out of the window in order to persuade her to sing the aria 'Falsa imagine'. Described by Burney as an expressive and pathetic singer, she demonstrated all the insecurities typical of a prima donna. Although of an unprepossessing appearance, her singing in *Ottone* caused such a stir that a footman was compelled to shout out from the gallery 'Damme, she has a nest of nightingales in her belly'.[37]

Not content with this success, the academy ventured further into the field, and in September 1725 the *London Journal* announced that 'Signora *Faustina*, a famous Italian Lady, is coming over this Winter to rival Signora Cuzzoni'.[38] Johann Joachim Quantz, the German flautist and composer, who was in London in 1727, described Faustina's singing as 'expressive and brilliant' which, combined with her natural beauty and common sense, made her 'born for singing and acting'.[39] In his next opera *Alessandro*, Handel now had the task of writing exactly equal, but contrasting, parts in the first opera to feature both women, a task he accomplished brilliantly. With players such as Geminiani, and the brothers Pietro and Prospero Castrucci, who represented the next generation of Italian violin virtuosi, the orchestra at the Haymarket Theatre was at its peak. Handel's rivalry with Bononcini was renewed, and added to by a third composer, Attilio Ariosti. Opera was truly the talk of the town, and the sixteen performances of Handel's next opera *Admeto* played to fuller houses than ever. As a contemporary satirical pamphleteer wrote:

> it is not now, (as formerly) *i.e.*, are you High Church or Low, Whig or Tory; are you for Court or Country, King *George*, or the Pretender: but are you for *Faustina* or *Cuzzoni*, *Handel* or *Bononcini* . . . and but for the soft Strains of the Opera, which have in some Measure qualified and allay'd the native city of the *English*, Blood and Slaughter would consequently ensue.[40]

With the help of rival noblewomen to champion the causes of Cuzzoni and Faustina, the pressure could not be sustained for much longer. Egged on by catcalling, hissing and applause on both sides, during a perform-ance of Bononcini's *Astianatte* on 6 June 1727, the two women resorted to an on-stage fight, bringing the season to a hasty close.[41]

The Royal Academy never recovered from the disrepute this incident brought about. The novelty of Italian opera had worn off, houses for the following season declined, and the academy's financial position was becoming precarious. The problems were further exacerbated by the pro-duction in January 1728 at Lincoln's Inn Fields of John Gay's *Beggar's Opera*. This ballad opera was a reassertion of the power and wit of the

English song and theatrical traditions, and its political satire, whose targets included the Royal Academy itself, gave it a relevance that Italian opera, based on historical or mythological subjects, could not approach. Jonathan Swift, writing in the *Intelligencer*, took the opportunity to score some points:

> This comedy likewise exposes, with good justice, that unnatural taste for Italian music among us which is wholly unsuitable to our northern climate, and the genius of the people, whereby we are over-run with Italian effeminacy, and Italian nonsense.[42]

The 1728 season was the Royal Academy's last, but the directors allowed Handel, in partnership with the impresario Heidegger, to continue to mount operas at the King's Theatre and to use the academy's props, costumes and instruments. Handel went to Italy to engage a new cast of singers, but failed to sign up the soprano castrato sensation, Carlo Broschi, known as Farinelli. Between 1729 and 1734, Handel continued to stage new operas, including *Partenope* and *Orlando*, but became unpopular as an entrepreneur when he tried to double the price of the tickets for a lavish performance. What was seen as an autocratic style of direction became unpopular with the singers – especially Senesino, who had returned to sing for Handel – and Handel's prominence as entrepreneur was resented in certain quarters of the nobility, who regarded musicians as servants. The result was the formation of a rival company, the Opera of the Nobility, which was patronised by George II's son, Frederick, Prince of Wales, thus beginning one of the most bizarre episodes in opera history in England.

While the Opera of the Nobility took over Handel's cast of singers, and also, after their first year, the King's Theatre in Haymarket, Handel moved his new company to John Rich's newly built theatre in Covent Garden. Senesino was initially the castrato star for the Opera of the Nobility, but within a year, they had also lured Farinelli to England. At his first public performance with Farinelli, in Hasse's *Artaserse* in October 1734, Senesino was so amazed by his singing that, 'forgetting his stage character, [he] ran to Farinelli and embraced him'.[43] Aware of the need to find a counter-attraction to the world's greatest singer, Handel contracted Marie Sallé, one of the leading French dancers of the time, for the 1734–5 season. The combination of this new dance influence and of competition – ever Handel's motivation – from the rival opera company stimulated him to write two of his finest operas, *Ariodante* and *Alcina* within a few months of one another.

Veracini was also back in town, first as a violinist in the rival company, but soon also leading the orchestra in performances of his own operas. Handel attended Veracini's *Adriano in Siria* in November 1735, and aroused the Italian composer's wrath, claiming that Handel had organised a claque at the first performance. In fact, the opera ran for twenty performances, and Veracini continued to produce operas for the Opera of the Nobility. Indeed, in his last opera, *Rosalinda*, performed in 1744, long after Handel had abandoned the genre, Veracini ventured into a field Handel never did, creating an opera based on a Shakespeare play, *As You Like It*.[44] This most un-British of musical visitors clearly had an interest in British culture, for he also used a Scottish ballad tune 'Tweed's side' in his Op. 2 violin sonatas. He left England for the last time in 1745, reaching Florence despite being shipwrecked.

By 1737, it became clear that there was not enough interest in opera in London to justify the existence of both companies, and the Opera of the Nobility folded, its purpose served. But Handel's appetite for opera was not yet exhausted, and he continued to stage operas until 1741, including two written in a lighter vein, *Serse*, which includes the picturesque aria 'Ombra mai fù', popularly known as Handel's 'Largo', and *Deidamia*. This, his last opera, received only three performances, and the cool response it received was the final straw for him, provoking rumours that he intended to leave England. By this time, however, Handel was thoroughly involved in a new and different enterprise.

4 Handel (2)

An Englishman by choice

Browsing along the bookshelves of any music library, the casual reader quickly becomes able to recognise in which language any one of the multitude of Handel biographies is written, simply by the spelling of the composer's name. The process of anglicising his name took some time, and until 1720, Handel's name was generally written as it was pronounced: Hendel (or Hendell, or Hendle, etc.). Only after this time did the familiar English spelling start to be used, and presumably his name start to be mispronounced, and Georg Friedrich became George Frederick.[1] Indeed, Mattheson in his *Critca Musica* of 1725 comments that 'the English have made a Handel out of Hendel'.[2] What one writer describes as the 'Battle of the *Umlaut*' was already under way.[3]

None of this would have bothered Handel himself, who in a letter of 1731 written in German, in which English, French and Latin words are thrown in, he signs himself George Friedrich Händel. Handel's impressive but idiosyncratic command of languages was often noted: the distinguished musical historian Charles Burney never forgot the impression made on him as a youth by Handel swearing in four or five languages. Burney also notes that Handel's 'natural propensity to wit and humour, and happy manner of relating common occurrences, in an uncommon way, enabled him to throw persons and things into very ridiculous attitudes'.[4] It is also interesting to find Handel writing in 1750 to Telemann, his fellow German, in French.[5] Handel's earliest surviving letter in English, which is rather halting, dates from as late as 1734.

Handel was tall and always well dressed, handsome in his younger days, and corpulent and bow-legged in later years, in a way that was ungraceful, even comic. Descriptions of his face emphasise its openness and animation, and of his character, dry humour and benevolence, with flashes of impetuosity and wit. Reports of his large appetite for food suggest an Epicurean nature, rather than a gluttonous one. He had a fierce sense of justice, gave generously to charity, and was strongly religious. Though essentially a private man, he could be convivial and generous with his time. Though unmarried, he preferred the company of women, with whom he would often play the harpsichord. Despite the chubbiness of his hands in later years, Handel's harpsichord-playing was much admired by Burney, himself a distinguished musician: 'his touch was so smooth, and the tone of the instrument so much cherished, that his fingers seemed to grow to the keys'.[6]

After more than ten years of a somewhat nomadic existence in London, Handel made the significant move in the summer of 1723 of purchasing a lease on a house in Brook Street, in the then new West End of London; he was to live there for the rest of his life. He had just been appointed as Composer to the Chapel Royal, and Brook Street was a convenient location both for those duties at St James's Palace and for his Royal Academy activities at the theatre in the Haymarket. The house, originally not numbered, but now number twenty-five, which in 2001 became the Handel House Museum, was part of a new development which was built and inhabited by 'People of Quality'. His neighbours included an MP, members of the minor aristocracy, and many of Handel's friends and professional acquaintances. The house served not only as living quarters, but also as rehearsal space, sometimes for large ensembles, and also for business purposes, such as the sale of his scores to subscribers.[7]

In 1727, Handel took the unusual step of applying for naturalisation as a British subject. George I, in one of his last acts before his death, gave royal assent. It is not clear why Handel chose this course: he never bought the Brook Street house, even though, as a British subject, he was now able to. The timing was however fortunate, as it enabled him to take part in the coronation of George II in October 1727, and to provide his most significant contribution yet to English choral music, the Coronation Anthems. One of these, *Zadok The Priest*, has been sung at every British coronation since then. Whether the entire performance was a success remains in doubt, however, the Archbishop of Canterbury's order of service being annotated thus in respect of *The King Shall Rejoice*: 'The Anthem in Confusion: All irregular in the Music'.[8]

With the accession of George II, Handel's involvement with the royal family was stronger than ever. Handel was a contemporary of the new king and Queen Caroline, and since Handel's time in Hanover, the queen in particular had been an enthusiastic supporter and patron of the composer. The choice of Handel as composer of the Coronation Anthems, instead of his rival Maurice Greene, seems to have been made by the king himself. Handel's opera *Riccardo Primo* of 1727 was written as a tribute to George I, who died before it could be premiered; minor modification was required to adapt it to a flattering comparison of the younger George with the eponymous lion-heart. Handel later was to provide music for the marriage of Princess Anne, the Princess Royal, to William of Orange in 1734, and also for the funeral of Queen Caroline, in 1737, with his melancholy masterpiece, the anthem *The Ways of Zion Do Mourn*.

Handel had been music master to the three royal princesses since 1723. A document from that year gives the daily timetable of Princess Anne,

the eldest, and demonstrates the level of accomplishment expected: 'from
4 to 5 either practice clavecin [harpsichord] or read; after that play music
with Hendel'.[9] We have the royal children to thank for the existence of
some of Handel's small-scale chamber music, including the beautifully
crafted figured bass exercises, and possibly the sonatas for recorder and
basso continuo.

4 The rehearsal and performance room in Handel's house, 25 Brook Street,
London, *c.* 1723

The early Hanoverians were a notoriously argumentative family, and Handel's fortunes were often bound up with internal royal politics. The Opera of the Nobility was formed partly as a way for Frederick, Prince of Wales, to get back at his father, whom he detested, and it was Frederick who was the focus for anti-Handel feeling. Nonetheless, Frederick was a regular supporter of Handel, and it was possibly the absence of any payment by the prince to Handel in the 1743–4 season that provoked the observation that 'Mr. Handel and the Prince had quarrelled, which I am sorry for. Handel says that the *Prince* is quite out of *his* good graces!'[10]

By the beginning of the 1730s, therefore, Handel was well on the road to becoming an Englishman. It was something of a chance incident in 1732, however, which set in motion the train of events which was to establish Handel for ever in the nation's affection and consciousness. In February and March 1732, Bernard Gates, Master of the Chapel Royal children, mounted three performances of Handel's English oratorio *Esther*, written in 1718, at the Crown & Anchor tavern in the Strand. The tavern, which was actually a smart and spacious four-storey building on the corner of Arundel Street, was often used by private musical societies for meetings and performances. *Esther* was such a success that an unauthorised performance was mounted at the York Buildings in Villiers Street. Handel, who was at this time engaged in his usual opera season at the King's Theatre, was encouraged by his friends to give a public performance of *Esther*. The Bishop of London forbade the children of the Chapel Royal to sing in a theatre, but with a chorus of some of the other singers from the Chapel Royal and Handel's usual cast of mainly Italian singers, six performances took place at the end of the 1732 season, to great acclaim.

The success of these performances encouraged Handel to introduce oratorio into his subsequent opera seasons, and for the next nine years, until he finally dispensed with opera, he ran the two side by side. At the end of the following season, having included *Deborah* in March of 1733, Handel set off with his company to Oxford in July, where he gave five performances at the Sheldonian Theatre, including the premiere of another oratorio, *Athalia*. Newspaper reports that 3,700 people were at the premiere must be exaggerated, but Handel's only public performances in England outside London proved a huge financial success and enhanced his reputation. Rumours that he was offered, and refused, an honorary degree from the university appear to be unfounded.

English oratorio had many ingredients in its favour. It contained many of the dramatic elements of Italian opera – conflicts between good and evil, love and honour – but was of course sung in English. Because it was not staged, no expensive costumes or props were necessary. The singers sang from scores, rather than from memory, thus avoiding expensive rehearsals. Crucially, this also allowed for the presence of a chorus, which was the key to its popularity. Oratorio also allowed Handel's mature cosmopolitan style to flower. The dramatic brilliance of the Italian vocal style combined with the melodic grace of French dance music, which had been the main stylistic features of Handel's operas, were supplemented by a contrapuntal rigour derived from the German Lutheran method of choral composition, and given a distinctly English, and especially Purcellian, flavour. Handel's role as performer was also much more prominent than in opera, and an oratorio typically featured an organ concerto as overture or interval music. His performances became an important feature, and were advertised to encourage the middle classes to come to see the oratorios.

Handel therefore pioneered two musical forms at once, English oratorio and the organ concerto. The concertos were so successful that six of them were published as his Op. 4 in 1736. Perhaps more important was that Handel now became the focus for suggestions from friends and literary acquaintances for new subjects and sources for his attention. His friend Newburgh Hamilton adapted Dryden's *Alexander's Feast*, an ode for St Cecilia. This was Handel's first attempt at setting the work of a famous English poet, and its first performance in February 1736 was his biggest success yet in the genre. Two more Old Testament themes were the basis for the oratorios *Saul* and *Israel in Egypt*, both premiered in 1739. These marked the beginning of Handel's collaboration with the librettist Charles Jennens, which was to prove the most fruitful partnership of all.

For Hamilton, Jennens and others, having a libretto set by Handel was of course a vehicle for their work reaching a potentially huge audience. The task itself was merely one of adapting an existing text, which these minor poets were happy to undertake, in order to encourage Handel to ever greater heights of artistic achievement, in the creation of consummate English artworks.[11] Indeed, in February 1740, this dream was achieved with *L'Allegro, il Penseroso ed il Moderato*, Handel's setting of Jennens's adaptation of two poems by John Milton. The popularity and the excellence of the work seem to have helped to rescue Milton's poetry from obscurity.

The autumn of 1739 also saw the writing of Handel's instrumental masterpiece, the twelve *Concerti Grossi*, Op. 6. Incredibly, all twelve were written in a single creative burst of just over a month and, although they were inspired partly by the need for interval music, they are superbly crafted classic works in the mould of Corelli. The publication of the set early in 1740 was planned on a subscription basis. It is easy to imagine that Handel was conscious of setting a new standard of excellence for English orchestral music and, unusually for him, of writing with posterity in mind.

Handel's adoption of more definably English musical genres somewhat helped to improve his standing with critical commentators of the time. Alexander Pope, who had warmly endorsed the success of *The Beggar's Opera* and in particular for the fact it dealt a body blow to Italian opera, praised Handel in his *The New Dunciad* of 1742 as the leader of the rebellion against opera. Horace Walpole, often merciless in his critique of 'the Handel phenomenon', grudgingly acknowledged that Handel's oratorio concerts were more popular than the operas staged by the new company of Charles Sackville, Lord Middlesex (later second Duke of Dorset), which had taken over the running of opera at the King's Theatre. Sir Isaac Newton, however, on seeing Handel play the harpsichord, had *'nothing worthy to remark but the elasticity of his fingers'*.[12]

English composers of the time continued to have a mixed reaction to their German rival. Handel's relationship with Maurice Greene, who repeatedly bore the brunt of Handel's competitive instinct, was openly hostile. Greene was repeatedly overlooked in favour of Handel when music was required for royal ceremonies, and Greene's first attempt at oratorio, *The Song of Deborah and Barak*, was immediately eclipsed by Handel's own setting, *Deborah*. Even the opening night of Handel's *Alexander's Feast* seems to have been timed to coincide with Greene's investiture of Steward at the Sons of the Clergy Festival. Thomas Arne was another who resented Handel's exalted status, regarding Handel as 'a tyrant and usurper'.[13] William Boyce, on the other hand, cheerfully referred to the delicate subject of Handel's borrowings, by saying 'he takes other men's pebbles and converts them into diamonds'.[14]

Perhaps the most peculiar, and most damaging, response from his colleagues was that of Handel's close friend, the French designer Joseph Goupy, with whom Handel had worked on several of the academy operas. In the late 1740s, Goupy produced several versions of a hideous caricature of Handel as a pig or boar, seated at the organ, entitled variously 'The Charming Brute' and 'The Harmonious Boar'. The picture cruelly satirised what Goupy saw as Handel's gluttony, vanity, liking for loud orchestral writing, and possibly his wealth through patronage. Clearly the two friends had fallen out, but Laetitia Hawkins, daughter of the music historian Sir John, relates a hardly credible account of the source of the dispute. Apparently, Handel had invited Goupy to dinner, having apologised for the necessary frugality of the meal:

> Soon after dinner, Handel left the room, and his absence was so long that Goupy at last, for want of other employ, strolled into the adjoining back-room, and walking up to the window, which looked diagonally on that of a small third room, he saw his host sitting at a table covered with such delicacies as he had lamented his inability to afford his friend. Goupy, to whom possibly such viands had little less relish than to his host, was so enraged, that he quitted the house abruptly, and published the engraving or etching . . . in which Handel figures as a hog in the midst of dainties.[15]

This insight into Handel's personal life, if true, is rare. His discretion, not to say secrecy, in private matters, which was a great advantage in the political gaming that surrounded his rivalry with Bononcini, the Opera of the Nobility and others, perhaps also contributed to eventual problems with his health. Curiously, Handel's health is the one area of his personal life about which a good deal is known. The 1736–7 season was a hectic one, in which no fewer than twelve works, five of them new, were performed, both opera and oratorio, and it was this season that finally saw off the challenge of the nobility's rival opera company. Handel, whose huge appetite for work was over-stretched by April 1737, suffered what was described as a paralytic disorder in his right side. He was treated with strong medicine, and spent six weeks at the vapour-baths in Aix-la-Chapelle (now Aachen, Germany) which effected a complete cure. He suffered similarly in 1743 and again in 1745, and some reports of his illness make reference to an associated mental disorder, even madness. These illnesses tended to coincide with periods of stress, and the decades of continuous work, much of it meeting deadlines and beating off competition, were beginning to take their toll.

By the beginning of the 1740s, Handel, legally an Englishman, living permanently in London, and thoroughly engaged in writing specifically English music largely accepted by an English audience, would struggle to be considered a musical visitor any longer, and, strictly speaking, we should leave his story here. However, three events of the 1740s – the writing of *Messiah*, military events at home and abroad, and the formation of the Foundling Hospital – were to ensure that Handel would become part of the fabric of musical and social life in England in his later years, and would have a profound influence on the future of English music.

Indeed, for all Handel's established position in London, and his rising status as a cult figure, the late 1730s and early 1740s had been unsettled times for him. As well as his battles with ill health, Handel was at severe financial risk, and his self-managed attempts to win back the affection of his opera audience had failed. Even the oratorios *Saul* and *Israel in Egypt*, despite their high quality and novel effects, failed to impress. Handel was also fighting with writer's block, and as much as four-fifths of the music for *Israel in Egypt* uses borrowed material. In addition, Handel was being pursued for the payment of the salary of one of his singers, Anna Maria Strada del Pò, and was saved from a court case and bankruptcy with the help of a benefit concert in March 1738 attended by nearly 1,300 people. In addition, the winter of 1739–40, one of the coldest on record, nearly forced Handel to abandon his season at Lincoln's Inn Fields, as did a group of his enemies, who employed ruffians to tear down posters and discourage audiences from venturing in.[16]

Rumours of Handel being a spent force, and of his intentions to leave England, had abounded since the late 1730s. Having finally left opera behind, Handel was theoretically less attached to London, and indeed, in the autumn of 1741, he left for Ireland, for Dublin. He had with him the newly composed score of *Messiah*, with libretto by Charles Jennens. The oratorio was Jennens's idea, and subtly combines scriptures from the Old and New Testaments to show how Jesus' coming was predicted in the Old Testament. There is no story as such, and no dramatic content: this was unusual for oratorio, but it meant there was virtually no room for recitative, and the 'action' consists only in arias and choruses, ideal for a British audience. Jennens wrote in July 1741: 'I hope [Handel] will lay out his whole Genius & Skill upon it, that the Composition may excell all his former Compositions, as the Subject excells every other subject. The Subject is Messiah.'[17] In his darkest hour, seemingly with the whole world against him, Handel delved deep within himself, and in the space of twenty-four days in August and September 1741, produced his masterwork.

Dublin was at this time Britain's second city, and the Lord Lieutenant, the king's representative, employed a band of musicians at the court at Dublin Castle. The musical household was run by the outstanding violinist Matthew Dubourg, a former pupil of Geminiani, and with two major public theatres and two cathedral choirs, the city had a lively musical scene. Handel chose for his concert season the recently opened Neale's New Musick Hall in Fishamble Street. Here he ran two highly successful subscription series in the winter season, before the premiere of *Messiah* on 13 April 1742, which was given in support of three charities. Handel donated all the proceeds to these charities, and 142 prisoners were freed when their debts had been settled by the Society of Relieving Prisoners. In order to accommodate the largest possible audience, ladies were requested to come 'without hoops' and gentlemen without swords.[18] The work was rapturously received by the packed house, and particular praise was given to the alto singer Susannah Cibber, sister of the composer Thomas Arne, for her performance of 'He was despised', and Handel declared himself happy with the standard of the playing in Dubourg's orchestra. Members of both the cathedral choirs took part, but not before Jonathan Swift, Dean of St Patrick's Cathedral, who was by this time close to mental breakdown, had forbidden his choristers to 'assist at a club of fiddlers in Fishamble Street'.[19]

Handel returned to London in August after a long Dublin season, confident that he could now survive without further recourse to opera. He resisted an offer to write operas for Lord Middlesex's company, despite considerable financial incentives and social pressures. *Messiah* was eventually given its English premiere at Covent Garden Theatre on 23 March 1743, but not before an article had appeared in a London newspaper, questioning the theatre's suitability as a venue for a religious work. Meanwhile, some Dissenters objected to their being performed in church, and the evangelical preacher John Newton delivered fifty sermons attacking the work. As a result, the work was advertised as 'A New Sacred Oratorio', and the three performances passed off without controversy. Its reception was only lukewarm, however, and Handel was reluctant to perform it for the rest of the decade.

Correspondence between Handel and Jennens reveals the extraordinary arrogance and high-handedness of the latter, whom Dr Johnson dubbed 'Solyman the Magnificent'.[20] Handel uniquely in his letters, other than those to royalty, adopts a humble, almost servile tone, but clearly understood Jennens's value to him. Although initially happy with the work, Jennens quickly reverts to type: 'in the main, a fine Composition, notwithstanding some weak parts, which he was too idle & too obstinate to retouch', and elsewhere, 'His Messiah has disappointed me ... I shall put no more Sacred Words into his hands, to be thus abus'd'.[21]

Indeed, Handel was by now receiving librettos to set in much the same way that current-day film stars receive scripts to read, and these resulted in a number of one-off collaborations. Even his close friend Mrs Delany tried her hand with an adaptation of Milton's *Paradise Lost*, which Handel however did not set.[22] Handel's productivity in the two years after his return to London was high, stimulated by competition, this time from Lord Middlesex's opera company. Despite fine new works, including *Semele* and *Belshazzar*, his last collaboration with Jennens, by the spring of 1745 Handel was struggling with an over-ambitious programme of subscription performances, some of which had to be cancelled.

Handel was lucky, though, that military and political events worked in his favour. The Europe of the 1740s was dominated by the War of the Austrian Succession, in which Britain experienced mixed fortunes. George II's victory at Dettingen in Germany in 1743, the last ever battle in which a British monarch led his troops, provided Handel with an opportunity to write a patriotic *Te Deum* and anthem. Perhaps because of the less than glorious manner of victory – George's horse apparently bolted, and created panic in the French ranks – the celebrations were muted, and Handel's music, which had been written for the expected large-scale thanksgiving at St Paul's Cathedral, was instead used for a service in the small chapel at St James's Palace.

Closer to home, the Jacobite rebellion of 1745, led by Bonnie Prince Charlie, caused alarm amongst Londoners. The 'Young Pretender', claiming the English throne for the Stuarts, made swift progress through Scotland and into England, and by December had reached Derby. Handel contributed some morale-boosting songs to the cause, including 'Stand round, my brave boys', but also quickly put together the *Occasional Oratorio*, which served as a prayer for the defeat of the rebellion.

At the same time, Middlesex's opera company had brought Christoph Willibald Gluck to London. Handel was no longer interested in opera, and so had no need to consider Gluck as a rival. He was reported, however, as having remarked that Gluck knew no more counterpoint than his cook. Gluck was a great admirer of Handel, and there appears to have been a good relationship between the two composers. Gluck also witnessed the new naturalistic style of acting of David Garrick, and much later, claimed that he owed the study of nature in his operas to his stay in England. Gluck was also drawn into the fervour of the time, and produced *La Caduta de' Giganti*, a tribute to the Duke of Cumberland, who was the commander of the king's forces. The work was not a great success and Handel is said to have advised Gluck about English taste: 'what the English like is something they can beat time to, something that hits them straight on the drum of the ear.'[23]

The defeat of the rebellion did not materialise until April 1746, when George II's younger son, the notorious Duke of Cumberland, routed the Jacobite rebels at the battle of Culloden. Handel's swift response was the composition of the oratorio *Judas Maccabaeus*, in which 'Butcher' Cumberland, as he became known, is effectively compared with the eponymous hero, who had led Jewish resistance to Syrian oppression about 160 BC. This work was a stirring and popular success from its first performance in April 1747, and was subsequently used in patriotic military celebrations across Europe. Such was the income it provided that Handel subsequently abandoned the subscription series in favour of tickets for individual concerts. His next two oratorios, *Alexander Balus* and *Joshua*, both performed in 1748, exploited the success of *Judas* in celebrating the deeds of biblical military heroes.

In October of the same year, the Treaty of Aix-la-Chapelle was signed, bringing to an end the protracted war in Europe, and even before this, plans were afoot to celebrate the peace with an elaborate display of fireworks. Nearly nine months' work was involved in planning the event, which was to be held in Green Park. An enormous wooden building was specially built, and Italian architects and designers were hired to plan the fireworks display. The music, which Handel was commissioned to write, was also planned on a huge scale; the overture was the longest single movement he ever composed, and was scored for twenty-four oboes, nine horns, nine trumpets, three sets of timpani, twelve bassoons and a contra-bassoon. Against the wishes of the king, who wanted only 'martial instruments' to perform, Handel also added strings to the band. Such was the public interest in the event that a rehearsal was held at Vauxhall Gardens on 21 April 1749, six days before the event itself; 12,000 people are said to have attended.[24] Though the music was a success, the event was marred by a part of the wooden building catching fire and causing a stampede.

In looking for a chance to perform the *Music for the Royal Fireworks* again, Handel chanced upon the new and fashionable world of charitable foundations, when he offered a performance of his music at the new Foundling Hospital, in Lamb's Conduit Fields, now Coram's Fields to raise money for the building of a new chapel. The hospital, which educated and oversaw the upbringing of abandoned children, required huge funds, and had already attracted the services of William Hogarth, who painted a portrait of the founder Thomas Coram. The concert took place in May 1749, and included an anthem *Blessed Are They that Considereth the Poor*, now known as the Foundling Hospital Anthem, which included the 'Hallelujah' Chorus. The following year, *Messiah* was given there, and was such a success – a thousand people attended – that it had to be repeated. Handel was made a governor of the hospital, and he presented an organ to the chapel. Most important of all, these performances of *Messiah* established the work in the popular consciousness, and set a new fashion for attending Handel's oratorios. At last Handel's music was beginning to reach a wider audience, and his reputation, for so long something he had to strive for, was now secure as 'the Great and Good Mr. Handel'.

The end of the 1740s was the final creative peak in Handel's long career, and physical decline began to take its toll. During the composition of his last oratorio *Jephtha* early in 1751, Handel was struck by blindness in his left eye, and forced to stop composing. There is a pathetic note to this effect from the composer on the corner of the page in the manuscript, written in German. Although he was able to resume work, he never regained his fluency of composition. Handel employed as amanuensis the organist and composer J. C. Smith the younger, who had been Handel's pupil. From 1754, when Handel could no longer direct performances, Smith took charge of the Foundling Hospital oratorio performances.

In his last years, Handel unsurprisingly became increasingly reclusive and was a much more regular churchgoer at the newly built St George's, Hanover Square. There are mixed reports of the now blind and infirm composer. Some emphasise the sense of loss experienced by an audience so well used to seeing Handel's strong and powerful presence. One such is the report of William Coxe, Smith's stepson, who observed that when the audience heard the aria from Samson,

> Total eclipse – no sun, no moon,
> All dark amid the blaze of noon.

and could see the blind composer sitting by the organ, many were moved to tears.[25] Other reports tell of Handel's harpsichord playing being better than ever and, before he quit public performance, he still played his organ concertos, but with improvised solo sections. Characteristically, he managed to invest the composition of *Jephtha* with his own struggles; indeed, the first instance of his blindness may have been brought on by the dark and terrible story of the Israelite warrior.

Handel was active in seeking a cure for his ills, and in the summer of 1751 he travelled to Bath and Cheltenham to take the waters. The series of eye operations he underwent were unfortunately unsuccessful, and the third and last of these, in August 1758 at Tunbridge Wells, was by the quack oculist, 'Chevalier' John Taylor, who had also operated on J. S. Bach. In the case of both composers, a brief recovery was followed by total blindness, and within a few months, perhaps not coincidentally, death. Handel died on 14 April 1759, and at his own request was buried in Westminster Abbey, where 3,000 attended his funeral.

If the praise heaped on him in the latter part of his life was extraordinary, the reverence with which he was treated after it and the attention his music merited was unprecedented. Within a year, Mainwaring's biography, the first of a composer in book form, appeared, and was translated into German and published in Hamburg, with some additions, by Johann Mattheson in 1761. George III, of whom Handel is supposed to have said, 'while that boy lives, my music will never want a protector', succeeded his grandfather as king in 1760, and the accuracy of Handel's prediction was borne out. The king also supported the idea of a complete edition of Handel's works, which was begun by Samuel Arnold in 1787, and lent his patronage to the Handel Commemorations of 1784 and following years. The 1784 event was intended as a centenary celebration of his birth (mistakenly inscribed as '1684' on the Roubiliac monument of Handel in Westminster Abbey), and was supposed to be 'a performance ... on so grand and magnificent a scale as no other part of the world could equal'.[26] More than 500 performers took part, before a vast audience, and the event, which was attended by the whole royal family, had all the pomp and ceremony of a coronation. The annual commemoration continued until 1791, when Joseph Haydn was in the audience and was so deeply moved by the experience.

Events such as these clearly had more to do with patriotic fervour than an appreciation of his music. But it could be argued that Handel's music was used after his death to help foster both a new sense of nationhood, and a new religious mainstream in Britain, and even a new popular role for the monarchy.[27] Unfortunately, the view of his music became increasingly skewed by oversized performances, particularly of *Messiah*. Most provincial musical festivals in the early nineteenth century featured a performance of the work, often in the adaptation made by Mozart. Huge Handel festivals took place at the Crystal Palace between 1857 and 1926, and the high water mark was achieved in the 1883 event with more than 4,500 performers taking part. George Bernard Shaw suggested making it a capital offence to perform a Handel oratorio with more than eighty performers. Also by the nineteenth century, fake Handel memorabilia were in abundance: not just the invented story of the 'Harmonious Blacksmith', but items of furniture and other relics supposed to have belonged to Handel, and his name was even attached to portraits not of him. Handel had, in effect, become the first merchandised composer.

But his most distinctive 'product', of course, was his music, and the distinctive sound of his religious and ceremonial music has influenced all such music subsequently written in England. More than any visitor to Britain before or since, musical or otherwise, Handel has come to be identified with his adopted country.

5 Wolfgang Amadeus Mozart

'I am a dyed-in-the-wool Englishman'

It may seem strange at first sight that Mozart, at the age of twenty-six, should boast to his father that he considered himself a 'dyed-in-the-wool Englishman' considering that he had only spent fifteen months in England as a young boy. This fondness was shared by his family, especially his sister Nannerl and to a large extent his father, Leopold.

The facts of Mozart's early life are fairly well known. Born Johannes Chrysostomus Wolfgangus Theophilus Mozart in Salzburg on 17 January 1756, he was the last of seven children; Wolfgang and his sister, who was four-and-a-half years his senior, were the only survivors. His early genius was soon recognised. At the age of four Wolfgang tried to teach himself composition, inventing his own system of musical notation, and also taught himself the violin.[1] By the age of five he had composed an *Andante* for piano, K. 1a. He was taught the harpsichord by his father, who was the deputy *Kapellmeister* and violinist at the archbishop's court; he took the children to Munich the following year to perform at court, and later travelled to Vienna to show off their skills before the Emperor Francis I. Leopold embarked on a more ambitious journey in 1763, a grand tour across Europe, which took them to Paris. They played at Versailles, in the presence of Louis XIV, with great success. The family stayed in Paris for five months, during which Wolfgang's early compositions, duos for harpsichord and violin, were published. Leopold wrote home to his landlord and friend, Lorenz Hagenauer, at this time: 'Picture to yourself the furore which they will make in the world, when people read on the title page that they have been composed by a seven-year-old child.'

There had been no definite intentions to go on to England when the tour was planned, though Leopold had long wished to do so. This became a reality through two English aristocrats at the French court, John Russell, fourth Duke of Bedford, and his son Francis who, much taken with Wolfgang's talents, encouraged the Mozarts to visit England. With the recent ending of the Seven Years' War, travel between the two countries was again possible. The Mozarts were recommended to the ambassador in London: the way was now clear for the visit.

Leopold's motives for bringing his family to England were mixed. He certainly wished to display the talents of Wolfgang and Nannerl to a wider audience, and also benefit from social esteem gained by performing in exalted circles.[2] Leopold also recognised the financial rewards which such a visit offered. He wrote later from London: 'I shall spend at least the whole winter here, and, God willing, I shall make in London my chief profit of some thousands of gulden.'[3]

He also relished the thought of being a pioneer: 'I am now in a city which no-one at our Salzburg court has ever yet dared to visit, and which perhaps no-one will ever visit in future.' Leopold had earlier taken the precaution of learning English – 'It will do no harm to have someone at the Salzburg court who speaks English: one never knows how handy it might be.'[4] He was encouraged, too, by the success of the late George Frederick Handel, who had gained popularity with all levels of society.

The Mozarts travelled to the French coast, and embarked at Calais on 19 April. Leopold grumbled 'whoever had too much money should just take a journey from Paris to London: for his purse will certainly be lightened'. After a rough crossing of the Channel which Leopold particularly found distressing, the family reached London. They spent their first night at the White Bear, Piccadilly, and then moved to accommodation owned by a barber, John Cousins, in Cecil Court, now No. 19, off St Martins Lane, conveniently situated for access to the musical activities of London. Leopold was anxious that his family should not be seen as foreigners. Accordingly, new outfits were purchased and he commented: 'You cannot imagine what my wife and little girl look like in English hats, and I and our big Wolfgang in English clothes.'[5]

Thanks to the fulsome letters of recommendation, within five days of their arrival the Mozarts were summoned to Buckingham House to perform before the young royal couple, George III and his wife, Queen Charlotte. They were both devoted to music: George played the violin, flute and harpsichord, and Charlotte was a reasonably good singer, and also a harpsichord player. Leopold was greatly impressed by the friendly way in which they were received. After performing, they were given a present of 24 guineas on leaving the king's apartment. A week later when the Mozarts were walking in St James's Park, the royal carriage passed them: the king opened the window, leaned out, waved and nodded to them, and especially saluted Master Wolfgang.

There was a second appearance at court on 19 May, before the king and queen, and the two princes, the Dukes of York and Gloucester, and Charlotte's brother. This time Leopold described in more detail the music which was played. The king placed before Wolfgang, to read at sight, works by Georg Christoph Wagenseil, Johann Christian Bach and Karl Friedrich Abel, and his favourite composer, Handel; this was readily accomplished. Wolfgang also played the organ, and accompanied the queen in an aria. Finally, he took the bass part of airs by Handel and extemporised new melodies for them. Every one was amazed at the boy's skills. 'What he knew when he left Salzburg,' Leopold noted, 'is a mere shadow compared with what he knows now. It exceeds all that one can imagine.'

Leopold's main objective was to give public concerts at which the children would perform, but this plan ran into difficulties because of Wolfgang's illness and the need to find a suitable date for the accompanying orchestra. Eventually, the first concert was held at the Great Room in Spring Gardens, St James's Park, on 5 June, the day after the king's birthday, when the cream of society would be in town. The programme included a double harpsichord concerto played by Nannerl and Wolfgang. Over 200 people, including the French ambassador, were present. Both artistically and financially, the concert was a success, Leopold remarking on 'the shock of taking in one hundred guineas in three hours'.

Leopold was a skilful publicist. In the advertisement in the press for the concert, he used purple prose. The concert, he stated, was intended 'to shew to the Public the greatest Prodigy that Europe or that even Human Nature has to boast of. Every Body will be struck with Admiration to hear them ... It surpasses all Understanding or all Imagination'.[6]

Leopold Mozart was a keen observer of the customs and the everyday behaviour in different countries, and his comments on England and the English at this time are often full of insight. Besides mentioning the opulence of Vauxhall, with its thousand glass lamps, and Ranelagh, on the north side of the River Thames, he was struck by their meritocratic nature. The admission fees – one shilling for Vauxhall and half-a-crown for Ranelagh – 'makes every man an equal – no standing with bare head before a lord'. Leopold was impressed by the working men's eagerness to seek information relating to issues affecting them and their freedom to lodge complaints.[7]

At a less serious level Leopold, on the topic of ill health, informed Hagenauer: 'I must tell you that in England there is a kind of native complaint, which is called "a *cold*". That is why you hardly ever see people wearing summer clothes. They all wear cloth garments.' He noted that the English seemed to have a kettle on the fire all day, that the beer was very strong, and that the 'Roasted Beef was the best in the world' but disliked the 'Plumb Pudding'. The dislike of France so soon after the ending of the war was noticed. 'If the street lads see anyone in Frenchified dress they shout *Buger French*.'[8]

As Nannerl and Wolfgang had been given no formal education, Leopold at least ensured that on their travels the children were taken to the well-known sights. Nannerl kept a diary while she was in London which gives a good idea of these broadening experiences. Besides the usual round of Westminster Abbey, the Tower of London, St Paul's Cathedral, Somerset

5 The house at 180 Ebury Street, Pimlico, where the Mozarts stayed during Leopold Mozart's recuperation from severe illness, 1764

House and the Monument, there were other impressive places: Kew Gardens, where a royal palace was situated, as well as the recently opened British Museum where they saw the library, many antiquities, birds, fish, insects, and fruit, globes of the world and the stars. Nannerl also describes a visit to a 'small park' where they saw a young elephant, and a donkey 'that has white and coffee brown stripes, and so even that no one could paint them better'.[9]

At the beginning of July 1764 Leopold had planned to take the family to Tunbridge Wells, Kent, by mail coach. As he explained to Hagenauer: 'There are wells there and it lies in the corner between the east and the south. In July and August many of the nobility assemble in Tunbridge, for now nobody who has means and leisure remains in London.'

This plan, to widen their circle of acquaintances, and possibly to improve opportunities for performance, was not carried out owing to the sudden serious illness of Leopold. On 8 July, the family were invited to a concert to be held at the house of Sackville Tufton, eighth Earl of Thanet, in Grosvenor Square. Unable to obtain a coach Leopold sent Nannerl and Wolfgang ahead by sedan chair, and he followed behind on foot. Within a few days his tonsils had swollen and he suffered stomach pains. Bleeding and purging had little effect but he was treated successfully by a cousin of Emanuel Sipurtini, a Dutch Sephardic Jew, who was a cellist and composer. As a mark of his gratitude, Leopold attempted to convert Sipurtini to Catholicism.[10]

For the next eleven weeks, Leopold was an invalid who needed constant care. In order to speed up his convalescence, the family moved on 6 August to a village two miles from London, Chelsea, which was noted for its healthy situation. 'I am now in a spot outside the town, in order to get more appetite and fresh strength from the good air. It has one of the most beautiful views in the world. Wherever I turn my eyes I only see gardens, and in the distance the finest castles.' The Mozarts took up residence at Five Fields Row (now 180 Ebury Street) which had its own delightful garden.

One of the consequences of Leopold's illness was the need for silence in the household. The clavier was not to be played and Leopold was not well enough to continue giving music lessons to the children. Thrown back on his own resources, the eight-year-old Wolfgang composed his first two or possibly three symphonies, K. 16 in E flat, K. 17 in B flat and K. 19 in D. These three-movement works show a remarkable maturity. Nannerl later recorded that whilst composing one of the symphonies Wolfgang said to her, 'remind me to give something good to the horn'.[11] He also passed the days sketching out little pieces in what is now known as the London (Chelsea) Notebook K.15a-ss.

Throughout Wolfgang's childhood he had been submissive to all of Leopold's demands. As his father and teacher, Leopold determined the pieces which Wolfgang should learn and all his orders were obeyed without question. Sometimes when Wolfgang had been practising all day, and Leopold later demanded that he resume, Wolfgang did so without protest. One early biographer claimed that, in order to avoid his parents' displeasure Wolfgang would not accept the smallest amount of food which was offered him at receptions, without permission. Leopold particularly used the psychology of reward and punishment to retain the maximum power over his son.

When Leopold had recovered from his illness the family moved back to London in September, renting accommodation from a corset-maker, Thomas Williamson, in Thrift Street (now 20 Frith Street) in Soho. There was now much lost ground to be made up after their enforced absence from the London music scene. Leopold grumbled to Hagenauer about this time: 'I shall have to use every effort to win over the aristocracy and this will take a lot of galloping round and hard work.' By November he calculated that the previous five months had cost him over 170 guineas. In addition to this he had had to bear the expense of engraving and printing six sonatas for keyboard and violin, or transverse flute, K. 10–15, which Wolfgang had written in the autumn. A number of Wolfgang's compositions were copied by Leopold, thus saving the high cost of a shilling a sheet demanded by London copiers. During the concert season there were fewer opportunities to perform as London was swarming with musicians at this time. But perhaps the biggest worry was the sudden cessation of royal patronage. Their third summons to Buckingham House to play before the royal couple on 25 October proved to be the last one, even though the Mozarts stayed on in London for another nine months. It has been surmised that at some stage Leopold had been offered a royal invitation for the family to settle in England, which he had rejected, and thus fell out of favour.[12]

One composer who made a lasting impression on the young Wolfgang at this time was Johann Christian Bach, the seventh and last son of Johann Sebastian Bach. He had held a number of posts in Berlin and Milan, but on receiving a commission from the King's Theatre, London to write two operas for the 1762–3 season, he settled in London. Christian spent the remaining twenty years of his life in England. He was soon appointed Music Master to Queen Charlotte, gave music lessons, accompanied George III on his flute, organised chamber concerts and directed the queen's band.[13] It has been claimed that it was due to Christian's influence that the Mozarts had received preferential treatment in performing before the royal couple, as visiting musicians were not likely to be introduced at court without his recommendation. Christian was a popular musician in the royal household. His keyboard concertos Op. 1 had been dedicated to the queen with the sixth concerto containing a set of variations on *God Save the King*. The Mozarts would have heard his popular *Vauxhall Songs*, and Bach had probably made the manuscript of his six symphonies Op. 3 available to the Mozarts before publication.[14] Christian was greatly taken with Wolfgang's musical ability. There was the famous occasion when, during

6 Ticket for the first Bach–Abel concert, the Great Room, Spring Gardens

the final appearance of the Mozarts at court, he took Wolfgang on his knee and the two played alternately bar by bar, on the same harpsichord, extemporising for two hours in the presence of the king and queen.

The older composer's influence on Mozart's musical style is obvious. Christian had published a set of six sonatas for harpsichord with violin or flute as Op. 6 the year before, thus providing a ready model for Wolfgang's six sonatas, K. 10–15, for the same combination. Leopold had written to Hagenauer: 'Wolfgang greets you from the clavier, where he is playing through *Kapellmeister* Bach's trios.' Again, Christian's Op. 3 Symphonies were probably the stylisic model for Wolfgang's B flat major Symphony K. 17 and the D major K. 19,[15] and particularly their instrumental style of 'almost feminine sweetness' and *andantes* of great beauty.[16] A few years later, Wolfgang arranged three of Christian's sonatas from his Op. 5 as keyboard concertos.

As early as May 1764 Leopold had observed that Wolfgang was becoming interested in composing an opera. In Christian's operas at the King's Theatre the castrato Giovanni Manzuoli was a sensation. Wolfgang took singing lessons from him and proceeded to write his first Italian operatic aria, *Va, da furor portata* K. 21 which was probably performed in London in 1765. On learning of Christian's death in 1782, Wolfgang paid him a touching musical tribute; in the andante main theme of his Piano Concerto No. 12 in A, K. 414, Wolfgang quoted from Bach's opera, *La calamita del cuor*, which he would have heard in London.[17] Wolfgang wrote to his father on 10 April 1782: 'You probably know already that the English Bach is dead? What a loss to the world of music!'[18]

A further source of inspiration to the young composer was the establishment of the Bach–Abel concert series which began in January 1765. Karl Friedrich Abel, the bass viol player and composer, had been one of J. S. Bach's pupils, and therefore knew Christian. Abel settled in England in 1759, and like Christian remained there for the rest of his short life. The two men shared lodgings in Soho and both held appointments as court musicians to the king and queen. They mounted a series of influential concerts at Carlisle House, Soho Square, near to where the Mozarts had moved. Many eminent instrumental and vocal artists appeared at the subscription series, which included such curiosities as an English musician Mr Davies, and his two daughters, Marianne and Cecilia, who performed on musical glasses: and a woman conductor, Mrs Chazal, who was also a composer, organist and singer.[19]

The first season of six concerts was so successful that the number was increased to fifteen in the following year. Large numbers of eager visitors had attended the concerts in the sumptuously appointed rooms but these were limited to 400 ladies and gentlemen in the second season. The Mozarts would dearly have wished to have participated, in order to restabilise their finances. As Baron Grimm, a friend of Leopold's in Paris, wrote to the king's brother, the Duke of York: 'If His Royal Highness would extend his protection to the Mozart children, their concert would certainly succeed and the problem would be resolved.'[20] It was to no avail.

Abel, who directed alternate performances and appeared also as bass viol soloist, like Christian, acted as mentor to Wolfgang. His influence on the young boy's compositions can also be seen. The Symphony in E minor K. 18, long attributed to Wolfgang, is in fact a copy of one of Abel's symphonies which was no doubt transcribed for study purposes.[21] Wolfgang must have admired Abel, for, on the latter's death, brought on by excessive drinking, he used the theme of the refrain from Abel's Violin Sonata Op. 5 No. 5 in the rondo of his own Violin Sonata K. 526.[22]

The six sonatas for harpsichord, violin or flute which Wolfgang wrote in the autumn and dedicated to Queen Charlotte had been engraved at some expense. On 19 January 1765, a copy was sent to the queen accompanied by a lengthy and flattering eulogy. The queen must have welcomed them, for Leopold reported that she had presented Wolfgang with 50 guineas.

Leopold complained that by postponing the summoning of Parliament by two months, the king 'had dealt upon the whole a severe blow at all the arts and sciences'. In addition, he claimed that 'this winter nobody is making much money except Manzuoli and a few others in the opera'. Leopold hoped that a public concert, given by Wolfgang and Nannerl at the Little Theatre, Haymarket, would help to restore the family's finances. In the event, the concert was twice postponed, from 15 to 18 February, and again until 21 February, when it took place. The concert was timed for 6 p.m., for as the advertisement stated: 'It will not hindering [*sic*] the Nobility and Gentry from meeting in other Assemblies on the same Evening.' The only known detail of the programme was that 'All the Overtures will be from the Composition of this astonishing Composer, only eight Years old'. The concert did not attract as many of the nobility as was hoped; receipts amounted to only 100 guineas.

Disillusioned, Leopold told Hagenauer that he had 'decided deliberately after mature reconsideration and several sleepless nights' to leave London at the beginning of May 'as I will not bring up my children in such a dangerous place, where the majority of the inhabitants have no religion and where one only has evil examples before one'. Faced with the need to build up funds for their departure, Leopold resorted to more desperate measures. He placed an advertisement in the press announcing the family's forthcoming departure, and offering the public a chance, at the cost of half a guinea, to attend a performance of vocal and instrumental music given by the children, and also to visit their lodgings in Thrift Street between midday and 3 p.m. every day to 'not only hear this young Music Master and his Sister perform in private; but likewise try his surprising

A Solo on the Viola de Gamba

Mr Abel

Published as the Act by E. Harding 132 Fleet Street July 1787

7 Caricature of Karl Friedrich Abel, 1787

musical capacity by giving him any Thing to play at Sight, or any music without Bass which he will write upon the Spot, without recurring to his Harpsichord'. This enterprise must have been of only limited success for by 9 April, another advertisement had announced that the price had been reduced to five shillings, and the public were invited to call any time.[23]

The final public appearance of Wolfgang and Nannerl was on 13 May at Hickford's Great Room, Brewer Street. It seems likely that they performed a concerto written for two claviers by Wagenseil but performed on one instrument, in an arrangement by Leopold Mozart. It was played on a superb two-manual harpsichord built for Frederick the Great by the eminent harpsichord maker, Burkhardt Tschudi, better known by his Anglicised name Burkat Shudi, another London resident. However, the highlight of the programme was a performance of Wolfgang's sonata for four hands, K. 19d, played on one instrument, which Leopold claimed was the first such sonata of its kind. One Salzburg newspaper publishing an account of the concert, probably written by Leopold himself, described 'Tschudi's extraordinary instrument played for the first time by the most extraordinary clavier player of this world, namely, the very celebrated nine-year-old maestro of music, Wolfgang Mozart . . . It was quite enchanting to hear the fourteen-year-old sister of this little virtuoso play the most difficult sonata on the clavier with the most astonishing dexterity'.

In view of his extreme youth, we have to rely on other people's accounts of Wolfgang's personality, behaviour and musical talents. Leopold's descriptions were obviously aimed to make the maximum impact on the reader. However we are fortunate in having an objective and detailed record of Wolfgang written by an Englishman, the Honourable Daines Barrington, after visiting the boy at Thrift Street in June 1765. Barrington, a lawyer who had practised at the Admiralty Court, compiled an account which was later published by the Royal Society in its *Transactions* for 1770.

After describing Wolfgang's early history in Salzburg and his appearances in Vienna and other places, Barrington stated:

> If I was to send you a well attested account of a boy who measured seven feet in height, when he was not more than eight years of age, it might be considered as not undeserving the notice of the Royal Society.
>
> The instance which I now desire you will communicate to that learned body, of as early an exertion of most extraordinary musical talents, seems perhaps equally to claim their attention.

Barrington had attended Wolfgang's public performances and was well aware of his capabilities. He went on:

I carried to him a manuscript duet, which was composed by an English gentleman to some favourite words in Metastasio's opera of *Demofoonte*.

The whole score was in five parts, viz. accompaniments for a first and second violin, the two vocal parts, and a base. I shall here likewise mention, that the parts for the first and second voice were written in what the Italians stile the *contralto* cleff; the reasons for taking notice of which particular will appear hereafter.

My intention in carrying with me this manuscript composition, was to have an irrefragable proof of his abilities, as a player at sight, it being absolutely impossible that he could ever have seen the music before.

The score was no sooner put upon his desk, than he began to play the symphony in a most masterly manner, as well as in the time and stile which corresponded with the intention of the composer.

I mention this circumstance, because the greatest masters often fail in these particulars on the first trial. The symphony ended, he took the upper part, leaving the under one to his father.

His voice in the tone of it was thin and infantine, but nothing could exceed the masterly manner in which he sung.

His father, who took the under part in this duet, was once or twice out, though the passages were not more difficult than those in the upper one; on which occasions the son looked back with some anger pointing out to him his mistakes, and setting him right. He not only however did complete justice to the duet, by singing his own part in the truest taste, and with the greatest precision; he also threw in the accompaniments of the two violins, wherever they were most necessary, and produced the best effects. It is well known that none but the most capital musicians are capable of accompanying in this superior stile.

The visitor then tested Wolfgang on his compositional skills:

Having been informed that he was often visited with musical ideas, to which, even in the midst of the night, he would give utterance on his harpsichord; I told his father that I should be glad to hear some of his extemporary compositions.

The father shook his head at this, saying, that it depended entirely upon his being as it were musically inspired, but that I might ask him whether he was in humour for such a composition.

Happening to know that little Mozart was much taken notice of by Manzoli [*sic*], the famous singer, who came over to England in 1764, I said to the boy, that I should be glad to hear an extemporary *Love Song*, such as his friend Manzoli might choose in an opera.

8 Statue of Mozart, Ebury Street, by Philip Jackson, 1994

The boy on this (who continued to sit at harpsichord) looked back with much archness, and immediately began five or six lines of a jargon recitative proper to introduce a love song.

He then played a symphony which might correspond with an air compared to the single word, *Affeto* . . .

Finding that he was in humour, and as it were inspired, I then desired him to compose a *Song of Rage*, such as might be proper for the opera stage.

The boy again looked back with much archness, and began five or six lines of jargon recitative proper to precede a *Song of Anger*.

This lasted also about the same time with the *Song of Love*; and in the middle of it, he had worked himself up to such a pitch, that he beat his harpsichord like a person possessed, rising sometimes in his chair.

A rather touching aspect of Barrington's account is the difference between Wolfgang's advanced, mature musical ability and his normal behaviour for a boy of his age:

For example, whilst he was playing to me, a favourite cat came in, upon which he immediately left his harpsichord, nor could we bring him back for a considerable time.

He would also sometimes run about the room with a stick between his legs by way of a horse.

Finally, Barrington, in comparing the childhood achievements of Handel and Wolfgang, stated:

It may be hoped that little Mozart may possibly attain to the same advanced years as Handel, contrary to the common observation that such *ingenia praecocia* are generally short lived.

I think I may say without prejudice to the memory of this great composer, that the scale most clearly preponderates on the side of Mozart in this comparison, as I have already stated that he was a composer when he did not much exceed the age of four.[24]

It was Barrington who introduced the Mozarts to the Reverend Andrew Planta, the German-speaking Assistant Keeper of Printed Books at the British Museum. The museum, which had opened six years earlier in January 1759, was building up its collections, and Planta and the trustees urged the Mozarts to make gift copies of some of Wolfgang's compositions. Besides a copy of the published sonatas K. 6–15, and an engraving of the three Mozarts, Leopold presented the museum with a manuscript of the only work composed by Wolfgang with English words. The anthem *God Is our Refuge*, K. 20 is a four-voice *a capella* motet in the deliberately old-fashioned manner of English music, a touching and appropriate final gesture. The gift was the only one made by the Mozarts to any national institution.[25]

Although there were hints that the concert of 13 May brought in less income than was anticipated, Leopold delayed his departure from England. One reason perhaps was that he was still hoping to build up his finances before leaving. But there are at present many gaps in our knowledge of the activities of the Mozarts whilst they were in England, and there are indications that they were more successful than previously thought. It has recently been suggested, for instance, that in fact the Mozarts may have appeared in 1765 at one or more of the Carlisle House concerts, at the successful Manzuoli benefit concert on 21 February at Lord Clive's house in Berkeley Square, and at Lady Clive's concert, as well as many other houses of fashionable London society.[26]

By July, the family had resorted to hiring rooms at the Swan and Harp Tavern, Cornhill, where Wolfgang and Nannerl played every day for three hours; the admittance fee had been reduced to two shillings and sixpence per person. On 24 July the Mozarts were ready to leave London on the next stage of their journey. 'The very sight of the luggage we have to pack makes me perspire,' Leopold had told Hagenauer in April. 'Just think! We have been in England for a whole year. Why, we have practically made our home here, so that to take our departure from England requires even more preparations than when we left Salzburg.'[27] They travelled to Canterbury, spending a few days with Sir Horace Mann, the British envoy to Florence, on his estate at Bourn End in Kent. An advertisement for a concert to be given by them appeared in the local newspaper but it is not known if it ever took place.

The family spent a day at Canterbury Races and then they were on their way again. Whilst travelling from London on their way to Paris there were intercepted by the Dutch ambassador with an urgent request that they should proceed to The Hague to appear before Princess Caroline of Nassau-Weilburg. Leopold must have received a lucrative financial offer to have changed his plans at this stage: he accepted the invitation and on 1 August the Mozarts set sail from Dover to Calais. Their English sojourn was over.

Wolfgang's memories of England remained powerful, and there were a number of occasions when he planned to return. It is known that in the autumn of 1778 Leopold effectively prevented his son from making the journey. Four years later, feeling unappreciated in Vienna, Mozart told his father: 'If Germany, my beloved fatherland, of which I am Proud, as you know, will not have me, then in god's name let France or England become richer by another talented German – to the disgrace of the German Nation.' In the same letter he mentions that he had already taken three English lessons 'and in about three months I hope to be able to read and understand English texts quite well'.[28] Leopold was equally unhelpful when in November 1786 Wolfgang suggested that his father might look after their new-born son, Johann, and two-year-old Carl, whilst Wolfgang and his wife Constanze travelled to England for the next carnival.

Wolfgang made friends with several musicians from Britain. Thomas Linley of Bath was an exact contemporary who composed and played the violin well. The young men frequently played duos when they met in Italy. Linley was drowned tragically in a boating accident at the age of twenty-two. Wolfgang enjoyed a close friendship in Vienna with four musicians between 1784 and 1787. Michael Kelly from Dublin who sang Don Basilio in *Figaro*, Nancy Storace, Wolfgang's first Susanna, and her brother Stephen, and his favourite pupil Thomas Attwood. In February 1787 when the four departed for London, they promised to look for opportunities for Wolfgang in London, and to meet up again. Nothing came of this, though a Prague journal had reported in December 1786: 'Herr Mozart, the famous composer, intends to visit London next spring, having received most advantageous offers from there.'[29]

Two authentic offers were actually made to Wolfgang, but neither was taken up. In October 1790, Robert O'Riley, the manager of the Italian Opera Company in London, offered him £300 for two new operas, 'serious or comic', which would have required his presence. Two months later at a farewell dinner in Vienna to Haydn who was leaving for London, Johann Salomon, the German impresario, responsible for bringing Haydn to England, extended a similar offer to Wolfgang. A year later, on 5 December 1791, Wolfgang Amadeus Mozart himself was dead. He was buried on the following day in an unmarked grave in Vienna, aged thirty-five.

6 Haydn in London
'A constellation of musical excellence'

Haydn's two visits to London in the 1790s represent the crowning glory in the story of musical visitors to Britain. With London in the grip of 'the rage for music', and Haydn at the peak of his creative powers, it was the perfect partnership, and was an unqualified success for the composer, artistically, financially, socially and experientially.

Franz Joseph Haydn, always known as Joseph, was born in Rohrau in Lower Austria on 31 March 1732 into a family of craftsmen. His father, a cartwright, and his mother were keen musicians, and she would sing folk melodies while he accompanied her on the harp. Haydn later acknowledged the influence of these melodies on his own music. The young Joseph, one of twenty children from his father's two marriages, showed great musical promise as a child, and was enrolled at the choir school at St Stephen's Cathedral in Vienna at the age of eight.

Unlike his great friend, and much younger compatriot, Wolfgang Amadeus Mozart, whose visit to London preceded his by more than twenty-five years, Haydn's rise to fame was steady and gradual. He lacked nothing in ambition, however, and as a child was scolded for trying to compose for sixteen voices before he had even learnt how to write two-part music. After leaving the cathedral school at sixteen, Haydn began to make his living in Vienna teaching and composing. As well as discovering the keyboard works of Carl Philipp Emmanuel Bach, which had a deep influence on him, he became assistant to the venerable Italian opera composer Nicola Porpora. Porpora had successfully composed for and directed the Opera of the Nobility in London between 1733 and 1736, and it seems likely that Haydn would have heard about the richness, and potential riches, of musical life in London from his master.

Haydn's big break came with his appointment as *Kapellmeister* to the Esterházy court in 1761. The Esterházys were the richest and most powerful noble family in Hungary, great patrons of the arts, and employed a full-time orchestra. This orchestra gradually increased in size during Haydn's tenure, and of course became the powerhouse for Haydn's unique project and life's work: the development of the symphony. Haydn famously said of himself, 'I was set apart from the world ... and so had to be original'.[1]

Haydn's surviving correspondence with Prince Nicolaus Esterházy shows the rise in the composer's status. Employed initially as vice-*Kapellmeister*, Haydn naturally adopts a servile tone in his dealings with the prince. As Haydn gains confidence, however, he shows himself to be an adept politician, able to fight his own corner and that of his fellow musicians. Nicolaus soon understood the value to the Esterháza court of Haydn's service, and Haydn himself tells of whenever he mentioned the possibility of travelling to France or Italy, Nicolaus would press money into his hand, causing Haydn to abandon such thoughts. One of the best examples of Haydn's influence and diplomacy, as well as his renowned sense of humour, is in the story of the 'Farewell' Symphony No. 45, which ends with the performers leaving the stage and blowing out their candles one by one. At the first performance, the prince well understood the meaning of this piece of theatre, and immediately allowed the overworked musicians to have a holiday.

Though Haydn had never travelled out of his native Austro-Hungarian land, the originality of his music began to be noticed elsewhere. During the 1780s, Haydn, a shrewd businessman, secured deals with a number of publishers at home and abroad, and he had an eye on the foreign market. In 1783, Haydn stated that his Symphonies nos. 76–8 were written 'for the English gentleman', while four years later he wrote to John Gallini, a leading Italian impresario in London, of his intention 'to write a new opera and to assist at your concerts in Hanover Square'.[2] However, so long as Prince Nicolaus lived, Haydn was unwilling to contemplate leaving Esterháza.

Meanwhile, London concert life had undergone several changes since the time of Mozart's visit. The Bach–Abel concerts were succeeded by the so-called Professional Concert, which from its inception in 1785 was the most prestigious concert series in London, and specialised in performances of Haydn's symphonies. There was considerable competition from other promoters, including the German violinist, composer and impresario Johann Peter Salomon, and also from the concert series at the Pantheon, before it burnt down in 1792, under suspicious circumstances. Salomon, who for a time lodged with the Beethoven family in Bonn and was born in the same house as the great composer, in particular had a galvanising effect on the London concert scene. His concert series specialised in performances of string quartets, with Salomon himself playing first violin. An announcement in the *Public Advertiser* of 7 January 1791 boasting of 'a constellation of musical excellence', shows at least one concert or opera series taking place every night of the week throughout the winter season, a total of nine per week.[3] Perhaps the most significant development of the concert scene during the 1780s was the advent of the 'superstar composer', a real turning point in the balance of power in the musical world. Until this time, to be a musician of influence, it was necessary to be an instrumentalist or a singer. Now, thanks partly to the idolisation of Handel, the composer was master.

Salomon's impromptu journey to Vienna to secure Haydn's employment in London is one of those fabled moments that have changed the course of music history. Haydn had apparently considered other destinations, especially Naples. His Italian was good, and Italian opera had been a significant part of his output. But Mozart's operas reigned supreme there. England, on the other hand, where Mozart's music was barely to be heard after becoming briefly fashionable in the 1780s, had large orchestras and a high standard of instrumental playing. Money was to be made, and London audiences had an insatiable appetite for Haydn's music. Accordingly, when Salomon, who was in Cologne engaging singers for the Italian opera in London, heard of Nicolaus Esterházy's death, he had no hesitation in travelling to Vienna to find Haydn. Apparently his first words were: 'I am Salomon from London and have come to fetch you. Tomorrow we shall conclude an agreement.'[4]

Haydn, speaking to his biographer Dies, remembers the touching farewell he bade Mozart, who was concerned that Haydn, now fifty-eight, was too old to undertake his first foreign adventure. 'Papa! You have had no training for the great world, and you speak too few languages.' 'Oh!' replied Haydn, 'my language is understood all over the world.' On the day of Haydn's departure, 15 December 1790, Mozart would not be parted from his mentor. 'We are probably saying our last farewell in this life,'[5] he said, which both composers took to refer to Haydn's predeceasing Mozart. Haydn was later moved to remember that it was in fact Mozart who was to die only a year after this event.

After taking his leave from Mozart, Haydn travelled with Salomon and, after a rough channel crossing, arrived at Dover on New Year's Day 1791. Haydn's tough constitution served him well, and in a letter to his confidante Maria Anna von Genzinger, he boasts:

> Most of the passengers were ill, and looked like ghosts, but since I went on to London, I didn't feel the effects of the journey right away; but then I needed 2 days to recover. Now, however, I am fresh and well again, and occupied in looking at this endlessly huge city of London, whose various beauties and marvels quite astonished me.[6]

Haydn took lodgings with Salomon at 18 Great Pulteney Street, and a studio at the shop of Broadwood the piano-maker. Later in the year, he moved to the much quieter pastures of Lisson Grove, near Marylebone, which was then outside the metropolis. Here the eminent Bohemian composer and pianist Jan Ladislav Dussek lent Haydn his own piano.

Haydn was immediately launched into the hectic social life of the big city:

9 Jan Ladislav Dussek's Pianoforte Sonata, Op. 44, dedicated to his friend Muzio Clementi, 1800

My arrival caused a great sensation throughout the whole city ...
everyone wants to know me. I had to dine out 6 times up to now,
and if I wanted, I could dine out every day; but first I must consider
my health, and 2nd my work.[7]

Wherever he went in London, he was received with the highest honour,
as befitted the most famous composer in the world. For his part Haydn
was eager to experience this new and foreign land. This did not always
run smoothly; at a dinner party given by the singer and impresario
Madame Mara

Mr Salomon arrived and brought Haydn with him ... Haydn did not
know a word of English. As soon as we knew who he was, Crosdill
[a leading cellist] proposed that we should celebrate the arrival of
Haydn with 'three times three' [cheers]. This proposal was warmly
adopted and commenced, all parties except Haydn standing up. He
heard his name mentioned, but not understanding this species of
congratulation, stared at us in surprise. He was so confused by this
unexpected and novel greeting that he put his hands before his face
and was quite disconcerted for some minutes.[8]

Haydn's contract with Salomon stipulated that he should compose
amongst other works six symphonies and an opera. The opera, entitled
L'anima del filosofo was based on the story of Orfeo, and was to be
performed at Gallini's New Theatre. Haydn's biographer Dies takes up
the story:

The orchestra was already assembled to rehearse the opera *Orfeo* ...
hardly had forty measures been played through when official persons
entered and in the name of the King and of Parliament ordered that
the opera should under no circumstances be played, not even once in
rehearsal ... *Orfeo* was, so to speak, declared contraband.[9]

Just as J. C. Bach had done some years earlier, Haydn had fallen victim
to political intrigue surrounding the opera, over which Italians had a
monopoly. There were no such problems with concert performances however, and the first one of Haydn's visit took place on 11 March at the
Hanover Square Rooms, amid feverish excitement amongst the concert-
going public. Dr Charles Burney, composer and music historian, who was
an attentive companion and enthusiastic supporter, wrote: 'Haydn himself
presided at the piano-forte; and the sight of that renowned composer so
electrified the audience, as to excite an attention and a pleasure superior
to any that had ever, to my knowledge, been caused by instrumental music
in England.'[10] According to the inveterate concert-goer Mrs Papendiek,

the audience 'rose to a person and stood through the whole of the first movement',[11] and the Adagio had to be repeated, something which had never happened before in London.

Salomon's concert series was an unqualified success, and two of the newly composed 'London' symphonies, No. 95 in C minor and No. 96 in D, were premiered in the course of the season. The latter apparently had to be repeated three times. This symphony later acquired a nickname, as Haydn later recounted:

> When Haydn appeared in the orchestra and sat down at the piano-forte to conduct a symphony himself, the curious audience in the parterre left their seats and crowded toward the orchestra the better to see the famous Haydn quite close. The seats in the middle of the floor were thus empty, and hardly were they empty when the great chandelier crashed down and broke into bits, throwing the numerous gathering into the greatest consternation. As soon as the first moment of fright was over ... several persons uttered the state of their feelings with loud cries of 'Miracle! Miracle!' Haydn himself was deeply moved and thanked the merciful Providence that had allowed him in a certain way to be the cause for or the means of saving the lives of at least thirty people.[12]

At the end of the 1791 concert season in June, Haydn was immediately re-engaged by Salomon for the following year, much to the displeasure of his patron at Esterháza. It was at Burney's suggestion that Haydn be awarded an honorary Doctorate of Music from Oxford University. At the concert given as part of the ceremony, Haydn gave his Symphony No. 92 in G major, which despite being written some three years previously, became known as the 'Oxford' Symphony. Haydn was obliged to pay one-and-a-half guineas for having the bells rung and a further half a guinea for the hire of a robe. Haydn told Dies,

> I looked quite funny in this gown, and the worst of it was, I had to go about the streets in this masquerade for three days. Still, I owe much in England, in fact I might say everything, to this doctorate. Through it I became acquainted with the foremost gentlemen, and gained entrance to the greatest houses.

Dies continues,

> Haydn said this with his characteristic naturalness, so that I can scarcely imagine how it is possible for a genius like him to be so completely unacquainted with his own power and to attribute every-thing to the doctorate and nothing to his art.[13]

Haydn spent five weeks at the house of the banker Nathaniel Brassey in Roxford, Hertfordshire, in August and September. Here he worked on his new symphonies, and once again we find his disarming nature having an effect on his English associates. Haydn was telling Brassey a story of his experiences when Brassey suddenly

> sprang up as if possessed, uttered the most frightful oaths, and swore that if he had a loaded pistol, he would shoot himself on the spot ... because he had never known misfortune ... but ... was still not happy, because he knew only eating and drinking.[14]

Haydn made full use of his free time in England and his strong constitution to travel around the country and to treat the experience as an adventure as perhaps no musical visitor before him had done. In the months before his departure for Austria at the end of June 1792, he visited a variety of places – what we might now regard as tourist sights – around the country, and noted his experiences. In November 1791, he passed through the 'little town of Cambridge', where he admired the 'stuccoed' ceiling of King's College Chapel which, he says, everyone 'thinks is not more than 10 years old, because of the firmness and peculiar whiteness of the stone'.[15] The following June, he went to Windsor Castle, Ascot races, and paid a visit to William Herschel, the Astronomer Royal, at his home in Slough. Haydn was given a demonstration of Herschel's telescope, 40 feet long and 5 feet in diameter, which was 'so ingenious that a single man can put it in motion with the greatest ease'. Haydn also notes that Herschel was himself a musical visitor to England, having deserted from the Prussian army, in which he was an oboist. On his arrival in England, he supported himself as a musician before turning to astronomy. 'Sometimes he sits for 5 or 6 hours under the open sky in the bitterest cold weather.'[16]

Haydn also writes of his invitation in November 1791 from the Prince of Wales, later George IV, to Oatlands, the country home of his brother, the Duke of York. This marked the beginning of a close relationship between the composer and members of the royal family. In a letter to Maria Anna von Genzinger, Haydn gives a glowing account of the attention he and his music received. The Duchess of York, who was the daughter of the King of Prussia,

> is the most delightful lady in the world, is very intelligent, plays the pianoforte and sings very nicely ... she remained continually at my side from 10 o'clock in the evening, when the music began, to 2 o'clock in the morning ... and the sweet little thing sat beside me on my left and hummed all the pieces from memory ... The Prince of Wales is the most handsome man on God's earth; he has an extraordinary love of music and a lot of feeling, but not much money.[17]

It had been a bad year for the Professional Concert, their concert series overshadowed by Haydn's appearances in Salomon's concerts, and the directors were busy planning their riposte. They hired the renowned violinist Wilhelm Cramer to replace Salomon as first violinist, then tried pitting Clementi against Haydn as symphonist. According to Dies, this plan backfired when a new Clementi symphony was played in the first half of one of the Professional Concerts, and an 'already known' Haydn symphony in the second. Haydn's music triumphed, and reinforced his unrivalled status. The Professional Concert then tried to persuade Haydn to work for them, offering more lucrative terms than Salomon's. Haydn refused. They then began a 'dirty tricks' campaign against Haydn in the press, claiming he was old and weak, and that his creative powers had deserted him. In a final attempt to oust Haydn, they hired his former star pupil Ignaz Pleyel for the 1792 season.

Pleyel's music was at this time riding a tide of popularity across Europe, his fluid melodic style perfectly suiting contemporary musical taste. The Professional Concert's idea was to drive a wedge between master and student, and to pit them against one another in competition. They did not count on the older man's confidence: 'I'm not afraid, because last year I made a great impression on the English and hope therefore to win their approval this year, too.'[18] Haydn also refused to let any bitterness develop between them, and on Christmas Eve 1791, the day after Pleyel's arrival, the two composers dined together.

Though the Professional Concert's motives were selfish, the rivalry with Pleyel probably spurred Haydn to even greater compositional heights. 'A bloody harmonious war will commence between master and pupil,' writes Haydn,[19] and indeed, on hearing Pleyel announce that he would present a new work every evening, Haydn declared that he would likewise produce twelve different new pieces. Although he complained of the effect this had on his health, he remained generous towards his rival: 'Pleyel's presumption is sharply criticised, but I love him just the same. I always go to his concerts, and am the first to applaud him.'[20] Indeed, Haydn's most famous musical moment, the 'surprise' in Symphony No. 94, was intended not only to make a startling effect, but also, as Haydn told his biographer Griesinger, to ensure 'my student Pleyel ... should not outdo me ... Pleyel himself complimented me on my idea'.[21]

The 'surprise' movement itself, which quickly became known as the Andante with the Drum Stroke, was criticised in some quarters for being coarse and making women faint. Though Haydn denied it, it seems likely that it was intended as a joke at the expense of some members of his audience. Haydn's symphonies were placed in the second half of concerts and, as Dies writes, some of the men, full of food and drink, 'were so overpowered by the magic of the music that a deep sleep overcame them'.[22]

In amongst the hectic schedule of writing and performing his own music, Haydn showed great interest in aspects of London musical life. He attended

10 Joseph Haydn by Thomas Hardy, 1791

the last of the Handel Commemorations in Westminster Abbey in May
1791, and was so touched by the opening of the 'Hallelujah' Chorus from
Messiah he is reported to have burst into tears and exclaimed, 'He is the
master of us all'.[23] Like Berlioz after him, he also heard a huge gathering
of orphans, perhaps as many as 4,000, sing a song at St Paul's Cathedral.
'No music ever moved me so deeply in my whole life.'[24] It is difficult to
believe that these two experiences did not contribute to Haydn's enthusiasm
for embarking on writing oratorios and other choral works after his
English visits.

To judge from the notebooks he kept whilst in London, Haydn was more often amused than moved by his observations of music in England. At a banquet given in honour of the Lord Mayor, Haydn passed from one room to another, unable to bear the excruciating dance music, which was either Polish style minuets or 'English' dancing, accompanied by a drum. What he found barely credible was that 'part of the company went on dancing without hearing a single note of the music, for first at one table, then at another, some were yelling songs and some swilling it down and drinking toasts amid terrific roars'.[25] Haydn also visited Covent Garden to see William Shield's opera *The Woodman*. Apart from observing 'THE ORCHESTRA IS SLEEPY', he was fascinated by the etiquette of the English theatre:

> The common people in the galleries ... set the fashion with all their unrestrained impetuosity, and whether something is repeated or not is determined by their yells ... That was just what happened this evening, with the Duet in the 3rd Act, which was very beautiful; and the pro's and contra's went on for nearly a quarter of an hour, till finally the parterre and the boxes won, and they repeated the Duet. Both the performers stood on the stage quite terrified, first retiring, then again coming forward.[26]

Haydn's London notebooks provide a unique and fascinating insight into a foreigner's experience of English life, and his witty, perceptive and often dry observations, all imbued with his characteristic cheerfulness, present a colourful view of London and its inhabitants. He of course presents his own experiences, musical – 'I accompanied [Madame Mara], all by myself at the pianoforte, in a very difficult English Aria by Purcell'[27] – and non-musical: 'On 17th March 1792, I was bled in London.'[28] Snippets of gossip, 'Madam Mara was hissed at Oxford because she did not rise from her seat during the "Hallelujah" Chorus',[29] mingle with comprehensive lists of leading musicians in London – divided into singers, composers, pianists, violinists, cellists, oboists and doctors, the vast majority of them visitors.

Haydn cannot resist a wry look at English customs. Religion is one target: 'Once when an Archbishop of London asked Parliament to silence a learned public preacher of the Moravian religion, the Vice President answered that it could be easily done; just make him a Bishop, and he will remain silent the rest of his life.'[30] Women provide a talking point: 'In France the girls are virtuous and the wives are whores; in Holland the girls are whores and the wives are virtuous: in England they stay proper all their lives.'[31] The weather is also mentioned: 'On 20th May 1792, there was a thunderstorm in the evening. An unusual thing in London.'[32] 'On 5th Dec. the fog was so thick that you could have spread it on bread.'[33]

Most charmingly of all is perhaps the mass of facts, figures, even little sayings that litter these notebooks, mostly in German, but some in English and even Latin, all infused with a detachment and an almost childlike enthusiasm. 'The national debt of England is estimated to be over two hundred millions';[34] 'During the last 31 years, 38,000 houses were built in London';[35] 'L'Isle of Whight [*sic*] is 64 miles in circumference.'[36] Recipes for punch and a cocktail sit alongside the price of poultry, the colour of Portuguese oranges, and a method for preventing milk curdling; Haydn even notes down some jokes.

Of an entirely different nature is the section of the notebooks where Haydn made copies of letters from Rebecca Schroeter, to whom Haydn had given piano lessons. The widow of the German pianist and composer Johann Samuel Schroeter, who had succeeded Johann Christian Bach as music master to Queen Charlotte, Rebecca was herself an excellent pianist, to whom Haydn dedicated three of his finest piano trios. Her letters speak of a passionate but innocent love affair, and Haydn later reminisced that they might have married had he been free. But Haydn, renowned for being attentive to women, was far from free. He and Frau Haydn had for a long time been virtually estranged, and her venomous letters to him, and his wishful references to her death show a relationship in total break-down. When in London, he received a letter from her requesting the money to buy a house in Vienna which she would occupy when she was a widow![37] Meanwhile, letters to his former mistress, the singer Luigia Polzelli, playing down the employment prospects for Italian singers in London, show that Haydn was having to work hard to dissuade her from coming from Italy to join him in England.

In addition to all these, Haydn became friends with Anne Hunter, whose poems inspired him to compose English songs. Anne was the wife of John Hunter, a famous surgeon of the time. Hunter had inspected the nasal polyp, which had afflicted the composer for many years, and Haydn had half agreed to the operation. Shortly before Haydn's departure from England in 1792, Hunter

> sent to ask me for pressing reasons to come to him. I went. After the first greeting several big strong fellows entered the room, seized me, and tried to seat me in a chair. I shouted, beat them black and blue, kicked till I freed myself, and made it clear to Mr Hunter, who was standing all ready with his instruments for the operation, that I would not be operated on. He wondered at my obstinacy, and it seemed to me that he pitied me for not wanting the fortunate experience of his skill.[38]

Haydn left London in the summer of 1792 fully expecting to return for the 1793 season, and on his travels back to Vienna, he stopped in Bonn where he was introduced to a young and brilliant German composer,

Ludwig van Beethoven. Beethoven was engaged by the older composer to accompany him on his next trip to London. Towards the end of the year, however, the political situation across Europe had become very unstable, with the Napoleonic Wars making travel hazardous. In addition, Haydn was suffering greatly with the nasal polyp he still had, and was also under pressure from Prince Anton Esterházy to remain in Austria. Beethoven instead travelled to Vienna to have composition lessons with Haydn, an arrangement which suited neither man.[39]

Meanwhile in England, the disappointment over Haydn's absence from Salomon's 1793 concert season was ameliorated by the arrival of the composer and brilliant violinist Giovanni Battista Viotti, who had fled from France. Billed as Europe's greatest violinist, Viotti helped to ensure that this season was the first to bring financial success to Salomon. For the following two seasons, Salomon's concerts benefited from the presence of high-quality soloists: Viotti, the pianist Dussek, the singer Madam Mara, the double bass virtuoso Dragonetti, and many others.[40]

After managing to persuade Prince Anton to release him, Haydn finally set off for London in January 1794, with much of symphonies 99, 100 and 101 already complete. He was accompanied on this second visit not by Beethoven, but by Johann Elssler, his valet and musical copyist. On his way, he stopped at an inn in Wiesbaden in Germany, where he heard the Andante from the 'Surprise' Symphony being played on the piano.

> He found several Prussian officers, all great admirers of his music, who, when he finally, made himself known, would not take his word for it that he was Haydn. 'Impossible! Impossible! You Haydn? – Already such an old man! – That doesn't rhyme with the fire in your music!'[41]

Haydn was forced to produce a letter from their king to prove his identity.

Haydn took lodgings at No. 1 Bury Street, in St James's, in the heart of the fashionable West End of London. Soon after his arrival, the Symphony No. 99 had its premiere in the first Salomon concert of the season, and was notable for being his first symphony to use clarinets. In the following weeks, the Symphonies No. 101, the 'Clock', and No. 100, the 'Military' were premiered. Each in turn was considered by critics to be Haydn's finest work yet. The 'Military' in particular captured the mood of the time, and surpassed even the 'Surprise' Symphony in popularity. One commentator has noted that Haydn's audience and critics were becoming aware that they were witnessing musical history in the making, and that each symphony was entering the permanent repertoire on its debut.[42] Salomon was also featured as performer in the premieres of Haydn's Op. 71 and Op. 74 string quartets which, although written in Vienna the previous year, were clearly aimed at the London audience.

For these works, which were later published in London, are much more brilliant and less conversational in style, and allowed Salomon to shine in the virtuosic first violin parts.

The Professional Concert had folded after the 1793 season, and Haydn's reign in London was unchallenged. Such was the extent of his success that the story of his musical triumphs is almost predictable. Perhaps Haydn began to feel this too, and the adulation he experienced at each new premiere, without even the obstacles of a Pleyel to compete against or the Professional Concert to outdo, began to pall. This change is reflected in his notebooks, and his characteristic dry humour verges on the sarcastic, especially when he refers to other musicians.

However, Haydn's appetite for travelling in England remained undimmed. In the summer of 1794, he visited Hampton Court, and then travelled down to Portsmouth, Gosport and the Isle of Wight. Fascinated by French warships that had been captured by the British fleet under Lord Howe, he was nevertheless forbidden from visiting the dockyard at Portsmouth, as he was a foreigner. After a visit to the Isle of Wight, where, he notes, 'the people look just like the Germans and mostly have black hair'[43] Haydn travelled back to London via Southampton, 'a little town on a peninsula'[44] and Winchester, where he admired the cathedral. In August, he undertook a journey to Bath and Bristol with Charles Burney. In Bath, which he describes as 'one of the most beautiful cities in Europe'[45] he witnessed the building of the Pump Room, and describes in detail the Royal Crescent. Here he paid a visit to the *castrato* singer Venanzio Rauzzini, for whom Mozart had written the motet *Exsultate, jubilate.* Rauzzini had lived in Bath for some years, and had built a monument in honour of his best friend, his pet dog. Haydn secretly composed a four-part canon on the words inscribed on the monument: 'He was not a man – he was a dog.' Rauzzini was so pleased with the canon that he had Haydn's music carved on the monument in honour of Haydn and the dog. Later in August, Haydn travelled to Waverley Abbey in Surrey, and in an expression of emotion rare in his notebooks, and with a fascinating mixture of the devout and the Romantic, he describes his experience:

> Here there are the remains of a monastery which has already been standing for 600 years. I must confess that whenever I looked at this beautiful wilderness, my heart was oppressed at the thought that all this once belonged to my religion [i.e. the Catholic faith].[46]

It is interesting that it was not until February 1795 that Haydn made the acquaintance of King George III and Queen Charlotte, at a musical soirée given by the Prince of Wales. Haydn was the guest of honour and, as well as playing the pianoforte, he was required to sing some of his songs. The queen made very complimentary remarks, and the king, who until that time would only listen to Handel's music, received Haydn's music enthusiastically. A conversation between the two was overheard by the oboist William Parke: 'his Majesty said (in English) "Doctor Haydn, you have written a great deal." To which Haydn modestly replied, "Yes, Sire, a great deal more than is good." To which the King neatly rejoined, "Oh no, the world contradicts that."'[47] From this point on, Haydn was a frequent guest of the royal family, most especially of the queen. Griesinger takes up the story:

> The King and the Queen wished to keep him in England. 'You shall have a place in Windsor in the summers', said the Queen, 'and then,' she added with an arch look toward the King, 'we shall sometimes make music tête à tête.' 'Oh!' replied the King, 'I am not worked up over Haydn, he is a good honest German gentleman.'[48]

They failed of course to prevent Haydn from returning home, and he believed that it was because of his refusal to stay on that the royal family never offered him any money. On his return to Austria, Haydn was persuaded to send the Prince a bill for a hundred guineas for his time, which had included directing twenty-six musical soirées. The money was sent to him immediately.

Perhaps it should not be a surprise that this royal connection gave Haydn no particular pleasure. As he said to this biographer Griesinger: 'I have been in the company of emperors, kings and many great gentlemen, and I have received many a compliment from them: but I do not wish to live on terms of intimacy with such persons and prefer to be with people of my class.'[49] It is noticeable from his notebooks that Haydn's acquaintances range from the noble to the ordinary, seemingly without him making any differentiation between them. For example the following entry in his notebook:

> Mister March is a dentist, *Carossieur* [coach-maker] and dealer in wines all at the same time: a man 84 years old. Keeps a very young mistress. Has a 9-year-old daughter who plays the pianoforte quite respectably. I often ate at his house.

Haydn then goes on to discuss March's profits, the cost of the coaches, and observes that he 'drags himself around on two crutches, or 2 wooden feet'.[50]

While Haydn is often dismissive of the abilities of his fellow musicians, he could also be generous. 'Field a young boy, which plays the pianoforte Extremely well.'[51] English musicians of course saw 'Papa' Haydn as a figure of authority, and on occasion sought his opinion. At a dinner party, a dispute arose between three doctors of music as to which of them should conduct the orchestra for the Handel anthem that was to be performed at the wedding of the Prince of Wales. Haydn's answer was that one should conduct the singers, a second the orchestra, and the junior organist play the organ. 'But this they would not have. I left the fools and went home.'[52] In the event they did exactly as Haydn had advised.

The 1795 season was Haydn's last in London, and took place under different management, Salomon having joined forces with the Opera. Viotti took charge of this new Opera Concert series for the season, and had a huge orchestra of sixty players. Haydn's last three symphonies were performed during this season, the 'Drum Roll', No. 103 being a particular success. A benefit concert was given for Haydn in May, and was the crowning event of his time in England. His Symphony No. 104 was premiered, as was his finest cantata, *Berenice, che fai*, performed by some of the leading singers in Europe. 'The whole company was thoroughly pleased and so was I. I made four thousand Gulden on this evening. Such a thing is only possible in England.'[53]

Haydn's compositions on his second visit show greater variety than the first. As well as the quartets and symphonies, Haydn wrote several of his finest piano trios, including the famous *Gypsy Rondo*, wrote his last three piano sonatas for another young woman of his acquaintance, Theresa Jansen, and set many songs. He first set a hundred Scottish folk songs in 1791 for the violinist William Napier, who had contracted gout and turned to music publishing. A second set of fifty followed, together with two sets of 'Six Original Canzonettas', with words by Anne Hunter.[54] Haydn proudly lists in his notebooks, in English, all his works written in and for England, together with the number of pages filled. A total of 768 sheets, where each sheet is a four-page bifolium, converts to over 3,000 pages of music – a remarkable testimony to the creative power of a man in his sixties.

Haydn considered staying on after the 1795 season, but his unerring instinct for making the appropriate career move dictated that he move on. He had benefited hugely from the rage for music, and particularly the rage for his music, but he knew it could not last. Indeed, he had written in a letter in 1791 that 'I don't hate London, but I would not be capable of spending the rest of my life there, even if I could amass millions'.[55] Haydn did in fact earn 24,000 gulden, the equivalent of twenty years' salary at Esterháza, in his three years in London. And yet it was news from Esterháza that was crucial in making up Haydn's mind: Prince Anton had died in 1794, and his successor, Prince Nicolaus II resolved to reform the orchestra, with Haydn as *Kapellmeister*. As Dies pointed out, 'nothing bound him to the princely house except love and gratitude'.[56] In addition, war was raging in Europe, and Haydn was keen to seek the relative security of life in his native Austria.

Therefore, after spending two months completing the last few works of his English stay, and overseeing publications of various compositions, Haydn left London on 15 August 1795. He took with him a variety of parting gifts, including a goblet of coconut shell with silver trimmings

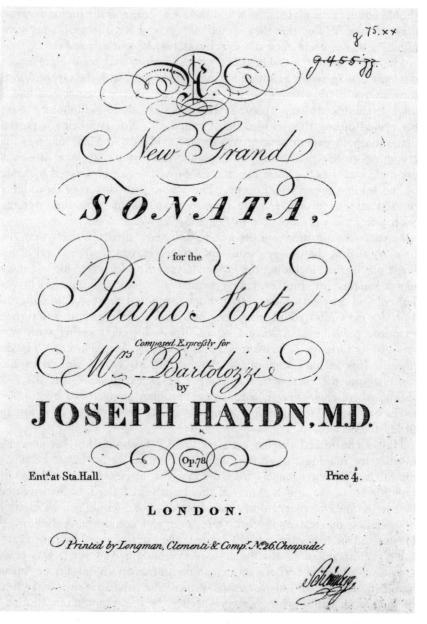

11 Haydn's Pianoforte Sonata, Op. 78 Hob. XVI/52, 1799

from Clementi, and a talking parrot (which outlived Haydn), and even some 'musical stockings' embroidered with extracts from some of his best-known works. Haydn said later that his days in England were among the happiest of his life.[57] He was also convinced that he only became famous in Germany because of his time in England, and even Emperor Joseph II began to take notice of him.[58]

England missed Haydn too. The four concert seasons in which he took part were among the most successful and glamorous ever to have been enjoyed by London audiences. The concert scene subsequently went into decline and in a sense was never the same again. Certainly until 1813, when the Philharmonic Society was formed, England, beset by war, had neither the appetite nor the possibility of staging another such feast of musical activity.

More significant still in terms of the course of musical history was the interest in oratorio England had given Haydn. His friend Lord Abingdon had tried to persuade Haydn to write an oratorio, but his lack of understanding of the English language had prevented the project from proceeding. On his departure from England, Haydn had been given a copy of a libretto entitled *The Creation of the World* by Salomon, which had apparently been written for Handel to set. On his return to Vienna, Haydn showed the text to Baron Gottfried van Swieten, who had earlier commissioned vocal works from Mozart, and was later to advance Beethoven's career. Van Swieten translated the text into German, and it was Haydn's idea to publish, indeed to conceive, the work in two versions, German and English. *The Creation* was a huge success from the moment of its premiere in Vienna in 1798, a worthy successor to Handel's *Messiah*, whose popularity it far exceeded Europe-wide. Like the earlier work, *The Creation*'s appeal was universal, with its particular combination of the philosophical and sublime, and was truly a work of its time.

Haydn also composed *The Seasons* to a text based on the famous poem by the English poet James Thomson, again adapted by van Swieten, and the *Missa in angustiis*, the so-called 'Nelson Mass', written while the battle of the Nile raged. Nelson was an admirer of Haydn and, with Lady Hamilton, visited Haydn twice, in Eisenstadt and in Vienna; the Mass probably acquired its nickname when it was performed before the admiral. Haydn and Nelson are said to have exchanged gifts: the composer gave the pen he used to write the Mass, and the admiral his gold watch. Whilst in England, Haydn had composed a setting of 'God Save the King', now lost, and when in late 1796 he was asked to compose a similar song for an Austrian anthem, he produced the 'Emperor's Hymn'. Described in a letter from Charles Burney as 'in imitation of our loyal song, "God save great George our King"',[59] the tune was so popular that it became the German national anthem. Haydn also used this melody in his String Quartet Op. 76 No. 3.

Towards the end of the composition of *The Seasons* in 1800, Haydn probably suffered a stroke, and wrote very little after this. During his fading years, he talked most of his days in England. After a long decline, amidst war-torn and French-occupied Vienna, he died on 31 May 1809. Amongst the medals placed in front of the catafalque was an ivory tablet, bearing the composer's name, which had given him free admission to the London concerts.

7 Interlude

The London Pianoforte School

The rise of the pianoforte coincides with a fascinating episode in musical history in London, and with a cluster of musical visitors, many of them drawn to England by the innovations connected with that instrument. The German Jacob Kirckman and Swiss Burkat Tschudi (or Shudi) had dominated harpsichord-making in England in the eighteenth century, but it was Shudi's apprentice, the German Johannes Zumpe, whose instruments first gained popularity in England. Although it was Johann Christian Bach who, in 1768 gave the first public pianoforte concert, probably the first anywhere in the world, on a square pianoforte of Zumpe, it was Muzio Clementi, who was often referred to as the 'father of the pianoforte', who is credited with the founding of what is known as the London Pianoforte School.

The story of Clementi's arrival in England is a bizarre one. Born in Rome, Clementi's playing came to the attention of Englishman Peter Beckford, who was in Italy on the Grand Tour, and Beckford, in his own words, 'bought' Clementi from his father, and brought him back to England. There he was a virtual prisoner in Beckford's Dorset mansion at Stepleton Iwerne where he practised the harpsichord for eight or more hours a day for seven years, until he was twenty-one. Clementi thereafter spent most of his life in London, with occasional extended foreign tours. On the first of these, he was pitted into a pianoforte battle with Mozart in 1781, from which the two composers gained contrasting impressions of one another.

Perhaps Clementi, described by Mozart as 'a charlatan, like all Italians',[1] was hampered by the different design of the pianofortes in Vienna. Whereas the Viennese instrument was light and delicate, the English pianoforte, developed chiefly by the Scottish pianoforte-maker John Broadwood, was noted for its brilliance and power. Broadwood, who had been apprenticed to Shudi, and who married Shudi's daughter, made several modifications to the pianoforte: adding more strings per note and iron braces to the wooden frame and introducing a sustaining pedal, instead of a hand-controlled stop.

Broadwood also worked closely with pianist–composers, and in particular with the Bohemian Jan Ladislav Dussek. Dussek, who fled to London from Paris at the time of the French Revolution and took up residence in a grand house in Dean Street, Soho, was a colourful and controversial character, and a brilliant pianist. On an earlier visit to Russia, he had been implicated in a plot to kill Catherine the Great; subsequently in Paris, his pianoforte-playing came to the attention both of Marie Antoinette and Napoleon. When in London, Dussek met Haydn, who wrote to Dussek's father, 'you have one of the most upright, moral, and, in music, most eminent of men for a son'.[2] It was Dussek who was the first to place the pianoforte side-on to the audience – a practice that has been universally accepted in recitals since then – which emphasised Dussek's trademark profile. Dussek's collaboration with Broadwood resulted in extending the compass of the pianoforte keyboard from five to five-and-a-half octaves in 1791, and to six octaves in 1794. Dussek's works published at this time boast that they are written for pianoforte 'with additional keys'.

The London Pianoforte School, which consisted almost entirely of foreign visitors like Dussek, had an identifiable musical character, reliant on dramatic effects, song-like melodies and keyboard virtuosity. Much of the output of the school is dominated by technical brilliance, and J. B. Cramer, a German composer, who was taught by Clementi, developed the genre of the study, or *Studio*, as he called it. The acme of this develop-ment was Clementi's three-volume masterwork *Gradus Ad Parnassum*, a collection of a hundred of his works assembled over a forty-five-year period, published from 1817 to 1826; it is still part of the canon for pianistic technique today.[3] The music of the school, however, is also rich in character pieces, many of them based on national, sometimes national-istic, airs of the host country. As a typical example, the Austrian Johann Nepomuk Hummel, when a twelve-year-old boy prodigy on tour in Britain wrote variations on 'The Plough Boy', a piece he reset nearly forty years later in his visit of 1829. Like several other composers, he also wrote vari-ations on both 'God Save the King' and 'Rule Britannia'. In 1793, Dussek wrote a narrative pianoforte piece entitled 'The Sufferings of the Queen of France', in which he portrays the sound of the guillotine in the music. Four years later, he published a pianoforte sonata with the extraordinary title of 'The Naval Battle and Total Defeat of the Dutch Fleet by Admiral Duncan, 11 October 1797'. Beethoven in particular was influenced by the works coming out of the London Pianoforte School, and developed further the intense and thrilling dramatic possibilities of pianoforte music.[4]

The pianoforte also powered the movement that arguably gave rise to what is now called the music industry. The Irish boy prodigy John Field, who later created the nocturne, was apprenticed to Clementi, and he accompanied his master on his European tours, largely for the purpose of demonstrating the instruments which Clementi was now involved in making. Clementi, a clever businessman, took in several business partners,

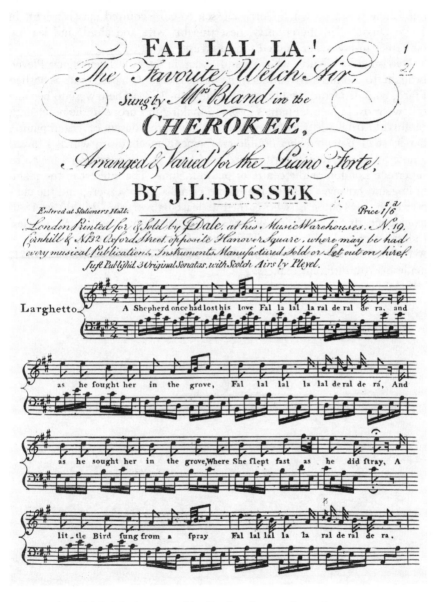

12 Dussek's 'Fal Lal La!' arranged by Stephen Storace from the opera
The Cherokee, staged at Drury Lane, 20 February 1794

and Clementi & Co. operated both a music-publishing and a pianoforte-making and selling business. Meanwhile, Dussek had married the daughter of the publisher Domenico Corri, and the two men started an ill-fated publishing business: when Corri, Dussek & Co. acquired massive debts in 1799, Dussek fled the country, deserting his wife and child, and leaving his father-in-law to be gaoled for bankruptcy.

Two other key figures who visited London in the 1790s were Ignaz Pleyel, brought to London to conduct the Professional Concert, and Sébastien Erard, who fled from the French Revolution in 1794. These were to become the two most influential names in piano-making in Europe in the nineteenth century. Erard made use of Broadwood's innovative design of 'grand piano', but in 1821 patented the 'double escapement' mechanism, which allowed a note to be repeated at great speed, and from this time on, Paris began to supersede London as the centre of piano-making. The interest in the piano in England however ensured that piano virtuosi thrived there, and the concert tours of Thalberg (who earned at least half of his £24,000 in 1840 from concerts in England), Liszt, and the visits of Chopin, Moscheles, Kalkbrenner and others, were highlights of nineteenth-century musical life. A remarkable 178 pianos were shown at the Great Exhibition of 1851, made by 102 different makers.

8 'That's Weber in London!'

On 10 August 1825, two Englishmen, the actor-manager Charles Kemble, and the musical director of Covent Garden, Sir George Smart, arrived at the spa town of Ems in Germany after a three-and-a-half-hour walk from Koblenz. Their mission was to visit the ailing Carl Maria von Weber, who was there to take the waters, and confer with him about his proposed journey to England and the payment for his promised new opera, *Oberon*.

Weber, born in Utin, north-west Germany, on 10 December 1786, had suffered from ill health from childhood. He was born with a diseased hip bone and did not walk until he was four years old. He was left with a limp for the rest of his life. His father, Baron Franz Anton von Weber, an uncle of Mozart, was a musician, playing at such functions as weddings and court balls. Dissatisfied with his lot, he established a troupe of strolling players who performed in provincial German towns. The young Carl led a nomadic existence, with little formal education, but he soon acquired an intimate knowledge of the theatre and stage production. Franz Anton had set his heart on making Carl a child prodigy and he became an outstanding pianist. Lessons in composition were given by Michael Haydn in Salzburg and the Abbé Vogler in Vienna.[1]

Carl found employment with the Duke Eugen Frederick, ruler of Karlsruhe, was later appointed conductor of the opera in Prague and in 1816 became *Kapellmeister* at the Royal Theatre in Dresden. Whilst conducting many different operas by other composers, he had composed a number of his own, *Peter Schmoll*, *Abu Hassan* and *Silvana*. He had married in 1812 Caroline Brandt, who had played the leading role in *Silvana* and who inspired him to write such piano pieces as his *Invitation to the Waltz*.

Weber longed to establish an essentially German opera which reflected the aspirations of the nation, especially if it could be rooted in the folk-lore tradition; he was able to include Beethoven's *Fidelio* and some operas by lesser of his countrymen. The planned opening of a new opera house in Berlin, by his employer, Count Carl von Brühl, provided the perfect opportunity. As early as 1819 Weber had been working on his opera *Der Freischütz* (The Marksman). Based on a text by Friedrich Kind, it contained all the elements of a superb composition: an overture which distilled the essence of the opera, a well-crafted libretto, stunning visual effects, the introduction of supernatural elements, and a score which contained some outstanding music. Given its first performance at the Schauspielhaus on 18 June 1821, it was immediately popular with the public, though Weber was hurt by the reception from the critics. However, further performances in Dresden and Vienna confirmed its success. More significantly for his later career, the opera was greeted with great acclaim when it was performed at the English Opera House in London in 1824.

Shortly before the first performance of *Freischütz*, Julius Benedict, a young musician and future conductor and composer, had been accepted as one of Weber's pupils. He later described the composer at this time:

> I shall never forget the impression of my first meeting with him. Ascending the by no means easy staircase which led to his modest home on the third storey in the old Market Place, I found him sitting at his desk, and occupied with a pianoforte arrangement of his *Freischütz*. The dire disease which but too soon was to carry him off had made its mark on his noble features; the projecting cheek-bones, general emaciation, told their sad tale; but in his clear blue eyes, too often concealed by spectacles, in his mighty forehead, fringed by a few straggling locks, in the sweet expression of his mouth, in the very tone of his weak but melodious voice, there was a magic power which attracted irresistibly all those who approached him.[2]

In November 1822 Weber was asked by an Italian impresario, Domenico Barberia, to write a successor to *Freischütz* for Vienna. Weber had contacted Helmina von Chezy, a Dresden poetess, to provide a suitable libretto for the project. Chezy was a highly eccentric figure, and the material she submitted on the subject of *Euryanthe* showed enormous incompetence. However, despite the criticisms of his literary friends, Weber persisted with Chezy.[3] *Euryanthe*, Weber's only grand opera without spoken dialogue, was based on a medieval French romance. The first performance in Vienna of 25 October 1823 drew the applause of the audience, but gradually the absurdity of the plot and the excessive length of the work told against it.

Benedict noted that Weber's appearance now dramatically changed. 'He seemed to have grown older by ten years in those few weeks; his former strength of mind, his confidence, his love for the art, had all forsaken him. Sunken eyes, general apathy, and a dry hectic cough bespoke clearly the precarious condition of his health.' For seventeen months, from October 1823 to January 1825, Weber stopped composing entirely, except for one short song.

Some three weeks before the first performance of *Euryanthe*, on 5 October 1823, Weber was invited to visit Beethoven, who was then residing at

Baden, not far from Vienna.[4] Weber had been apprehensive about the reception which he might gain, but these fears proved groundless. The deaf composer had admired the score of *Der Freischütz*. 'I could never have believed it of the poor weak little mannikin', he was heard to say, banging on the score with his fist. 'Weber must write operas now; nothing but operas, one after the other!'[5]

Weber described the meeting to his wife in a letter the following day:

> He embraced me six or seven times heartily and cried out enthusiastic-ally: 'Yes, you are a devil of a fellow, a really fine fellow.' We spent the afternoon together merrily. This rough repellent man actually paid court to me, served me at table with politeness as if I had been a lady etc. In short, this day will always remain memorable in the highest degree to me and to the others.[6]

Beethoven complained bitterly about his financial situation, the theatre and concert directors. He was at the time working on the Finale of the Ninth Symphony, for which he was being paid £100 by the Philharmonic Society of London.[7] Weber suggested that Beethoven should tour Germany to augment his income. Beethoven made a pantomime of pianoforte-playing in reply, and shook his head. 'Well, then,' said Weber, 'go to England.' 'Too late!' cried Beethoven, and taking Weber's arm under his own, led him to the local hotel when they dined. On parting, Beethoven and Weber embraced, Beethoven promising to come to the first night of *Euryanthe* if he could. The two men never met again.

Following *Euryanthe*, Weber had to struggle not only with writer's block but also with increasing physical frailty. On 2 July 1824 whilst conducting a concert, Weber burst into a flood of tears and later collapsed. Rest was prescribed but he did not improve. He now experienced a presentiment that he was soon to die, and sank into gloom. 'I never could have believed that I could ever feel this disgust for work,' he wrote to Caroline. 'I feel as if I had never composed a note in my life.'[8] A month before, he had received offers from Paris to write operas and to conduct, but Weber hesitated. Now he received another offer, this time from England, which tempted him.

When he retired in 1820 the theatre manager, John Philip Kemble, made over his eighth share in the Theatre Royal, Covent Garden, to his brother Charles. The latter had ambitious plans to found a national theatre, training actors to perform in British plays. Kemble took a lease of the English Opera House, Covent Garden with this in mind, but four years later was deeply in debt.[9] However, after abandoning drama, he had staged *Der Freischütz* in July 1824, which was an outstanding financial success, running for fifty-two performances. Other unauthorised versions quickly appeared at rival theatres, such was the opera's popularity. At this point,

Kemble wrote to Weber offering him £500 to compose a new opera for Covent Garden, and to conduct the performances himself.

Weber was advised by his friends, particularly Moscheles, to accept Kemble's offer. Before concluding such an agreement, Weber consulted his physician, Dr Hedenus, on the advisability of making the journey to England. According to Benedict, the doctor replied: 'If you give up any idea of conducting or composing, start at once for Italy and remain in idleness for at least one year, you may live five or six years longer.' 'And if not?' asked Weber. 'Then,' was the stern reply of the doctor, 'it can be only a question of months, nay, maybe of weeks.'

Weber swore the doctor to secrecy about this warning and then decided the matter. Caroline was pregnant with their second child, and there was need to provide for his growing family; a son, Max, had been born two years earlier. In spite of the universal popularity of *Der Freischütz*, it yielded little income because of the many unauthorised performances. A successful expedition to London, Weber calculated, would be of great benefit to his family in the event of his death. He thus wrote to Kemble accepting his offer. The manager was delighted and increased the sum offered from £500 to £1,000, suggesting a German opera on perhaps the Faust legend or Oberon.

No doubt Weber had in mind also the richly rewarded visit by Rossini to England between 13 December 1823 and 26 July 1824. At the age of thirty-one he had arrived in London after a triumphant five weeks in Paris. Rossini and his wife had been given a letter of introduction from the Duke of Devonshire and they were accommodated at 90 Regent Street, in Nash's Quadrant, from the roof of which he enjoyed watching the flow of people in the street below.[10] He was very well known in London as no fewer than twelve of his operas had been performed and Rossini was to conduct some of them in the coming season.

A fortnight after his arrival, Rossini travelled to Brighton to the Royal Pavilion to be presented to George IV, where he accompanied himself at the king's request in one of his *buffo* arias, singing in a falsetto voice. The king also accompanied Rossini in a song, though his erratic rhythm spoiled the effect. Rossini soon discovered that there was much to be gained simply by singing and playing at the homes of the rich. A peer is reputed to have paid him £200 for one appearance, and he also received many valuable gifts. He later told Hiller: 'I never earned enough from my art to be able to save anything except for my stay in England. And in London I made my money not as a composer, but as an accompanist.'[11] Many wealthy ladies begged him to give them singing lessons, but when asked why he charges such high fees, Rossini replied: 'Because not even £100 per lesson could compensate me for the tortures that I suffer while listening to those ladies, whose voices creak horribly.'[12]

Besides the fees for conducting operas, Rossini was honoured with two benefit concerts at the Almanack's Assembly Rooms when most of the artists gave their services. The tickets were priced at £2 each and proved a lucrative addition to Rossini's already growing income. There was a topical touch at the last concert where Rossini's cantata on the death of Lord Byron, who had recently died in Greece, was performed.

The invitation to the Thursday morning *musicales* held in the house of Prince Leopold, the future king of the Belgians, was further acknowledgement of his celebrity status. At one of these Leopold sang some solos, as well as duets with his sister, the Duchess of Kent, mother of the future Queen Victoria; from time to time both George IV and Rossini joined in the singing. There were two final engagements to fulfil in England. The first was an appearance at the annual Cambridge University Music Festival at which Rossini accompanied singers on the organ of Great St Mary's Church and sang various arias at Senate House, including *Largo al factotum* from the *Barber of Seville*. The second was a large rout, held at the Duke of Wellington's house, which the king attended. Rossini left London for Paris towards the end of July, highly satisfied at his profitable venture. His five months' sojourn had earned him an extraordinary £7,000.

It was without doubt the outbreak of *Freischütz* mania in London in 1824 which had induced Kemble to invite Weber, as well as a hope that it would restore his own fortunes. Weber, similarly, might have considered that it would be possible to emulate Rossini's financial and artistic triumph in England. In this, he was somewhat over-optimistic; he was not a good negotiator, insisting on matters of detail, such as the cost of his accommodation falling on the management. Weber, who personally liked Kemble, wrote on 7 October 1824 to accept the offer to write a new opera, direct performances of *Der Freischütz* and *Preciosa*, and to appear at other musical events which would raise funds for himself. The plan was for Weber to spend three months in England in the spring of 1825.

Kemble had asked for a 'German opera' and Weber wished to compose a Romantic opera in the mould of *Der Freischütz* or *Euryanthe*. Weber selected Christoph Martin Wieland's epic poem *Oberon*, written in 1780, but known in England through a translation by William Sotheby, made some eighteen years later. The characters ranged from Shakespeare's Oberon, Titania and Puck, to Charlemagne, Sir Huon of Bordeaux and Reiza, daughter of Haroun el Rashid, which allowed for a number of different settings within the opera, such as a deserted island in the Mediterranean and the Caliph's palace in Baghdad.

Kemble chose for the librettist James Robinson Planché, who had collaborated with him at Covent Garden for several seasons. Planché had already produced a libretto for Sir Henry Bishop's opera *Cortez, or The Conquest of Mexico*, which was a failure. Besides writing historical adaptations, he was the author of such melodramas as *The Vampire, or The Bride of the*

Isles and *Abudahior, the Talisman of Oromanes*, which included ballads. Planché seemed an ideal choice for *Oberon* which he tailored to meet the current English theatrical taste: spectacle was paramount, the pantomime element was important and the plot was necessarily one which would appeal to a popular audience, not connoisseurs. *Oberon, or The Elf King's Oath* as Weber's opera was entitled, was thus conceived, partly in the *Singspiel* tradition, with musical numbers interspersed with dialogue and with speaking parts outnumbering those of the singers.

The project roused Weber from his long-standing apathy. In order to prepare himself he began to take English lessons, and by the time he arrived in London, he had had no fewer than 153 sessions. He made rapid progress with the language. On receipt of the libretto for Act I from Planché on 30 December 1824, he managed to write in broken English:

> I can only congratulate myself to share in toils of an author who displays so much feeling and genius in his fluent verses. The cut of an English opera is certainly very different from a German one. The English is more a drama with songs, but in the first Act of *Oberon* there is nothing that I could wish to see changed except the finale . . . Pardon my making use of your condescending permission.[13]

This letter, written on 6 January 1825, coincided with the birth of Caroline's second son, Alexander. Twelve days later, Act II of the libretto had reached Weber, who was now becoming more anxious. 'The cut of the whole is very foreign to all my ideals and maxims,' he told Planché. 'The intermix of so many principal actors who do not sing, the omission of the music in the most important moments – all these things deprive *Oberon* of the title of an opera, and will make him unfit for all other theatres in Europe, which is a very bad thing for me.'

Weber also expressed his anxiety at Kemble's tardiness in finalising the terms of his visit:

> Russia, Sweden, Holland, France, Scotland and England have brought on the boards my performances without their being entitled to it; for my works have not been printed; and though I do not value money to take no notice of it, the world forces me at last.[14]

There was another link forged between Weber and Britain at this time. George Thomson, an Edinburgh music publisher and collector of folk music, approached the composer to make some arrangements of Scottish folk songs, following in the steps of Haydn, Pleyel, Hummel and Beethoven. Setting to work, he had soon completed a set of twelve melodies, scored for flute, violin, cello and piano; they were not published until twelve years after his death.[15]

Weber began work on the opera in early 1825 and he had composed Huron's *scena*, 'From boyhood trained in battlefield', by the end of February. But by now, as he was suffering from consumption, he became quite ill. He took a country house in order to relax as much as he could when his official duties allowed. He also informed Kemble that he must postpone his visit to London until the following spring of 1826. Weber had asked for £2,400 for his labours. Kemble offered him terms well below this: £500 for the score of *Oberon*, for conducting twelve performances of the opera £225, and five other concerts at £25 each, making a total of £850, only a third of the sum which Weber expected.[16]

His health gave increasing cause for concern and he agreed with the doctors to go to Ems for a rest in July. It was here that the meeting took place, mentioned at the beginning of this chapter, with Sir George Smart and Charles Kemble. Weber reluctantly agreed to Kemble's terms. He had aggravated his condition on his way to Ems by stopping at Weimar to meet Goethe, who had summarily dismissed him. On recovering, Weber's time was largely spent on his official duties, but he was able to resume work on *Oberon* in September. He finished Act I by 18 November and almost the whole of Act II by 3 December, apologising to Planché for the delay: 'You must have indulgence with a very much toiled and moiled poor man as I am.'[17] Whilst he composed, wrapped in furs in a heated room with swollen feet and wearing velvet boots, Weber had an incessant cough and suffered from depression. When he was in Berlin in December to

13 The Argyll Rooms, Regent Street, London, 1806, where Liszt, Weber and Mendelssohn performed

conduct *Euryanthe*, he told the playwright, Friedrich Gubitz, who had advised him not to undertake the London journey: 'Whether I can or no, I must. Money must be made for my family. I am going to London to die there. Not a word! I know it as well as you.'

There was better news from Kemble about the contract for *Oberon* and in January 1826, Weber received a letter from Sir Charles Smart, offering him accommodation at his London house until he was otherwise fixed up.[18] By 6 January, Weber, working with feverish haste, had virtually finished Act III of the opera, reusing two pieces from his early opera *Peter Schmoll*. With the journey to England now imminent, Weber began to put his affairs in order and consult his legal friends. His appearance was changed: his voice had almost gone; he coughed incessantly, and he would fall asleep unaccountably when in company. Caroline pleaded in vain with him not to go, for the sake of the family, as well as for himself. On 16 February 1826, a carriage drew up at Weber's house in Dresden and after bidding a fond farewell to Caroline and the children, Weber, accompanied by his friend the flautist Anton Fürstenau left for England.

Weber was in better mental and physical condition on his journey. He spent a week in Paris, meeting leading poets and musicians, having long sessions with Boieldieu, Cherubini, Hérold and Rossini. The last described Weber as 'very pallid, breathless for having climbed my stairs, for he was already very ill'. He believed Weber to be a genius: 'I felt an emotion not unlike the one I had felt earlier upon finding myself in the presence of Beethoven.'[19] Rossini became one of the many people who tried to dissuade Weber from continuing his journey: 'He would be committing a crime ... suicide.' Weber, however, felt obliged to fulfil his contract. Fürstenau and Weber reached Calais on 4 March and arrived in London the next day.

The carriage journey, via Rochester, was a pleasant one. 'The meadows are of the loveliest green,' wrote Weber, 'the gardens full of bright flowers, and the houses of an elegance and neatness which contrast in the most incredible way with the dirt of France.' He arrived at Sir George Smart's home at 91 (now 103) Great Portland Street and was very happy with the living arrangements. He wrote immediately to Caroline:

> Here, in Smart's house, I am excellently well taken care of. Every possible comfort is provided – a bath-room in the house. We dined at six; and by ten o'clock, I was in my good bed, where I slept charmingly till seven. Fürstenau is lodged close by. I found a host of visiting-cards awaiting my arrival. One of the first piano-makers has provided me with an admirable instrument, which, in a charming note, he begs me to make him happy by using during my stay ... I am allowed to be alone the whole day until five; then we dine out and go to the theatre, or into society.[20]

One of the houses frequently visited by Weber and Smart was that of Charles Kemble at 5 Soho Square. His two daughters, Fanny and Adelaide, had awaited Weber's arrival with eagerness. Fanny had been fascinated with the production of *Der Freischütz* the previous year and saw the opera several times. She admitted to a great feeling of affection for the composer and wore a small engraving of him in a locket round her neck, but when she met Weber, she was shocked at his appearance:

> He was a little thin man, lame of one foot, and with a slight tendency to a deformed shoulder. His hollow, sallow, sickly face wore an expression of habitual suffering and ill-health, and the long, hooked nose, sallow cheek bones, light, prominent eyes, and spectacles, were certainly done no more than justice to in the unattractive representation of my cherished portrait of him.

Smart, in introducing the sisters to Weber, assured him that both Fanny and Adelaide and all the young girls in England were head over heels in love with him. Weber, who was not noted for his sense of humour,[21] did not spare the young women's embarrassment. Fanny continued:

> With my guilty satchel round my neck, I felt ready to sink with confusion, and stammered out something about Herr von Weber's beautiful music, to which, with a comical, melancholy smile, he replied, 'Ah, my music! It is always my music, but never myself!'[22]

Weber was anxious to begin work, and on the day of his arrival in London he went, hoping to be unobserved, to Covent Garden to see the theatre, where *Marco Polo* was being performed. However, when he was recognised by the audience there were shouts of 'Weber! Weber!'; the performance was suspended whilst the overture to *Der Freiscshütz* had to be played, and this was followed by thunderous applause. 'I was deeply affected,' he wrote to Caroline. 'Could it be the English, generally called so cold, who received me? It seemed incredible.'[23]

An even greater triumph awaited him at the first of the Oratorical Concerts, 'Grand Performances of Ancient and Modern Music', at which he was to conduct a selection from *Der Freischütz*. The whole house rose up on his entry, and the applause continued for a quarter of an hour before he was able to begin. Weber was coughing noticeably during the performance, and subsequently Great Portland Street was besieged with jellies, lozenges and cough cures. When the first of the sixteen rehearsals for *Oberon* was held on 9 March there were many problems. John Braham, the veteran tenor who took the part of Huron and called by Planché 'one of the worst actors ever seen', found some of the arias too high for him. Mary Paton as Reiza, although in Benedict's opinion was gifted with a good voice, was 'wayward, capricious, made frequent alterations and abbreviations in her part'. At one rehearsal, Weber stopped her in the middle of an aria, asking: 'My dear lady, why give yourself so much trouble? I do not wish you to sing so much more notes than I have written.' More bluntly, Kemble declared, 'That woman's an inspired idiot', while Weber limped up and down the room, silently wringing his hands. Further, according to Planché, none of the actors could sing and only one singer, Lucia Vestris as Fatima, could act.

Weber was happy to write new arias for Braham and even granted the request of the stage manager, John Fawcett, for a singing part. On the other hand he could be quite fierce when he considered the musical integrity of the opera was in danger of being eroded. When the mermaid, Mary Gouard, could not keep time with the orchestra, Fawcett shouted: 'Cut it out!' At this, to everyone's surprise, Weber sprang over the balustrade into the orchestra, picked up the baton and cried: 'What do you mean? I'll show you how it will go', and saved the day.[24]

Away from the opera house there were other forms of music-making in which Weber took part. He was not of the temperament of Rossini, whose showmanship and entrepreneurial skills won him both admiration and wealth. Over-sensitive and lacking the common touch, Weber was uneasy in aristocratic company. On one occasion he performed on the piano at Lord Hertford's house in the presence of over 500 guests. Weber described the event thus:

> The noise and chatter of the throng of people was appalling. There was an attempt to get a little quiet while I played, and about a 100 people gathered interestedly about me. What they heard, God alone knows, because I didn't hear much. I thought busily of my thirty guineas and so kept my patience. Eventually at 2 o'clock everyone went into supper and I excused myself.[25]

On another occasion, Lady Guilford asked him to play the *Freischütz* overture: 'That's not piano music, Madam,' he replied. When she pointed to the cover of his own piano arrangement he remarked bitingly: 'You are quite right to remind me of that mistake. I'll play it to punish myself.' On the other hand he was pleased to be invited to perform in royal circles by Prince Leopold and the Duke of Clarence. He was twice received at family meetings at the Duchess of Kent's, where he accompanied her in his own compositions; the duchess's daughter, the seven-year-old Princess Victoria, was present and enjoyed the music.

Weber's heavy musical commitments made great demands on his weak constitution. Apart from the rehearsals and performances of *Oberon* there were Oratorio concerts, the Philharmonic Society concerts, and two benefit concerts as well as performances in aristocratic houses. In addition, he had not finished composing Act III of *Oberon*, two extra arias for Braham and the overture; the last parts were completed three days before the opening night. By early April he was suffering from extreme nervous irritability, chest constriction, fever and swollen feet; his hand shook visibly and he was spitting blood. Weber was also suffering from homesickness. Nevertheless, he fulfilled the majority of his commitments even though on one occasion when attending a dinner given by a Member of Parliament in his honour, he had to be carried upstairs to the drawing room.

The premiere of *Oberon* on 12 April was eagerly awaited by the public; all twelve performances of the opera had already been sold out. Weber's appearance at the conductor's desk was greeted with a standing ovation by the audience and orchestra. The overture had to be encored, as were individual numbers, and an attempt was made to encore the whole of the second act. At the end of the performance there were shouts for Weber which continued until the frail and exhausted composer appeared on the stage. The audience's enthusiasm was not shared by the music critics the next day, who complained at the lack of melody and the difficult nature of the music. Weber himself had compromised in producing a work which consisted of a hotchpotch of a plot, with an emphasis on visual effects and comedic interludes. Planché records that he met Weber on the stage the following morning who embraced the librettist most affectionately and remarked: 'Now we will go to work and write another opera together, and *then* they shall see what we can do!'[26]

The effort of conducting the opera exhausted him. The fog depressed him and the spring weather was extremely cold. 'This is a day on which to shoot oneself,' he told Caroline on 18 April.[27] He was cheered when the weather improved, and he made a few excursions to parts of London and the surrounding country. He was delighted with Hampstead, Richmond and Chelsea and, as with other composers before and after him, fascinated by the mass of shipping at Greenwich.

Weber's continuing ill health left him too weak to compose, and some of the conducting engagements turned out to be unexpectedly arduous. One particular concert provides an interesting insight into both the hazards of music-making and musical taste in England at this time. Weber had promised to conduct at Braham's benefit concert on 18 May. Moscheles, a good friend of Weber, left an account of the proceedings. Braham, after singing several sea-shanties and popular songs, was followed by Lucia Vestris, who treated the audience to songs from operettas, and some nursery rhymes. These were well received by those in the gods, but when in the second half, with Weber conducting his overture to *Ruler of the Spirits* and other works of a more serious character, the mood of the audience changed. The music was drowned out by shouting from the gallery, and it was only with the resumption of popular melodies and sea-shanties at the end that order was restored.[28]

Weber was too unwell to attend the annual festival of the Royal Society of Musicians where it was customary for the invited composer to present

NEVER ACTED.

Theatre Royal, Covent-Garden,

Tomorrow, WEDNESDAY, *April* 12, 1826,

Will be performed *(for the first time)* a Grand Romantic and Fairy OPERA, in three acts, (Founded on WIELAND's celebrated Poem) entitled

OBERON:

OR,

THE ELF-KING's OATH.

With entirely new Music, Scenery, Machinery, Dresses and Decorations.

The OVERTURE and the whole of the MUSIC composed by

CARL MARIA VON WEBER,

Who will preside that Evening in the Orchestra.

The CHORUS (under the direction of Mr. WATSON,) has been greatly augmented.
The DANCES composed by Mr. AUSTIN.
The Scenes painted by Mess. Grieve, Pugh, T. and W. Grieve, Luppino, and assistants.
The Machinery by Mr. E. SAUL. The Properties by Mess. BRADWELL,
The Dresses by Mr PALMER, Miss EGAN, and assistants.

Fairies.

Oberon, *King of the Fairies,* Mr. C. BLAND;   Puck, Miss H. CAWSE.
Titania, *Queen of the Fairies,* Miss SMITH.

Franks.

Charlemagne, *King of the Franks,* Mr. AUSTIN,
Sir Huon, of Bourdeaux, *Duke of Guienne,* .... Mr. BRAHAM,
Sherasmin, *his Squire,* .... Mr. FAWCETT,

Arabians.

Haroun-Al-Rashchid, *Caliph of Bagdad,* Mr. CHAPMAN,
Baba-khan, *a Saracenic Prince,* Mr. BAKER;   Hassan, *Master of a Vessel,* Mr. J. ISAACS,
Ismet, Mr. EVANS;   Amrou, Mr. ATKINS,
Reiza, *Daughter of the Caliph,* .... Miss PATON,
Fatima, Madame VESTRIS,
Namouna, *Fatima's Grandmother,* . Mrs. DAVENPORT.

Tunisians.

Almansor, *Emir of Tunis,* ...... Mr. COOPER,
Abdallah, *a Corsair,* Mr. HORREBOW,   Slave, Mr. TINNEY,
Roshana, *Wife of Almansor,* .... Miss LACY,
Nadina, *a female Slave,* Mrs. WILSON.
Officers, Soldiers, Slaves, &c. of the different Courts,——Fairies, Sprites, &c.

Order of the Scenery:

OBERON'S BOWER,

With the VISION.   Painted by Mr. Grieve.

Distant View of Bagdad, and the adjacent Country on the Banks of the Tigris,
By Sunset.   Grieve

INTERIOR of NAMOUNA's COTTAGE,   T. Grieve

VESTIBULE and TERRACE in the HAREM of the CALIPH, overlooking the Tigris.   W. Grieve

GRAND BANQUETTING CHAMBER of HAROUN.   F. Grieve

GARDENS of the PALACE.   Pogh

PORT OF ASCALON.   T. Grieve

RAVINE amongst the ROCKS of a DESOLATE ISLAND,
The Haunt of the Spirits of the Storm.   Pugh

Perforated Cavern on the Beach,

With the OCEAN—in a STORM—a CALM—by SUNSET—
Twilight—Starlight—and Moonlight.   T. Grieve

Exterior of Gardener's House in the Pleasure Grounds of the Emir of Tunis. Grieve

Hall and Gallery in Almansor's Palace.   W. Grieve

MYRTLE GROVE in the GARDENS of the EMIR.   Pugh

GOLDEN SALOON in the KIOSK of ROSHANA.   W. Grieve.
The Palace and Gardens, by Moonlight.   Grieve.
COURT of the HAREM.   Pogh.

HALL of ARMS in the Palace of Charlemagne. Grieve & Luppino

☞ *Books of the Songs to be had in the Theatre, price 1s.d.*

To which will be added (23d time) a NEW PIECE, in one act, called

THE SCAPE-GOAT.

Old Eustace, Mr. BLANCHARD,   Charles, Mr. COOPER,
Ignatius Polyglot, Mr. W. FARREN,   Robin, Mr. MEADOWS,
Molly Maggs, Miss JONES,   Harriet, Miss A. JONES.

W. REYNOLDS, Printer, 9. Denmark-Court, Strand

14 Weber's opera *Oberon*, first conducted by the composer at Covent Garden,
12 April 1826

a new work, but he dictated a march to Fürstenau for the performance. His main hope for financial success lay in a benefit concert he was to give at the Argyll Rooms on 26 May. The leading artists gave their services in a concert devoted mainly to Weber's own music. Catherine Stephens, a popular soprano, was to sing a song specially composed for her by Weber. He had so little strength that he was able only to write out the vocal line and accompanied her on the piano without music. It was to be his last composition.

The programme was a full one. He had arranged his *Jubel-Cantate* to be sung in English at *The Festival of Peace* which he rehearsed seated in a large chair. There were arias by Braham and Mary Paton, flute solos by Fürstenau and the overtures to *Oberon* and *Euryanthe*. The concert was an artistic success but a financial failure, raising only £96 11s. The hall was only half full due to heavy rain and competition from the Oaks at Epsom. However, the main reason was that the tenor Pierre Begrez gave his own benefit concert at the Duke of St Albans's house on the same day, attracting the cream of high society. When the *Euryanthe* overture was finished Weber was in despair as he was led by friends to lie down on a sofa. As they gathered round him he murmured: 'What do you say to that? That is Weber in London!'[29]

After a slight improvement in his health the painful symptoms had returned. He promised his colleagues to give up any more conducting engagements as well as a further benefit concert. Weber though was still optimistic and hoped to be with his family by the end of June. He planned to clear up personal matters, purchase presents for Caroline and the children, and leave England on 6 June. He wrote at this time: 'Thank God the end of it all is fast approaching.'

Returning from Mary Paton's benefit concert at the end of May he was out of breath and coughing blood. He was urged to delay the journey but he was determined to leave. On 4 June he lay exhausted in an armchair surrounded by his friends, Smart, Fürstenau, Goschen and Moscheles. The latter bid him goodnight, Weber saying that he hoped to see him again on the morrow. Moscheles, who was concerned at Weber's condition, wrote later:

> Sir G. Smart told me that on no account would Weber suffer any one to sit up with him; that every night he locked the door of his bedroom, and that only today he had yielded to the earnest entreaties of his friends, and promised to leave it open, adding that he had peremptorily refused to allow anybody, either friends or paid attendant, to watch beside him.[30]

After being helped to undress by Fürstenau, Weber said, 'Now let me sleep'. The next morning, 5 June, a maidservant tried his door but found it locked. She woke Smart and, alarmed, sent for the locksmith along with Moscheles. On breaking open the door, they saw Weber lying with his head on his left arm, dead as if peacefully asleep.

The news of Weber's death quickly spread and there followed musical tributes to his memory at Drury Lane, the Philharmonic Society and Covent Garden. His friends had hoped for a requiem at St Paul's Cathedral but as Weber was a Roman Catholic, this request was turned down. After repeated delays the body was conveyed to the Moorfields Catholic Chapel where he was interred in the vaults on 21 June. The route was lined with a great number of mourners. Eighteen years later, in 1844, subscriptions were raised in order to convey Weber's remains to Dresden. Due to the efforts of the young Richard Wagner, then *Kapellmeister* in the city, this was accomplished. At the ceremony, he delivered a moving oration over the composer's grave. Weber was in his fortieth year when he died.

The *Musical Times*, in a lengthy tribute to the composer nearly seven decades later, remarked:

> The old house in Great Portland Street will, in course of time, be no more; and the passer-by, who, in looking up at those second floor windows gives a kindly thought of poor Weber, will miss his familiar landmark. But a great musician's best memorial is his music. Of this, Weber has left us a goodly heritage; and therefore may we not say, 'He being dead yet speaketh.'[31]

9 Felix Mendelssohn

A genius recognised

Unlike many other musicians who visited England, Mendelssohn had not, in the first instance, intended to appear in public before audiences. His father, Abraham, a Berlin banker, had encouraged his gifted son to go 'into the world'. Travelling to countries such as Italy, France, Germany and England would broaden his view of culture, and making the acquaintance of musicians and artists would be a valuable experience. Felix himself had little inkling that his first visit to England in 1829 would be a great musical success in his triple role of composer, conductor and pianist.

There were several reasons why London was chosen to show off his talents. The Mendelssohn family had long been Anglophiles, with an especial liking for the English way of life. Many European composers and pianists, including Clementi, Dussek, Hummel and Moscheles were resident in the metropolis and had made their mark. It was likely, therefore, that his virtuosity as a pianist would be well received. Felix's financial and social position, unlike many other musical visitors, was also a great advantage. He found no difficulty in gaining access to the higher ranks of society who made up the majority of audiences in Britain. His introduction to the London musical scene was made easier by the presence here of two friends. Karl Klingemann, some eleven years older than Mendelssohn and secretary of the Hanoverian Legation, was welcomed in court circles. The other was the German-Bohemian pianist and composer Ignaz Moscheles, a former pupil of Beethoven. Moscheles had previously heard the fifteen-year-old Mendelssohn play the piano with a view to giving him lessons, but who had to admit: 'I can teach him nothing more.' Four years later, Moscheles received a letter from Abraham Mendelssohn asking for advice on whether the young man should visit London, bringing with him some of his compositions. Moscheles's opinion was encouraging. As he wrote later: 'Well, I thought and believed that the young man was a genius, so I counselled that he should come to us at Easter, and I promised with all my heart to introduce him to the great London world.'[1]

Jakob Ludwig Felix Mendelssohn was born on 3 February 1809 in Hamburg into a wealthy Jewish family which later settled in Berlin. His maternal great-grandfather was Daniel Itzig, who had been the second most important court Jew under Frederick the Great, and his paternal grandfather, Moses Mendelssohn, was a rabbi and distinguished liberal philosopher. Although Felix had been secretly baptised as a Christian in 1816, he was still proud of his Jewishness. When his father adopted the family name of Mendelssohn-Bartholdy, Felix refused to use it, preferring simply to be known as Mendelssohn.[2] His musical talents were recognised at an early age. By the time he left for England, he had composed two piano sonatas, a piano quartet, a string quartet, a string octet, a symphony, and the overture to *A Midsummer Night's Dream*. A month before, on 11 March 1829, he had conducted a performance of J. S. Bach's *St Matthew Passion*, a work which had not been heard for over eighty years.[3]

After a gruelling three-day voyage across the North Sea from Hamburg, Mendelssohn reached London on 21 April. Moscheles had arranged lodgings for the young man at the house of Friedrich Heinke, a German ironmonger, at 103 Great Portland Street. It was very comfortably appointed: there were two pianos for his use, and Mendelssohn was able to give dinner parties to select friends, including Dr Friedrich Rosen, Professor of Oriental Languages at University College, London. Heinke's son, Henry, later recalled:

> Mrs. Heinke [Mendelssohn's landlady] was *au fait* at making bread-and-butter puddings, and Mendelssohn was so fond of them that he asked her to keep a reserve of cold pudding in the cupboard in his sitting-room, to which he might help himself on his return from a late concert or social evening.[4]

Mendelssohn immediately threw himself into the social and cultural world which London offered. He was invited to parties by leading society hostesses at such places as Devonshire House and Lansdowne House. Within four days of his arrival in the capital he wrote to his father and sister Rebecka:

> It is fearful! It is mad! I am quite giddy and confused. London is the grandest and most complicated monster on the face of the earth. How can I compress into one letter what I have experienced in the last three days! I hardly remember the chief events, and yet I dare not keep a diary, for then I should have to see less of life, and that I do not wish. On the contrary, I wish to take everything that offers itself. Things toss and whirl about me as if I were in a vortex, and I am whirled along with them. Not in the last six months in Berlin have I seen so many contrasts and such variety as in these three days. Just turn to the right from my lodging, walk down Regent Street and see the wide, bright thoroughfare with its arcades (alas! it is again enveloped in a thick fog today) and the shops with signs as big as a man, and the stage-coaches piled up with people, and a row of vehicles left behind

by the pedestrians because in one place the smart carriages have crowded the way! See how a horse rears before a house because his rider has acquaintances there, and how men are used for carrying advertisements on which the graceful achievements of accomplished cats are promised, and the beggars, and the negroes, and those fat John Bulls with their slender, beautiful daughters hanging on their arms. Ah, the daughters![5]

His friend Klingemann took him to an English coffee house 'where, of course, I read *The Times*', and visited on two successive evenings the Italian Opera at the King's Theatre where the notable soprano, Maria Malibran, was making her English début. Mendelssohn was fascinated to observe that steamers on the River Thames were able to navigate the bridges because of a mechanism for lowering their funnels like masts. He even found a touch of his homeland in unlikely places:

The other day we walked home from a highly diplomatic dinner party at Buelow's, and were satiated with fashionable dishes, sayings and doings. We passed a very enticing sausage shop, in which 'German sausages, two pence each' were laid out for show. Patriotism overcame us, we each bought a long sausage, turned into Portland Streeet where it was quieter, and there consumed our purchases.[6]

His main purpose, however, was to advance his musical presence and in this he was initially disappointed. Soon after his arrival in London, Mendelssohn had called on the secretary of the Philharmonic Society with a view to having one of his new works performed. Because of a number of misunderstandings and intrigues within the society, he received no reply, but after, by chance, meeting two of its directors in a bookshop, he was immediately invited to conduct his First Symphony on 25 May. The occasion was to be the beginning of the long-lasting veneration of Mendelssohn in England.

He described to his father in detail the rehearsal and the concert. About 200 guests were present at the rehearsal. Mendelssohn had had made a little white baton for the occasion, and the concertmaster, John Cramer, showed him how the orchestra was placed. Upon being introduced to the orchestra, Mendelssohn noted, 'a few snickered, seeing a little fellow with a stick instead of the powdered and bewigged *Conductor* to which they were accustomed'. The occasion was one of the earliest uses of the baton in England and this soon became standard practice. The orchestra was particularly enthusiastic, tapping their bows and stamping their feet at the end of each movement.

The concert itself was a glorious occasion. The audience demanded a repeat of the symphony's adagio, which was ignored, but Mendelssohn had to repeat the scherzo, which was an orchestral version of the scherzo from his String Octet. The work was well received and at the end, as Mendelssohn wrote: 'I *handsshakte* till I left the hall.' As a mark of his gratitude, Mendelssohn dedicated the symphony to the society.[7] Near the end of his life, the composer stated that the 'universal English applause lifted a stone from my heart'.[8]

Within a week he was displaying his pianistic skills at a public concert at the Argyll Rooms as soloist in Weber's *Konzertstück* for piano and orchestra, which he played from memory. At a Philharmonic benefit concert on 10 June his symphony was repeated, and a fortnight later, Mendelssohn conducted *A Midsummer Night's Dream* overture for the first time in England. There was a grand finale to the season in July. On hearing from his uncle of the plight of the poor of Silesia who had suffered the effects of flash floods, Mendelssohn, together with a German soprano, Henriette Sontag, devised a four-hour long programme for the charity concert. For this, he gathered a number of celebrated musicians and composers, such as Clementi, John Taylor, Sir Thomas Attwood, who had been a pupil of Mozart, and Malibran. So many artists volunteered their services that there was not room for a single solo singer. Mendelssohn's part was to conduct his *A Midsummer's Night Dream* overture and to play, together with Moscheles, his Double Piano Concerto in E major. The concert was completely sold out and raised a sum of 300 guineas for the charity. In a short space of time, Mendelssohn had made his mark, both musically and socially, in London. He wrote later from Naples: 'There is no question that that smoky nest [London] is my preferred city and will remain so. I feel quite emotional when I think of it.'[9]

After the concert Mendelssohn left with Klingemann for a tour of Scotland. It was a hectic schedule with visits to Glasgow, Perth, Inverness and Loch Lomond. They travelled by coach to Edinburgh, arriving on 28 July, and they visited Holyrood Palace with its Mary Stuart connections, well known to them from the Schiller play. There was a pilgrimage to Abbotsford to meet Sir Walter Scott, whose works were celebrated in Germany. The visit was disappointing: the ailing author seemed indifferent to the company, resulting in 'a half hour of inconsequential conversation'. However, Mendelssohn particularly appreciated the Highland scenery, as witness the many delightful sketches with accompanying notes which he made at the time. Musically, he was less impressed, describing a bagpipe contest they had attended in unfavourable terms.[10]

On 7 August 1829, the two men set off by steamboat for the Isle of Staffa. As they sailed, the barometer fell and the seas rose. Klingemann wrote on their return:

> The ladies went down like ninepins, and one or two of the gentlemen followed their example. I wished my fellow-traveller in misery, Felix, had not been among them: but as an artist he gets along better with the sea than does his stomach ... We were put out into boats and

clambered past the hissing sea set on stumps of columns to the odiously celebrated Fingal's Cave. I must say, never did such green and roaring waves pound in a stranger cave. The many pillars made the inside resemble a monstrous organ. Black, resounding, and utterly without any purpose at all, it lies there, the broad gray sea inside it and in front of it.[11]

That same day, Mendelssohn told his family 'how extraordinarily the Hebrides affected me'. In the letter he sketched out the memorable opening bars of what was to become *The Hebrides* overture, given out on two bassoons. It is possible to see the enormous influence of the work on later European music, ranging from Niels Gade in Denmark to Mikhail Glinka in Russia. His sojourn in the north was also to provide ideas in years to come for his 'Scottish' Symphony.

On the way back to London before returning home, Mendelssohn decided to accept a standing invitation to stay with the mine-owner, John Taylor, and his family at Coed Du in North Wales. He broke his journey to travel by railway on the recently opened line from Liverpool to Manchester, with the train achieving a speed of 22 kilometres per hour. Mendelssohn enjoyed the scenery around Taylor's country estate and he was greatly taken with the three pretty musical daughters, Anne, Honoria and Susan. 'We have become friends, I think,' he informed his own sisters, 'and I am so deeply fond of the girls and I believe they like me too, for we are happy ... Yes, children, you may be scandalised, but I do nothing but flirt, and that in English!' One of the lasting souvenirs of his visit to the Taylors was a tribute to the three girls, a piano piece entitled *Trois fantasies*, which were musical portraits of the girls and their characters.[12]

Mendelssohn reached London on September 10 and resumed work on his E flat major String Quartet. He was looking forward to returning home for the wedding of his favourite sister Fanny on 3 October, and had composed wedding music especially for the occasion. He hoped too to find time upon his return to Berlin to begin his 'Reformation' and 'Scottish' Symphonies as well as *The Hebrides*. Unfortunately for him, before this could happen, Mendelssohn was knocked down by a cab and he damaged his kneecap. He was to be incapacitated for two months and he grieved at missing Fanny's wedding. As part of his recuperation, he spent a few days at Norwood, near London, the country seat of his old friend Sir Thomas Attwood. By November, he was able to return home in time for his parents' silver wedding, and composed a *singspiel* for them entitled appropriately *Die Heimkehr aus der Fremde*, The Return from Abroad.

During the next two years Mendelssohn travelled extensively throughout Europe, sightseeing, composing and giving concerts. It was in Rome in 1830 that he completed his third and final version of *The Hebrides* overture. His visit to Paris had not been an unqualified success. The Conservatoire Orchestra had rejected his 'Reformation' Symphony and whilst there he was saddened to hear the news of the death of Goethe, who had befriended Mendelssohn when he was a child. A further blow awaited him on his arrival in England on 23 April 1832, when he learned of the death of his tutor, Carl Zelter, who had taught him all aspects of musicianship and who had encouraged him to develop his own style. It was through Zelter that Mendelssohn was introduced to such outstanding musicians as Cherubini, Paganini and Spohr, as well as to Zelter's friend Goethe.[13]

Mendelssohn settled once again at his Great Portland Street lodgings. He was eager to show Moscheles his new compositions, and the day after his arrival Mendelssohn played for the first time some of his *Songs without Words* and the *Capriccio brillant* in B minor for piano and orchestra.[14] He was also busy as conductor and performer. The overtures to *The Hebrides* and *A Midsummer Night's Dream* were acclaimed, as well as his performance of his Piano Concerto No. 1 in G minor. An organ recital of Bach's music in St Paul's attracted a distinguished and enthusiastic audience and gave an opportunity of displaying his skills of improvisation.[15] The first volume of *Songs without Words* was published by Vincent Novello in London, but it made little initial impact. Only forty-eight copies were sold in the first year, and 144 in total after four years. Mendelssohn forfeited the rights on volumes 1 and 3 of the work, as well as three preludes and fugues and three choral motets, for a sum of £35.[16]

Whilst he was content to pursue his career primarily as a composer, his family had other ideas for him. Following the death of Zelter, there was a vacancy for head of the prestigious *Singakademie* in Berlin. Mendelssohn, against his better judgement, was persuaded to apply for the post but, largely because of the attitude of some committee members towards his Jewishness, it was given to a far less talented candidate.[17] He was deeply wounded by the rejection and he called the autumn of 1832 'the bitterest time which I can imagine and which I have ever experienced'; it is believed that a deterioration in his health from that time was triggered by this incident. But good news followed almost immediately. In November, the Philharmonic Society of London offered Mendelssohn a commission to write a symphony, an overture and a vocal composition for a sum of 720 rheinhalters. He was also delighted to hear that Moscheles and his wife wished him to be a godfather to their son, to be named Felix, and to be present at the ceremony.

He was back in England in good spirits on 25 April 1833. The highlight of the visit was the Philharmonic concert on 13 May, when the composer conducted the world premiere of his Italian Symphony No. 4 in A and he also performed Mozart's D minor Piano Concerto. The reception of the symphony was outstanding. However, there was little time to savour this success as, on the following morning, Mendelssohn had to leave for

Düsseldorf, where he had been appointed to direct concerts for the Lower Rhine Music Festival. He returned to London with his father Abraham on 3 June. As with many other visitors before and since, he noted the all-enveloping yellow fog which assumed larger dimensions as the day progressed: 'At four o'clock I had to move my table right to the window in order to see not *what* I was writing but *that* I was writing!' Abraham, who spoke no English, was shown off to many of Felix's friends. Like his son, he was fascinated by Malibran, whose private life was the subject of much speculation. When Abraham suffered a leg injury remarkably similar to that which Felix had incurred on his first visit, he was looked after with great solicitude by his son.

Felix, as we have seen, never denied his Jewish ancestry. In July he recorded, with some satisfaction, after attending a debate in the House of Commons:

> This morning they have emancipated the Jews; that pleases me tremendously. After a number of Jew-baiters, Mr Finn, Mr Bruce . . . and Inglis had twaddled unctuously, Mr Robert Grant, the sponsor of the bill, concluded with the question, whether they believed they existed in order to fulfil the prophecies of Scripture . . . and stated that he himself followed the word 'Glory to God and good will to men'. Thereupon followed ayes 187 and noes 51. This is quite noble and beautiful and makes me proud.[18]

One interesting aspect of Mendelssohn's social life at this time was the friendship which he struck up with the organist and composer, William Horsley, and his family. Mendelssohn became a regular visitor to their house in Church Lane, Kensington, then in the fields, and he was immediately taken with the charms of their three daughters, Mary, later wife of the engineer Isambard Brunel, Frances (Fanny) and Sophy. Together with his friends Klingemann and Rosen, he was a welcome visitor to their house. There he could relax, even in the presence of his father, as Fanny describes in a letter of 13 July:

> After tea we went into the garden and all played at Ghost except old Mendelssohn and I . . . Mendelssohn runs the quickest, but Dr. Rosen the most graceful. Mendelssohn and Sophy at my desire played the beautiful Ottetto; and the bass, though perhaps you won't believe it, was quite so good as the treble. Afterwards we had a quadrille . . . Mendelssohn engaged me before tea. He was very droll, in the highest spirits I ever saw, laughing at his own jokes, whirling round in pirouettes and all sorts of 'folies'.[19]

Sophy, the youngest of the sisters, reported, after calling on Mendelssohn: 'I have ever seen him look so handsome, but never, never, did I see such a blaze of light when he stood in the passage door; he appeared so perfectly happy.'

When Felix broke the news to the Horsley family that he had accepted the music directorship at Düsseldorf from October and that he would not be returning to England for two years, they were dismayed. Mendelssohn also seems to have been affected by the decision. Fanny describes one of his last visits, together with Klingemann, to the Horsleys:

> Sophy and I, who were sitting in the parlour, heard voices, a rushing up the steps and then the peculiar knock. Mama happily soon sent for us by Anne who came in with (she is by the way a great oddity) 'Miss Fanny, your Mama says you and Miss Sophy is to go up, as Mr. Mendisllum and Mr Liggimum is there'. We just stopped to correct her pronunciation and then proceeded to the drawing room where sat Felix and K. They stayed a full half hour and it was a very merry visit and we talked and laughed a great deal. F. sank once or twice behind a cloud, but I stirred him up with such a very long pole the instant that I saw the attack coming on, that his spirits rose and he went off quite elated.[20]

The final meeting with the Horsleys was shortly before the Mendelssohns left for Berlin on 3 August. Felix arrived for breakfast, then spent some time with Horsley in his study, looking at some Clementi manuscripts which his host presented to him. Returning to the family, Mendelssohn played his new *Rondo brillant* for piano and orchestra and the overture composed for the Philharmonic Society, *The Fair Melusine*. Before his departure, he drew up a solemn contract with the girls, promising by the end of September a piano duet arrangement of the overture for Fanny and Sophy. In return, their contract stipulated sending him a box full of Christmas presents. The family accompanied Klingemann and Felix to Apsley House in Piccadilly. Mendelssohn turned round at the gate and with a serious demeanour said: 'Oh pray, Mrs. Horsley, pray let me find no changes. Let all be the same as ever.' There were, in fact, to be a number of important changes in Mendelssohn's own life before he returned to England four years later.

The Düsseldorf appointment turned out to be a disenchanting experience. Mendelssohn's attempts to introduce reforms into opera productions met with opposition and, uncharacteristically, he gave up the post after only a few months. Shortly after this, he was approached to become *Kapellmeister* of the prestigious Gewandhaus Orchestra in Leipzig, the city of his beloved Johann Sebastian Bach, and he accepted the position. Whilst at Düsseldorf he had been working on his oratorio *Saint Paul*, a work which his father had urged him to complete. Abraham's death in November 1835 was a great personal loss for Mendelssohn; the first performance of the oratorio the following year was an act of homage to him.

Another important landmark in his life was his meeting with, and subsequent marriage to, Cécile Jeannrenaud, the daughter of a Reformed French Church pastor. They were married in March 1837 when she was nineteen and Felix was twenty-seven. Their honeymoon was spent travelling in Germany, though his musical commitments were always to the fore. Shortly after their marriage, Mendelssohn was approached by the organising committee of the Birmingham Triennial Festival through its director, Joseph Moore, to write a new work and to appear as performer. The festival, which dated back to 1784, was held over a period of four days in Birmingham Town Hall. Mendelssohn accepted the invitation.

He reached London on 27 August 1837, attended a performance of *Saint Paul* and gave a number of organ recitals. In contrast to his previous visits, Mendelssohn was in no mood for socialising. He wrote to his friend Ferdinand Hiller from London on 1 September:

> I am much too cross and melancholy today. It is nine days since I parted from Cécile at Düsseldorf; the first few were quite bearable, though very wearisome, but now I have got into the whirl of London – great distances – too many people – my head crammed with business and accounts and money matters and arrangements – and it is becoming unbearable, and I wish I were sitting with Cécile, and had let Birmingham be Birmingham, and could enjoy my life more than I do today. D—n it![21]

During his short stay in Birmingham, Felix was able to display many aspects of his talents. He gave an organ recital on the opening night and conducted a performance of *Saint Paul* on the second. His new work for the festival was his Second Piano Concerto in D minor, which he conducted from the keyboard. One local paper described the intense excitement of the occasion: 'As soon as he entered the orchestra the applause was almost uproarious.' Mendelssohn himself wrote afterwards: 'I had such a brilliant success ... The applause and shouts at the least glimpse of me really made me laugh.'[22] On the final night, after giving another organ recital, he immediately took a coach to London, thence to Dover, boarded a channel steamer and journeyed across France to Frankfurt where he joined Cécile. The journey had taken six days in all. After a short rest the couple proceeded to Leipzig where, four hours after arriving, he conducted another concert. If the fifth visit to England had been his shortest it had certainly been the most exhausting.[23]

The many different demands of Mendelssohn's activities took its toll. By the time of his next visit in 1840, he had composed three more string quartets, two more volumes of *Songs without Words*, including the famous 'On Wings of Song', the Second Piano Trio, and had started work on a

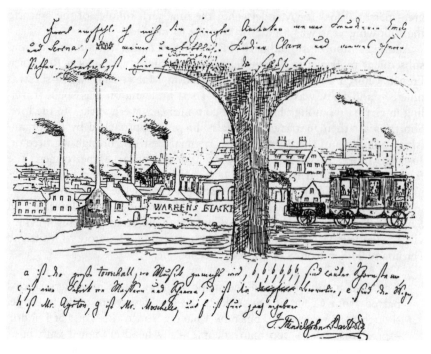

15 Drawing of Birmingham by Mendelssohn, 1846

violin concerto. In addition, his conducting commitments absorbed much of his time. His constitution, which was never robust, was undermined and he suffered from migraine and at times deafness. To add to his difficulties, Cécile, now the mother of two children, also suffered from delicate health. Despite his problems, Mendelssohn was anxious to accept a further invitation to perform at the 1840 Birmingham Festival. In August, shortly before leaving Leipzig, he played an organ recital in Bach's own church, the Thomaskirche, consisting entirely of the great master's music, in order to raise funds for a statue to the composer. Erected three years later, it still stands by the church today.

After Mendelssohn had landed in England on 17 September, he immediately made his way to the Moscheles's household where, as Mrs Moscheles reported: 'Felix junior had such a tremendous romp with his godfather, that the whole house shook.'[24] After two days, Mendelssohn and Moscheles travelled on the railway from London to Birmingham, and the former sent the Moscheles's children a sketch of the train arriving at Birmingham. Mendelssohn's newest work, which received its British premiere, was *The Hymn of Praise (Lobgesang)*, performed on 23 September and conducted by Moscheles. Although it was enthusiastically received, Mendelssohn was not satisfied with the piece and subsequently revised the second part. A week later, Felix was on his way back to

Leipzig. He was anxious to return home where Cécile was pregnant with their third child.

Mendelssohn's seventh visit two years later was perhaps the most memorable of them all, despite his many new responsibilities. He had been appointed director of the music section of the Academy of Arts in Berlin and had moved to the city whilst remaining notionally in charge of the Gewandhaus Orchestra in Leipzig, and still conducted at the Lower Rhine Festival. A visit to his beloved England in late May would be a relief from his other responsibilities, especially as Cécile would be accompanying him. At the first of the five Philharmonic Society concerts, for which he received £180, held on 3 June 1842, Felix conducted his 'Scottish' Symphony, No. 3 in A, in which he drew on memories of his visit to Scotland in 1829. As ever, the audience greeted his music with acclaim. At the same concert he was also the soloist in his own D minor Piano Concerto.

Mendelssohn's fame attracted the attention of royalty. The King of Prussia, Friedrich Wilhelm IV, had given him a letter of introduction to Prince Albert, who had aspirations as a composer as well as a performer. Accordingly, Felix was invited to Buckingham Palace early in June to make the acquaintance of Albert, and was asked again on the 16th of the month to play the organ there. As they were talking, Queen Victoria entered the room. She wrote in her journal:

> After dinner came Mendelssohn Bartholdy, whose acquaintance I was so anxious to make . . . He is short, dark, & Jewish looking – delicate – with a fine intellectual forehead. I should say he must be about 35 or 6. He is very pleasing & modest, & is greatly protected by the King of Prussia. He played first of all some of his *Leider ohne Worte* (*Songs without Words*) after which, his Serenade & then, he asked us to give him a theme, upon which he could improvise. We gave him 2, *Rule Britannia* & the Austrian National Anthem He began immediately, & really I have never heard anything so beautiful; the way in which he blended them both together & changed over from one to the other, was quite wonderful as well as the exquisite harmony & feeling he puts into the variations, & the powerful rich chords, & modulations, which reminded one of all his beautiful compositions. At one moment he played the Austrian Anthem with the right hand he played *Rule Britannia*, as the bass, with his left! He made some further improvisations on well known themes & songs. We were all filled with the greatest admiration. Poor Mendelssohn was quite exhausted, when he had done playing.[25]

Felix elaborated on the event in a letter to his mother:

Just as we were in the midst of a conversation, in came the queen, also quite alone and dressed in a house dress. She said that she had to leave for Claremont in an hour. 'My God, what a mess there is here!' she exclaimed, noticing that the wind had scattered single sheets of a large, unbound score which was lying on the organ ... and blown them into all corners of the room. So saying, she knelt down and began to gather up the sheets. Prince Albert helped, and I deigned to do likewise. The prince explained the various registers to me, and she said: never mind, she would straighten up the room all by herself. Then I asked the prince to play something for me so that I could boast about that in Germany. He played a Chorale by heart, pedalling nicely, cleanly, and without mistakes, so well that many a professional organist could have taken it as an example. The queen, who had finished her work, sat down and listened with pleasure. Now it was my turn to play, and I began my Chorus *Wie lieblich sind die Boten* from *St Paul*. Even before I had finished the first verse, both of them began to sing along. While I played, Prince Albert manipulated the registers skilfully; first a flute, then at the *forte* at the C-Major passage everything full, then an excellent *diminuendo*, and so on until the end of the piece, and everything by heart. I was enchanted and happy.[26]

The queen asked Mendelssohn if he had composed any new songs, as she loved to sing those already published. She was persuaded by Albert to sing the Spring Song, accompanied by Felix, and later, another song by his sister Fanny. When Victoria sang another Mendelssohn song, she confessed that she had been nervous performing in the presence of the composer. Felix recounted to his mother one amusing incident: 'Just as the queen was about to sing, she said, "But that parrot must be removed first, or he will scream louder than I sing"; upon which Prince Albert rang the bell and the Prince of Gotha said, "I will carry him out", upon which I replied, "Allow me to do that" ... and lifted up the big cage and carried it out to the astonished servants.'[27] Finally, he asked the queen for permission to dedicate his 'Scottish' Symphony to her, and she readily agreed. On 9 July, he once more played for the royal couple and again accompanied the queen. 'We thanked him very much,' Victoria wrote in her journal, 'and I gave him a handsome ring in remembrance.'

The Philharmonic Society had hoped to celebrate Mendelssohn's latest visit in a sumptuous manner but failed to do so. Instead, a whitebait dinner at Greenwich was hurriedly arranged, which both Felix and Cécile attended; in his speech, he promised to do all in his power to promote the interests of the Society.[28] The couple, happy at the success of their visit, left the following day for Frankfurt and then a well-earned rest in Switzerland.

It was his English friend, William Sterndale Bennett, the composer, pianist and a director of the Philharmonic Society, who invited Mendelssohn to conduct five Philharmonic Society concerts in May and June 1844. They were, financially and artistically, the most successful of all his ten visits to England. At one concert, he introduced the thirteen-year-old violinist Joseph Joachim to London audiences in the Beethoven Concerto. Felix also performed the newly written incidental music to *A Midsummer Night's Dream*. There was only one disappointment. Mendelssohn hoped to introduce the recently discovered Schubert Symphony No. 9 in C major, *The Great*, to English audiences. However, in rehearsal, the orchestra poked fun at the repeated triplets in the last movement; angered by the attitude of the musicians, Mendelssohn withdrew the piece. He once more visited Buckingham Palace, on 30 May, played some of his new works to the royal couple and presented them with a piano duet arrangement of a number of *Songs without Words*. Victoria enjoyed his company. 'He is such an agreeable, clever man,' she wrote, 'and his countenance beams with intelligence and genius.' Felix left England on 10 July. His next visit was to offer to the world his masterpiece, *Elijah*.

The Birmingham Festival Committee met on 11 June 1845 and passed a resolution 'that it appears to this committee desirable that the services of Dr Mendelssohn be obtained to act as conductor at the next Festival: and that he be requested to provide a new oratorio or other music for the occasion'.[29] The idea appealed greatly to Mendelssohn. He had, for some time, contemplated writing a large-scale oratorio on the subject of Elijah, but had been unable do so because of other pressing commitments. He now accepted the invitation, but only on condition that his conducting should be limited to the oratorio and the *Midsummer Night's Dream* music: Moscheles was to be the chief conductor for the festival.

By January 1846, Felix had started work on the composition. Nine years earlier he had considered Elijah as 'a prophet such as we could use again today – strong, zealous, angry, and gloomy, in opposition to the courtiers, the rabble and practically the whole world', and it is likely that there was a strong autobiographical element in the work.[30] By May, the first part had been set, and by July, a month before the festival, the last choral parts were despatched to Birmingham.

The Philharmonic Society Orchestra had been engaged for the occasion. When Mendelssohn heard that the festival director Moore intended not to employ those members of the orchestra whose behaviour on his previous visit had led to the abandonment of the performance of Schubert's Ninth Symphony, he protested, 'there is nothing I hate more than the reviving of bygone disputes', and the offending musicians were reinstated.[31] Every detail of the oratorio was scrutinised by Mendelssohn. The translation of the text from German into English was by William Bartholomew, an old friend, but the composer in many cases insisted on changes.[32]

16 Mendelssohn conducting the first performance of *Elijah*, Birmingham Town
   Hall, 26 August 1846

Mendelssohn arrived in London on 18 August and five days later travelled
to Birmingham with the performers. They consisted of a 125-strong
orchestra, a choir of 271 and the four soloists, together with members of
the press. Jenny Lind, for whom Mendelssohn had great admiration, had
promised to sing the soprano solos, but failed to appear at rehearsal. The
performance took place in Birmingham Town Hall on 26 August. It was
an outstanding success and the audience demanded that eight of the numbers
be repeated. The following evening he wrote to his brother:

> From the very first you have taken such a friendly interest in my
> *Elijah*, and thereby so stimulated my desire and courage to complete
> it, that I must write and tell you of its first performance yesterday.
> No work of mine ever went so admirably at its first performance, nor
> was received with such enthusiasm by both the musicians and the audi-
> ence, as this oratorio. It was quite evident at the very first rehearsal
> in London that they liked it, and liked to sing and play it; but I confess,
> I was far from anticipating that it would have such vigour and attrac-
> tion at the first performance. Had you only been there! During the
> whole hour and a half that it lasted, the big hall with its two thou-
> sand people and the large orchestra were all so concentrated on the
> subject in question, that not the slightest sound could be heard from
> the audience, and I was able to sway at will the enormous mass of
> orchestra and choir and organ.[33]

It is interesting to note that the festival programmes traditionally lasted for three hours, so the remainder of the time was filled with vocal pieces by Cimarosa, Handel and Mozart. Mendelssohn stayed for the rest of the festival and in an exhausted state returned to London and thence home. During the following months, he extensively revised the oratorio, and it is this later version which is usually performed today.

In spite of growing ill health, his relentless activity continued. He started work on his third oratorio, *Christus*, planned to write an opera, *Lorelei*, and continued with his teaching duties at the Leipzig Conservatory, an institution which he had helped to found. Mendelssohn's doctors were now seriously concerned about his condition, but he could not resist an invitation from the Sacred Harmonic Society in London to conduct his new version of *Elijah*.[34] Initially, only one performance was planned, though in the event this rose to four London performances at the Exeter Hall and one each in Manchester and Birmingham, all within a period of eight days.

Mendelssohn arrived on 12 April 1847. Queen Victoria attended the second London performance on 23 April and three days later she attended the Philharmonic concert which he conducted. Besides performing his 'Scottish' Symphony and the *Midsummer Night's Dream* music, he was a soloist in Beethoven's Fourth Piano Concerto. Jenny Lind, much to his pleasure, was also in the audience.[35] Even this did not complete the demands on his energy: he took part in several chamber music concerts, played at two receptions at the house of the Prussian ambassador, where he met the future Prime Minister, William Gladstone, and paid two visits to Buckingham Palace, playing again for the queen. 'Another exhausting week like this, and I am a dead man,' he told Klingemann.

He left London for the last time on 8 May. Only a few days later, he learned of the death of his beloved sister Fanny and he collapsed. Of her death he wrote: 'I will never, never be able to get used to it.' In August, Mendelssohn completed a string quartet in memory of her and its dark tone indicates his state of mind at the time. Shortly after going for a walk with Cécile on 28 October, he became paralysed following a severe stroke. On 4 November 1847 after telling his family that he was 'tired, very tired', he died peacefully. He was thirty-eight years old. A friend at the deathbed reported that 'the expression of his face was indescribably friendly and peaceful'.[36]

Mendelssohn's ten visits to England spanned a period of eighteen years. Apart from Haydn no other visitor made such an impact as conductor, performer and composer. In turn, few visitors were inspired to create such marvellous music based on their experiences in this country. In Queen Victoria and Albert, Mendelssohn was fortunate in finding not only eager patrons but also kindred musical spirits. Victoria summed up the feelings of the nation at the composer's passing:

We were horrified, astounded and distressed to read in the papers of the death of Mendelssohn, the greatest musical genius since Mozart, & the most amiable man. He was quite worshipped by those who knew him intimately, & we have so much appreciated & admired his wonderfully beautiful compositions. We liked & esteemed the excellent man, & looked up to & revered, the wonderful genius, & the great mind, which I fear were too much for the frail delicate body. With it all, he was so modest and simple.[37]

10 Berlioz and Wagner
A meeting of minds

'I am quite surprised at my knowledge of English,' Hector Berlioz told his father on 7 November 1847, three days after arriving in London for the first time. 'I can say almost all I want without too much accent, but I do not understand a half of what is said. There is a lot of work to be done.' Berlioz was then forty-four, badly in need of money, and had been enticed to England by the lucrative terms offered by the entrepreneur-conductor Louis-Antoine Jullien. He would be appointed as opera conductor of the Drury Lane Theatre for six years at £1,600 per annum, £400 extra for concerts and £800 for composing an opera.

The composer, some five feet four inches in height, with piercing grey eyes, an oval face and firm mouth, and a high forehead capped by a mass of hair, was already an internationally known figure. The previous year, he had toured Central European countries and had composed *The Damnation of Faust*, *Harold in Italy*, *Romeo and Juliet* and perhaps his best-known work, the *Symphonie fantastique*. Berlioz was happy to take up residence with Jullien and his wife in their house at 76 (now 27) Harley Street, behind Oxford Street. He was assured that it was only a few steps to Drury Lane, and was surprised to find that the walk took him three-quarters of an hour.

Unfortunately for Berlioz, Jullien's skill as an impresario left much to be desired, as he was careless in planning and unrealistic in money matters. Jullien was also a showman and liked nothing better than being in the limelight. When he conducted, he was dressed in striking clothes, wore white gloves, and wielded a jewelled baton which a footman handed to him on a silver salver before the performance.[1]

The opera season opened with Michael Balfe's *Maid of Honour* conducted by the composer and Donizetti's *Lucia di Lammermoor*, conducted by Berlioz. The former was well received by the audiences whilst the Donizetti, though hailed at its early performances, was not. This was largely due to the poor singing of the main roles and the fact that Jullien had taken away many members of the orchestra on his tour of the provinces. Berlioz remarked to a friend on 'the unwholesome lot of tenors with which we are generally afflicted, all of us, that is, who unhappily look for a mind behind the voice'.[2]

This was Berlioz's introduction as a conductor to the opera house and by January 1848, the hectic routine – rehearsals from twelve to four and performance from seven to ten or eleven in the evening – led to a week in bed with bronchitis and fatigue. To add to this, Jullien was by now heavily in debt, leaving Berlioz with no salary. Nevertheless, the season continued with Berlioz conducting another Donizetti opera, *Linda di Chamounix*, and Mozart's *The Marriage of Figaro*. The Mozart, given on 11 February, was enthusiastically received.

Just four days before this, he had mounted his first Grand Vocal and Instrumental Concert at the Theatre Royal, Drury Lane, which was entirely devoted to his own works. With an orchestra and chorus of 250 performers, the programme must have taxed the ear of the most inveterate concert-goer. The first part consisted of the *Carnival Roman* overture and the symphony *Harold in Italy*. Part two was devoted to the first two parts of *The Damnation of Faust*, and the third part, selections from his opera *Benvenuto Cellini*, the *Requiem* and the *Grande Symphonie funèbre et triomphale*. All the works were new to London. The success of the concert, which lasted over four hours, had other benefits. Five days later, Berlioz noted: 'Now when I appear at the conductor's desk at Drury Lane to conduct the Opera in the evening, I am always met by a burst of applause.'[3] One music critic commented:

> A more perfect and magnificent performance was perhaps never listened to ... M. Berlioz fully realised his continental celebrity as a *chef d'orchestre*; his beating was emphatic and intelligible, and the mass of instrumentalists followed the slightest indications of his *baton*, the minutest shade of expression which he desired to obtain, with marvellous accuracy ... Not a little of the unusual excellence of his performance is due to the highly favourable impression which M. Berlioz has known how to produce among the members of his orchestra, by his polished and courteous manners; no conductor that ever entered an orchestra was more affable in his demeanour, or more gentlemanly in his conduct.[4]

By February, though, Jullien's inability to pay the artists was leading to open revolt. The horn-players threatened not to turn up for a performance of *Figaro* and a leading soprano refused to go on stage until she received an assurance that she would be paid. The negotiations were completed by the end of Act I and she took part in the remainder of the opera. In spite of these setbacks, when the season closed on 25 February it had been an artistic, though not a financial, success.

With the season behind him, Berlioz could relax. He wrote to a friend:

> I get up at midday and at one o'clock visitors arrive: friends, new acquaintances and musicians who've come to introduce themselves

whether I like it or not; that's three hours lost. From four to six I work. If I don't have any invitations, I go out for dinner some way away from here. I read the papers, after which it's time for theatres and concerts: I stay and listen to whatever music there is until 11.30, then at last three or four of us musicians go off together to have supper in some tavern and smoke till two in the morning. So much for the external details of my life here.[5]

Berlioz had considered settling in London and when news came of the uprising which had taken place in Paris in February and which led to the proclamation of the Second Republic, he was not anxious to return immediately. He was also enjoying being a celebrated figure, receiving hospitality in a number of great London houses and met people such as Thackeray, Charles Dickens's wife, and musicians including the conductors Charles Hallé and Julius Benedict. He found London an awesomely large city, though not always a friendly one. Walking round Trafalgar Square in March 1848, Berlioz's 'nice tie-pin' was snatched from his cravat. He witnessed the great Chartist meeting on Kennington Common and was impressed by the comparative orderliness of the crowd. He was also present in the audience at a number of musical events. On the day he landed in England, his adored friend Mendelssohn had died in Leipzig. After attending a Memorial Concert in Exeter Hall at which *Elijah* was performed, Berlioz was overwhelmed by a 'great emotional experience'. He was later present in the same hall when Mendelssohn's 'Italian' Symphony received its first British performance, and he considered it 'a masterpiece, struck in a single instant, like a gold medal'.

It was at this time that Berlioz decided to begin writing his *Mémoires*. He was able to complete four chapters in just under three weeks, spanning the period from childhood to the age of seventeen. Ten days later, on 20 April, the bailiffs arrived at Jullien's Harley Street house, where Berlioz was still asleep, and took possession. He had to plead with them not take his clothes and rapidly moved to 26 Osnaburgh Street (now demolished), near Albany Street, Regent's Park. Separated since 1844 from his wife, the Shakespearean actress Harriet Smithson, Berlioz was joined by Marie Recio, an undistinguished mezzo soprano, whom he married after Smithson's death ten years later. One of the hobbies Berlioz indulged in was a study of the harmonic resonance of church clocks. He was pleased to add to his collection a 'new' interval, a major third, in the clock of nearby Holy Trinity Church in Marylebone Road.

Although Jullien continued to promise to pay Berlioz for his services, nothing came of it. But by now, Berlioz's contribution to the London musical scene was widely recognised. As a tribute to him, a grand final concert was arranged at Hanover Square Rooms on 29 June, at which the orchestra, made up of players from Her Majesty's Theatre and Covent Garden, refused to accept any payment. The concert consisted of, besides

Berlioz's own works, pieces by Bellini and Mendelssohn. It was a great success, with the audience demanding four encores. The only disappointment, as Berlioz told the audience, was the absence of cymbals and drums in the rousing *Hungarian March*, in deference to the inhabitants of Hanover Square.

The civil war still continued in Paris. Berlioz was becoming restless, and with no other engagements to fulfil in London, it was time to return to Paris. On 13 July 1848, after eight months in the capital, he left for Folkestone and crossed the Channel. Shortly before he departed, he observed to a Russian friend: 'Would you believe it, the English are now really musical people; they like fine things and despise trivialities.'

Berlioz's second visit three years later was on quite different business. In April 1851, to his surprise, he was informed by the French Minister of Commerce that he had been appointed as one of ten distinguished men who would form a jury to hear and judge a whole range of musical instruments, which had been submitted by their makers, at the Great Exhibition in Hyde Park. This was to be held in the Crystal Palace, a glass structure designed by Joseph Paxton which was later taken to Sydenham and subsequently destroyed by fire in 1936. Berlioz arrived in London on 8 May and took rooms close to Jullien's old house, at 27 (now 58) Queen Anne Street, which was within walking distance of Hyde Park. Below him was the rehearsal room and concert hall of the excellent Beethoven Quartet Society; by opening his door, Berlioz could hear the strains of music drifting up the house.

The Music Committee of the Exhibition, with the task of deciding to whom to award medals, was chaired by Sir Henry Bishop, and included Sterndale Bennett, Cipriani Potter and Sir George Smart. The Committee met six days a week and continued in session until July. Berlioz took the work very seriously, financing the last few weeks of his stay himself. He wrote to his sister, Adèle Suat: 'No one can imagine the appalling drudgery of my particular task. I have to *listen* to the wind instruments, both wood and brass. My head is bursting from hearing hundreds of these foul machines, each more out of tune than the last, with three or four exceptions.'[6]

One of the undoubted exceptions was the submissions of Adolphe Sax, the Belgian-born instrument-maker. Sax, after whom the saxophone is named, was a close friend of Berlioz and like him, a romantic visionary.[7] He was to supply the composer with a sopranino saxophone in one version of *The Trojans*, and he made a special triangle for a performance of *Harold in Italy*. Not surprisingly, Sax, with his instrument-making ability, was a medallist, along with Theobald Boehm from Munich, the composer and flute-maker.

In June, Berlioz attended the annual Charity Children's Concert in St Paul's Cathedral at which some 6,500 orphans took part. Tickets were scarce, so Berlioz managed to obtain one through the organist, but only as a member of the choir:

> When I got to the organ loft [he wrote] reserved for the choir ... I was given a copy of the bass part which they asked me to sing with the rest, also a surplice which I had to put on ... Disguised thus as a cleric, I awaited the performance with a sort of vague emotion roused by the spectacle.

Berlioz was overwhelmed by the performance, as was Haydn before him: 'My feelings overcame me, and I had to use my music, as Agamemnon did his toga, to hide my face.' He left the cathedral in a dazed state.

In the evenings, Berlioz made several visits to the opera at Covent Garden and Her Majesty's Theatre. He saw *Fidelio* three times, *The Marriage of Figaro* and *Der Freischütz*. 'There is no city in the world, I am convinced, where so much music is consumed as in London.' He also enjoyed the variety and vivacity of the London street musicians, noting that 'several talented artists have found that the lot of the itinerant musician is incomparably less laborious and more lucrative than that of the orchestral musician in an opera house'.

Plans for a Crystal Palace Music Festival, which Berlioz tried to mount, with the participation of music societies from London, Liverpool and

17 Hanover Square Rooms, London, opened in 1774 and later home of the Philharmonic concerts

Manchester, failed to materialise. However, a more ambitious venture was advanced by him. A Philharmonic Society had been formed in 1813 to promote the performance 'in the most perfect manner possible of the best and approved instrumental music'.[8] The conservative nature of the programmes and the standard of playing left much to be desired. Berlioz, with the music publisher Frederick Beale, discussed the formation of a new organisation, the New Philharmonic Society, which was to create an orchestra consisting of many leading instrumentalists. Berlioz was engaged to organise and conduct concerts at Exeter Hall the following year, 1852, between March and June. There would be some 300 performers in all. On the strength of this development, Berlioz rented an apartment at 10 Old Cavendish Street and left for Paris on 28 July.

The 1852 season proved to be the highlight of his conducting career in England. Exeter Hall, on the site now occupied by the Strand Palace Hotel, attracted large audiences to the concerts. The first, given on 24 March, included four parts of his *Romeo and Juliet* Symphony, and a *fantasie* for double bass, composed and played by the virtuoso Giovanni Bottesini, who was a member of the orchestra. The success of the concert attracted an even larger audience for the second one three weeks later. Beethoven's Fifth Symphony was in Berlioz's estimation '*the* performance of the night', though he complained at the lack of rehearsal allowed for an inferior composition in the programme, a masque by Edward Loder, *The Island of Calypso*. He had already commented on 'the haste shown in all musical matters in England, and the artists' hatred of rehearsals. Their affection for what is nearly right, but not quite, for scratch performances, may ruin everything'.[9]

The third concert gave rise to new tensions for Berlioz. Camille Pleyel, who had married the son of the famous piano manufacturer and publisher, also called Camille, was engaged to perform in Weber's *Konzertstück* for piano and orchestra. More than two decades earlier, Camille Moke, as she was then, had been the object of Berlioz's passion, and he had hoped to marry her; but whilst the composer was studying in Rome, she had married the fifty-eight-year-old Pleyel. Berlioz thereupon resolved to disguise himself as a chambermaid, kill Camille and her mother, and then poison himself. He had travelled as far as Genoa on this mission, but there fell off the ramparts into the sea and abandoned his original plan. Camille's career as a concert pianist flourished subsequently but she never forgave Berlioz for publishing a short story about the courtship in which she was readily identifiable. At the concert, she claimed that Berlioz had deliberately set out to spoil one of her solo passages. Her revenge came in the final concert in the series when she decided to play solo pieces by Liszt and Rossini whilst Berlioz and the orchestra were merely passive listeners.

The young Dutch pianist and composer Edouard Silas visited Camille in her rooms in Regent Street during her London visit, and described the scene thus:

When I got there, she came in and said: 'I must take off my bonnet, it interferes with my smoking.' I thought I had misunderstood her; but when she presently brought out a box of big strong cigars, her meaning became clear. She offered me one, took one herself, lay down on the sofa and exclaimed 'Now play me something'. I soon saw that I'd found more than my match in the consumption of big and strong cigars. Mme Pleyel is a fine woman, an excellent pianiste, has led rather a wild life and has all sorts of scandals attached to her name, but – I liked her nevertheless.[10]

The next concert proved to be of historic importance for music-making. Beethoven's Ninth Symphony, the 'Choral', then barely known in England, was performed. It was ironic that the old Philharmonic Society, who had commissioned the work from Beethoven and owned the score, had only ever rehearsed it. The soloists included Clara Novello and Sims Reeves and the performance made a great impression on the audience. Berlioz was called back to the platform six times and a crown was thrown to him from the galleries.[11] The music critics were full of praise, that of *The Times* pointing out that justice had at last been done to the work.

Two more concerts remained. The first on 28 May contained two works by Mendelssohn: the Fourth Symphony, the 'Italian', and his Violin Concerto, followed by Berlioz's own version of a Weber's *Invitation to the Waltz*, which required eight harps, an extravagance for one short item in a lengthy programme. Because of its outstanding success, the Beethoven 'Choral' Symphony was repeated at the final concert on 9 June and was received once more with great enthusiasm.

Returning to Paris twelve days later, Berlioz still had high hopes of being invited back to London for a further series with the same orchestra. Although his concerts had been a success, the Philharmonic Society had made a financial loss, mainly because of the forces required for the Beethoven symphony. Furthermore, Berlioz was aware of moves to replace him. Writing in December 1852 to a friend, he commented:

They are busy at the moment arranging three concerts for me in April. I don't know whether it will be possible to remove certain obstacles which have just presented themselves owing to a Doctor Wylde, a professor at the Conservatoire, the friend of a millionaire, and an imitator of Handel. I'll let you know the end of this little intrigue, which is worthy of Paris.[12]

Dr Henry Wylde, a co-founder of the society, who had taught harmony at the Royal Academy of Music, was a mediocre composer and an ineffectual conductor. He had shared the rostrum with Berlioz at the fourth concert of the series where two of Wylde's choral pieces were performed. Wylde regarded Berlioz as a rival composer and conductor. By appointing Wylde in Berlioz's place, the society would save extra expense. With the retirement of Frederick Beale, the Society's manager, the way was open for Wylde to take over.

So far, the opportunity had not arisen for Berlioz to present his then sole opera *Benvenuto Cellini* to a London audience. It had had a chequered history. Completed in 1837, it was performed the following year at the Paris Opéra. In Berlioz's own words in his *Mémoires*: 'The overture was extravagantly applauded; the rest was hissed with exemplary precision and energy.' After its fourth performance in 1839, it lay neglected until Liszt revived it at Weimar thirteen years later, whilst Berlioz was in London.

As Berlioz anticipated, the new Philharmonic Society did not reappoint him for 1853 but an opportunity to produce the opera at Covent Garden appealed to him. Frederick Gye, the opera house manager, had begun negotiations with Berlioz in March 1853, with a view to mounting a performance in June. The composer arrived in London on 14 May, taking lodgings at 17 Old Cavendish Street, well aware of the very short time available for producing the large-scale opera.

He had also been approached by the old Philharmonic Society to conduct a half of one of their concerts at Hanover Square Rooms on 30 May. Berlioz offered the *Symphonie fantastique*, which had never been performed in England, but the committee preferred *Harold in Italy*, together with part of *The Flight into Egypt* (which became the second part of *L'Enfance du Christ*) and the *Carnival Roman* overture. Berlioz received a fee of ten guineas for his efforts. He boasted to a friend afterwards: 'I was tremendously applauded in spite of the fury of four or five intimate enemies who, I am told, shrivelled up in a corner.' He told the influential *The Times* music critic, J. W. Davison: 'It is a splendid preparation for the big affair at Covent Garden.'

Berlioz was pleased with the progress of the rehearsals of *Benvenuto Cellini* and worked intensively with the leading singers. The omens seemed good for the opening night. He had dined with several music journalists and the public's interest and curiosity had been aroused. The news that Queen Victoria and Prince Albert, together with the King and Queen of Hanover would attend, added extra excitement.

On the opening night, Berlioz himself conducted the orchestra. From the first notes of the overture to the end of the opera, there was hissing from a claque whom Berlioz took to be a few Frenchmen from Paris. The performance was ruined and, as Berlioz noted later: 'They were sure to continue the following evening, consequently I had to withdraw my work the next day.' Marie Recio had also been warned before the opera began that there would be disruption by Italians from the rival Her Majesty's Theatre, who would be paid for their efforts. There were others present who did not enjoy the opera. Queen Victoria called it 'one of the most unattractive and absurd operas I suppose anyone could ever have composed'. She added in her journal: 'There was not a particle of melody, merely disjointed and most confused sounds, producing a fearful noise ... The first two acts kept us in fits of laughter, owing to their extreme foolishness.'[13]

The experience depressed Berlioz but there was wide public support. This was demonstrated the following day when a committee headed by the piano manufacturer Broadwood was formed to sponsor a concert at Exeter Hall early in July for Berlioz's benefit. Some 200 musicians from both Covent Garden and Her Majesty's Theatre, together with the Covent Garden choir, offered their services without payment and a substantial sum of money was collected for the tickets within a few days. In the event, it proved impossible to find time for the performance. Berlioz refused to accept the money and instead proposed that it should be devoted to financing an English publication of *The Damnation of Faust*.

Although the possibility of reviving the opera was mooted, nothing came of the project. It was another century before it was performed in London again. Berlioz returned once more to Paris on 9 July 1853 after eight hectic and eventful weeks.

Berlioz's fifth and last visit to England almost exactly two years later proved to be perhaps the most satisfying experience of them all. Much had changed in his life since his previous stay. His wife, Harriet, had died, paralysed and speechless, in March 1854. The unhappy marriage was summed up by Berlioz in a letter to his sister after the funeral, which he was too distraught to attend: 'We could neither live together nor leave each other.' Six months later, he married the shrewish Marie Recio, who caused Berlioz much embarrassment by her displays of jealousy towards his colleagues.

Artistically, he had witnessed a great triumph in Paris with his new oratorio *L'Enfance du Christ* and the *Te Deum* which he had dedicated to Prince Albert. In London, the old Philharmonic Society offered Berlioz a season of eight concerts, with the proviso that he should conduct for no other body. Unfortunately for him, he had already agreed to perform two concerts for the new Philharmonic Society, and his old rival, Wylde, refused to allow Berlioz to break the contract. Arriving in London 8 June 1855, Berlioz and his wife took up lodgings at 43 Margaret Street with Mary Pannier, a dressmaker. Only five days later, he conducted his first concert, at Exeter Hall. It was, as usual, an enormously long programme, consisting of two overtures, Mozart's 40th, Beethoven's 'Emperor' Concerto, arias by Mozart and Rossini, and three movements from his own *Romeo and Juliet*. The choral parts of the latter had to be omitted because Berlioz discovered that some members of the choir had failed to attend even a single rehearsal with the orchestra, and the parts were extremely difficult to sing. To show their resentment at this action, some members of the choir hissed Berlioz at the concert. In spite of this, it was well

18 Berlioz and his orchestra, caricature by Grandville, 1846

received by the audience, and one of the movements was repeated. Unfortunately, a cloud was cast over the event by the news from the Crimea, where the war was in its second year, of the unsuccessful attempt to capture Sebastapol. *The Times*, which was covering the campaign at length, could not find space to print a review of the concert.

One of the most memorable events of the stay was the meeting in London with Richard Wagner. Wagner had been appointed to conduct the eight concerts with the old Philharmonic Society which Berlioz had originally been offered. This was not Wagner's first visit to England. In July 1839 he had had to flee from Riga to avoid his creditors, and after a terrible sea journey with his first wife Minna, he arrived in London in August. The ordeal left its mark. Having found accommodation at the King's Arms in Old Compton Street, according to Wagner, 'every time we shut our eyes we sank into frightful abysses, and springing up again, cried out for help'.[14]

For some time before this, Wagner had been working on a scheme for a grand opera, *Rienzi*, based on the work of the celebrated writer, Sir Edward Bulwer-Lytton. Whilst in England, Wagner was anxious to meet him and, as Bulwer-Lytton was an MP, Wagner made his way to the House of Commons hoping to meet him there. The composer's total ignorance of English did not help, but on ascertaining that the author was not present, he listened to a debate in the House of Lords on the Slave Trade Suppression Bill, led by the Prime Minister, Lord Melbourne. He also experienced 'a ghastly London Sunday', saw the statue of Shakespeare in Westminster Abbey, and visited the Chelsea Hospital, where a pensioner addressed him in Saxon.[15] After only eight days in England the Wagners left for Boulogne.

During Wagner's subsequent eighteen months' stay in France, spent mainly in Paris, he became acquainted with Berlioz and his music. Listening to a performance of *Harold in Italy* which delighted him, the *Symphonie funèbre et triomphale*, which he found equally impressive, and *Romeo and Juliet*, for which he expressed less admiration, Wagner admitted in his autobiography, 'it is a fact that at that time I felt almost like a little schoolboy by the side of Berlioz'. The latter, then aged thirty-six, was a successful composer of six major works. In contrast, Wagner, some ten years younger, was a virtually unknown, struggling musician. Wagner lived in poverty during his time in Paris. He was reduced to taking on musical hack work and like Berlioz before him even sought employment as a chorister in a popular theatre. The conductor who tested him discovered that Wagner could not sing at all and he failed to get the appointment.

The two men met again in Dresden in 1843 when Berlioz was conducting concerts in several German towns. At Dresden Wagner assisted him with his rehearsals which Berlioz noted 'he did with both zest and goodwill'. Berlioz described how Wagner 'had the audacity to embark upon and the good fortune to complete the composition of both the words and music of a five act opera, *Rienzi*. This work had a brilliant success in Dresden'. Berlioz also attended a performance of *The Flying Dutchman* which had received its premiere the previous month and he heard the last three acts of *Rienzi*. Wagner met Berlioz again briefly on his visits to Paris in 1849, 1850 and 1853. Although there was only a little correspondence between them, Berlioz and Wagner were aware of the other's activities through their letters to and from Liszt.

By the time of his second London visit in March 1855, Wagner was a political exile in Zurich, and had composed three more operas, *Lohengrin*, *Tannhäuser* and *Die Walküre*. In London the £200 fee which the Philharmonic Society offered him rapidly disappeared with the cost of accommodation, coal and cabs. Moreover he was depressed by the thick London fog and the unfriendly people. He accused *The Times* music critic, Davison, of hostility towards him on account of his (Wagner's) essay *Judaism in Music*, and complained of the inadequacy of the rehearsal time allowed by the Philharmonic Society. One consolation was the reception he received from Queen Victoria and Prince Albert at his penultimate concert on 11 June, where the queen expressed a wish to hear the *Tannhäuser* overture and then demanded a repeat of it.

Shortly before this concert, Berlioz had also arrived in London, and at the concert he gave on 13 June, Wagner was present. Subsequently Wagner wrote to his great friend, Franz Liszt: 'I heard a concert of the New Philharmonic under his (Berlioz's) direction and was, it is true, little edified by his performance of Mozart's G minor Symphony, while the imperfect execution of his *Romeo and Juliet* Symphony made me pity him.'[16] Berlioz, for his part, reported that 'Wagner conducts in a free style, the way Klindworth plays the piano ... such a style is like dancing on a slack rope ... *sempre tempo rubato*'.[17] It seemed likely, therefore, that when the two men met again, there could be difficulties. Liszt, however, had no doubt that the meeting would be an amicable one. He told Wagner: 'Of all contemporary composers, he is the one with whom you can converse in the simplest, and most interesting manner. Take him for all in all, he is an honest, splendid, tremendous fellow.'[18] Wagner, in his critical works, such as *Oper und Drama* (1851), had made disparaging remarks about Berlioz's works. Their dispositions were very different. Ferdinand Praeger, a German music teacher living in London at the time, though not always a reliable witness, compared the two as follows: 'Hector Berlioz was of an excitable temperament but could repress it. Not so Wagner. He presented a striking contrast to the polished, refined Frenchman, whose speech was almost classic through his careful selection of words.'[19]

In fact when Wagner and Berlioz met on 16 June at the former's lodgings at 22 Portland Terrace, Regent's Park, both men enjoyed the occasion. Berlioz had not read Wagner's criticisms and the latter, some ten years younger, admitted to admiring some of Berlioz's music. As late as January 1879, Wagner told a visitor: 'There are themes of his I remember. One of them in the Adagio of *Romeo* is wonderful.'[20] Karl Klindworth, the composer–conductor and a pupil of Liszt, who was also present at the time, recalled: 'Wagner said to me, "When Berlioz comes in to the room, play something from his *Romeo and Juliet*," which I did.' Wagner gave his own account of the first of the meetings:

> When I saw him, a man considerably my senior, coming here merely in the hope of earning a few guineas, I could deem myself perfectly happy, and almost floating on air, by contrast . . . His whole being expressed weariness and despair, and I was suddenly seized with deep sympathy for this man whose talent so far surpassed that of his rivals – for this was as clear as daylight to me. Berlioz seemed to be pleasantly affected by the attitude of gay spontaneity I adopted with him. His usual short, almost reserved, manner thawed visibly during the friendly hours we passed together.[21]

Berlioz was equally happy with the encounter. He wrote of Wagner to Liszt: 'His ardour, warmth and courage are superb, and I confess that even his violence delights me . . . There's something remarkably attractive about him and if we both have our rough edges, at least they dovetail.'[22]

There were two further meetings, one at the house of Prospere Sainton, the leader of the Philharmonic, in Hinde Street, Manchester Square, and the third took place before Wagner's final concert engagement on 25 June. They found much to discuss which was of mutual interest, particularly the standard of British orchestral playing, the lack of adequate rehearsal time and the extremely lengthy programmes they were given to conduct. Not unexpectedly, there were also differences of opinion. Wagner, speaking in fluent French, began explaining to Berlioz his Schopenhauerian artistic theories in an abstract manner which, according to Wagner, Berlioz dismissed with a patronising smile. Another matter of disagreement was their attitudes towards Mendelssohn, whom Berlioz adored. He wrote to Liszt: 'I'd say Wagner is wrong not to consider the puritan Mendelssohn as a fine and powerful individual voice.'[23] They had supper together before the concert, and afterwards drank punch until three o'clock in the morning at Wagner's house. The following day, Wagner returned to Zurich, not visiting England again for another twenty-two years.

In the ten days Berlioz remained in London after Wagner's departure, he had a number of commitments to fulfil. He negotiated with the publishers Novello for an English edition of his *Treatise on Modern Instrumentation and Orchestration* with a supplement, *The Conductor's Art*, which was published the following year. He visited the Crystal Palace which had recently been removed to Sydenham and considered it 'one of the wonders of the world. I thought of Aladdin's palace, the Gardens of Semiramis . . . It is a dream'.[24] Berlioz was delighted to be offered the conductorship of a series of concerts which would be held there, though this project was not to be.

His last Philharmonic Society concert was on 4 July, where works by ten composers were performed. Berlioz's own contribution was to conduct a performance of *Harold in Italy*. Another composer, Giacomo Meyerbeer, was in the audience. Berlioz's final musical engagement two days later was at Covent Garden, Mrs Anderson's Annual Grand Morning Concert, of which the queen was patron. Mrs Anderson, the wife of the Master of the Queen's Music, had been Queen Victoria's piano teacher and had also taught some of the royal children. The concert, under Berlioz's direction, was a glittering occasion. Almost every great opera star took part, including Luigi Lablache, Giovanni Mario and Antonio Tamburini, and there was an aria from *Benvenuto Cellini* and a performance of *La Captive*. The concert ended with a dazzling performance of Rossini's *Stabat Mater*.

The choice of Berlioz as conductor of this prestigious concert was a clear demonstration of his high standing in England. Negotiations were already in progress for him to return for concerts at St Martin's Hall, Long Acre, the following spring. He wrote to a close friend, Auguste Morel, a fortnight later: 'I had a brilliant excursion to London where I am getting more and more in the swim. I shall go back there this winter, after a tour I am arranging in Bohemia and Austria.' Nothing came of this but in 1859 when the old Philharmonic Society decided to make Berlioz an honorary member, he wrote that he was 'very happy and proud' to accept. However, he never returned to England again and died in 1869, after several days in a coma, at the age of sixty-five.

11 Frédéric Chopin

'My good Scottish ladies'

There can be few musical visitors to Britain who enjoyed the experience less than Frédéric Chopin. Born in Warsaw on 1 March 1810, Chopin's childhood and youth were spent in a comparatively privileged family. His father, Nicholas, was a tutor to a Polish countess and the Chopins lived in an apartment in the wing of the palace. Nicholas gained entry into the circle of Warsaw intellectuals and the aristocracy; when there were signs of Frédéric's early precociousness as a pianist, there was ready support available for him.

By the age of nineteen, he had performed two concerts in Vienna. His competence as a composer was acknowledged the following year, when he played his recently written second Piano Concerto in F minor, Op. 21 and his first in E minor, Op. 11 at two concerts in Warsaw in 1830. Seeking wider opportunities, Chopin left Warsaw on 1 November that year for Vienna, little knowing that it would be his last sight of his native country. After a seven-month stay in Vienna, where he became friendly with fellow composer–pianists, such as Czerny, Hummel and Thalberg, he left on 20 July for Paris. Whilst passing through Stuttgart he learned that the Polish revolution against the Russian authorities which had broken out earlier in the year had been crushed, with Warsaw being occupied in September 1831.

Chopin was greeted in Paris by the substantial Polish community and there were many opportunities for employing his musical talents. He was helped by many fellow pianists in the capital, particularly Friedrich Kalkbrenner, who procured Chopin's first public engagement there, and his playing was admired by such contemporaries as Liszt and Berlioz. His main source of income however was from giving piano lessons to the aristocracy, and holding private performances in salons. He also began to publish his own compositions from 1832, consisting mainly of nocturnes, mazurkas and études, which were well received by the public. His fame spread as his works were published in England, France and Germany. His playing had a great effect on his contemporaries, as can be seen from their written accounts. Charles Hallé, the German-born pianist, who had arrived in Paris in 1836 to improve his own technique, found himself at a dinner party seated next to Chopin:

The same evening I heard him play, and was fascinated beyond expression. It seemed to me as if I had got into another world ... I sat entranced, filled with wonderment, and if the room had suddenly been peopled with fairies, I should not have been astonished. The marvellous charm, the poetry and originality, the perfect freedom and absolute lucidity of Chopin's playing at that time cannot be described. It was perfection in every sense. He seemed to be pleased with the evident impression he had produced, for I could only stammer a few broken words of admiration, and he played again and again, each time revealing new beauties, until I could have dropped on my knees to worship him.[1]

By this time, Chopin had met one of his father's former boarding-school pupils, Felix Wadzinski, and he fell in love with Wadzinski's sixteen-year-old sister, Maria. In the summer of 1836 Chopin had spent the time holidaying with Maria and her parents, Count and Countess Wadzinski, and had proposed marriage. Chopin waited anxiously to hear the outcome, and by the middle of 1837, with no further news, his friend Camille Pleyel, son and partner of Ignaz, the founder of the piano firm, persuaded Chopin to accompany him for a short break in England. They arrived on 11 July when they were met by an old friend, Stanislus Kozmian. Pleyel and Kozmian had the task of raising Chopin from his gloom. The unseasonable weather did not help. Soon after arriving, Chopin wrote home, mentioning some admirable features of English life as well as some of the worst: 'this sooty *Italian* sky can scarcely support such columns of grey air ... As for the English women, the horses, the palaces, the carriages, the wealth, the splendour, the space, trees – everything from soap to razors – it's all extraordinary, all uniform, all very proper, all well-washed BUT as black as a gentleman's bottom!'[2]

Kozmian noted Chopin's poor appearance due to his state of health, for he was already ill from tuberculosis. Pleyel and Kozmian did their best to cheer him up, but Chopin was plunged into despair when he received a letter from Maria's mother her telling him that no marriage could be contemplated. Chopin probably stayed at the superior Sablonniere and Province Hotel at the corner of Leicester Square and Cranborne Street, a convenient and comfortable base for sightseeing. During this time, the three men went to Windsor, Richmond, Blackwall for a fish dinner, and attended operas by Bellini and Cherubini and a concert in aid of the Beethoven memorial at Bonn.

Chopin made no attempt to meet Moscheles and Mendelssohn who were at the Beethoven concert. Mrs Moscheles wrote after the visit: 'Chopin was the only one of the foreign artists who did not go out, and wished no one to visit him, for the effort of talking told on his consumptive frame. He heard a few concerts and disappeared.'[3] He did, however, make one exception to this rule. One night, he was taken by Pleyel for dinner to 49 Bryanston Square, the home of the piano-maker James Shudi Broadwood. Chopin was introduced as 'M. Fritz', preferring to remain incognito. Later in the evening, some of the guests took turns to play the piano; Chopin, unable to resist, joined in. After he had played two or three bars, the guests realised that the exquisite touch was that of no ordinary mortal and Chopin's identity was revealed.[4] The visit to England was a brief one and in less than a fortnight he was back in Paris.

Another event which had added to Chopin's unsettled state stemmed from his meeting some months earlier, in October 1836, with the novelist George Sand. Noted for her eccentric manner – she dressed in men's clothes and smoked cigarettes in public – she was well known for her out-spokenness on many matters. Sand was in many ways very unlike Chopin, whom she later described as 'modest by principle and gentle by habit', but she admitted that she shared neither his interests, ideals nor political principles.[5] Chopin's initial reaction on meeting her was: 'What an unpre-possessing woman that Sand is. Is she really a woman? I am inclined to doubt it.' Six years older than him – Sand was thirty-two and he twenty-six – she had separated from her husband though she looked after the two children. Sand was attracted to Chopin, but they were not to meet again until April 1838 when they subsequently became lovers. Over the follow-ing years, although the sexual aspect of their relationship cooled, to be replaced by years of maternal devotion, Sand was to play an important part in Chopin's life. It was at her country mansion at Nohant, where he wrote some of his most important works. Their friendship came to an end with an angry exchange after Chopin had sided with Sand's daugh-ter after an unfortunate wedding in July 1847. Chopin and Sand met briefly by accident at a friend's house in Paris on 4 March 1848, scarcely exchanging greetings.[6] Emotionally, he never recovered from his liaison with Sand.[7]

Whilst Chopin was pouring out his heart in letters to friends in February 1848, a significant political upheaval in France was shortly to bring him to England once more. Following a big demonstration by workers, students and others in Paris, the king, Louis Philippe, abdicated on 24 February and the Second Republic was proclaimed. Although this event finally determined Chopin's course of action, there is evidence that he was con-templating such a step before this, with the Paris newspapers announcing his imminent departure.[8] Jane Stirling, a Scotswoman who had lived in Paris for some years and a great admirer of the composer, had deter-mined to become one of his pupils. She not only succeeded in this mission but was able to persuade Chopin that this would be a good time to visit England and Scotland, where she had a number of useful contacts and relatives. She was assisted by her widowed elder sister, Katherine Erskine;

Chopin was soon to discover that the sisters were inseparable. Accordingly, on 20 April 1848, Chopin arrived in London.

The Stirlings had made all the necessary arrangements for Chopin's comfort. For a few days, he lodged at 10 Bentinck Street, Cavendish Square, before moving to better accommodation at 48 Welbeck Street. Every detail had been carefully planned, including the provision of Chopin's favourite drinking chocolate. There were no fewer than three pianos in the apartment, lent for his use by Pleyel, Broadwood and Erard, but he was very depressed by the weather and the need to adjust to a new environment and did not make much use of them. A fortnight after his arrival he wrote to a friend: 'I have at last managed to get a foothold in this abyss called London. I have only just begun to breathe more freely these last few days now that the sun has begun to shine.'[9] Chopin was deeply worried about the situation in Poland. One of his first visits was to Kingston-on-Thames where many of the entourage of the exiled French king had settled, and where he discussed the Polish Question. There were many other sympathisers among English politicians and members of society who helped Chopin to become more at ease in his new surroundings.[10]

He was well placed to make the visit a success. His reputation in England was high: for some ten years all his works had been published by a London firm and his music was being performed by a growing number of pianists. Moreover, the London season was about to begin with its opportunities for public and private performances. On the other hand, London had acted as a magnet for many continental musicians, such as Berlioz, Hallé, Kalkbrenner and Thalberg, whose livelihoods had also been threatened by revolution.[11]

One of the earliest offers to perform came from the prestigious Philharmonic Society of London, as his two piano concertos were already in the repertoire. Chopin curtly refused this offer after hearing the orchestra perform. '[It is] like their roast beef and turtle soup, strong and efficient but that is all.' More seriously, he objected to the fact that there would be only one rehearsal, and a public one at that. This snub did not enhance his reputation in official circles and may account for the fact that he was never invited as he much hoped to perform at Buckingham Palace. It was at a christening party at Stafford House given by the Duchess of Sutherland that Chopin met and played before the queen and Prince Albert 'and all the cream of the Garter', as he put it. His playing evidently made little impression on the queen, who noted in her journal: 'There was some pretty music, good Lablache, Mario and Tamburini singing, and some pianists playing.'[12]

There were other invitations to perform at many of the great London homes. By the beginning of June, Chopin had visited such houses as those of Lady Gainsborough, the Duchess of Somerset and the Duke and Duchess of Westminster. The constant theme in Chopin's correspondence at this time concerns the question of fees:

The Duke of Westminster is close-fisted, so they don't pay ... Old Lady Rothschild asked me how much I *charged*, because some lady who had heard me had asked her about it. As Lady Sutherland had given me 20 guineas, and as Broadwood, on whose piano I play, had suggested that price, I answered: 20 guineas. The good lady, obviously kind, thereupon told me that it is true I play very well, but that she advises me to take less, as moderation is necessary this season.[13]

His activities were to some extent limited by his physical condition. He wrote: 'If I could run around for whole days from one end of London to the other, if only I had not been spitting blood the last few days; if I were younger and if I were not, as I am, up to the neck in social obligations – then I might start my life over again.'[14] He also met and dined with many musicians, writers and artists, including Dickens, the historian George Grote and Thomas and Jane Carlyle. Thomas Carlyle wrote to a colleague: 'If you see M. Chopin, pray offer him my hearty regards. I hope we shall get some language to speak in by and by, and then get into more plentiful communication.'[15] Chopin never bothered to learn English though he could converse in French.

One particular friendship which he valued was with the 'Swedish Nightingale', Jenny Lind. Shortly after his arrival in London, Chopin attended a performance of Bellini's opera, *La Somnambula* at Her Majesty's Theatre. 'This Swede is indeed an original from head to foot,' he wrote afterwards, 'she does not show herself in the ordinary light, but in the magic rays of an *aurora borealis*. Her singing is infallibly pure and true; but above all I admire her *piano* passages, the charm of which is indescribable.'[16] A few days later he paid her a visit; it was a great success with both parties expressing their admiration for the other, playing and singing together till midnight. Lind never forgot Chopin. She married subsequently a former student of Chopin, and she included in her recitals a *Recueil de Mazourkas*, a selection from his works with Italian words.[17]

Whilst Chopin was enjoying a full social life he was greatly aware that he needed money, not least to pay the rent of his apartment. He had little difficulty in attracting pupils for piano lessons. Within a few days of his arrival in London he was giving lessons to five women, three of whom were titled. It seems surprising that he gave only two semi-public concerts in London during his first stay of five months. On 23 June 1848, he gave a matinée performance at the house, 99 Eaton Place, of his old friend Adelaide Sartoris, née Kemble. Tickets were one guinea each and all 150 were sold the day before the concert took place. Chopin who was ill and out of sorts, played a selection of études, mazurkas, nocturnes, waltzes and the Berceuse Op. 7. He had a supporting artist, an Italian operatic singer, Giovanni Mario. One observer in the room noted his 'death-like appearance'.[18]

There was a second concert on the 7 July at 2 St James's Square, the home of the eccentric bachelor, Lord Falmouth. Chopin, who was now slightly better than on the previous occasion, again filled the venue. This time there were two women singers. Artistically, as current newspapers show, it was a success, but after deducting the cost of publicity and some other items, Chopin doubted if he had made as much as 100 guineas out of it.

During these few months in London, he had been well looked after by Jane Stirling and Katherine Erskine. Chopin wrote in June: 'My good Scottish ladies show great friendship here. I always dine with them when I am not invited out. But they are used to roving around and being shaken in a carriage while rushing all over London with visiting-cards. They would like me to visit all their acquaintances although I am more dead than alive.' Such was his state of health that when Chopin went to Broadwood's to try out the piano before his matinées, he had on both occasions to be carried upstairs to the piano room.[19]

The London season was now over; work opportunities were fewer and his meagre savings were diminishing. (Chopin claimed that one lady had left London owing him for eight lessons.) By mid-July he was increasingly worried about his health. 'Often in the morning I think I am going to cough myself to death.' Chopin had been engaged to play two concerts in Manchester at the end of August and was uncertain how to fill the time before then. Jane Stirling persuaded him to stay with her brother-in-law, Lord Torphichen, at Calder House, his country seat in Midlothian, twelve miles from Edinburgh. Thus on 5 August, Chopin set off from Euston Station for Edinburgh, Henry Broadwood having booked three first-class seats for the journey, one for Chopin, one for his Irish manservant, Daniel, and one for Chopin's feet.[20]

Chopin found the country air and the grounds of the mansion to be very invigorating and at first he was in reasonably good health. Musical inspiration, however, had deserted him. 'Not a decent musical idea,' he wrote soon after his arrival. 'I am out of my rut – I am like, shall I say, a donkey at a fancy-dress ball – a violin E string on a double bass – amazed, bewildered.' He was soon complaining that he could not breathe and that 'all that is left of me is a long nose and a fourth finger out of practice'.[21] Jane Stirling and her sister were also staying with him. He noted how kind they had been to him. Jane had brought up to Scotland a Pleyel piano for his use and his every wish was soon satisfied, including the appearance of Parisian newspapers every day. Nevertheless, Chopin felt smothered by their attention. Already in July he had told a friend: 'My Scots ladies are dear and kind, but they sometimes bore me to distraction.'

There has been much speculation about Jane Stirling's deep feelings for Chopin. He had dedicated the two Nocturnes Op. 55 to her four years earlier, and she became one of his most fervent admirers; after Chopin's death she dressed in widow's tweeds. Jane's love for him was not reciprocated. Chopin is alleged to have told a friend: 'They have married me to Miss Stirling: she might as well marry to death.'[22] For one thing, he still missed George Sand[23] and he was also preoccupied with the state of his own health. Jane and her sister urged him to stay at different Scottish houses, wrote him letters daily, which he did not answer, and Jane tried to be with him on every possible occasion. When Chopin finally returned to London in November, he wrote to his friend Grzymala about Jane's manoeuvres, which had given rise to rumours about a possible wedding:

> Perhaps that has given someone the notion that I am getting married, but there really has to be some kind of physical attraction, and the unmarried one [Jane] is too much like me. How could you kiss yourself? Friendship is all very well, but gives no right to anything further. I have made that clear.[24]

Chopin travelled to Manchester for his appearance at a Gentleman's Concert on 28 August. He stayed with Salis Schwabe, an emigrant German Jew, whom he knew in Paris and who had settled in Manchester early in the century. Schwabe, together with Hermann Léo, had been responsible for creating a strong musical tradition in the city. Chopin was impressed by Schwabe, a leading manufacturer, for owning the tallest factory chimney in Manchester, which had cost £5,000 to build. The composer stayed with him for three nights at his home at Crumpsall House, a fine building in its own extensive grounds.[25] His stay was extended because, to his delight, Jenny Lind was a fellow guest. The concert hall accommodated an audience of 1,200. He was due to play two groups of solos; the rest of the programme comprised orchestral music and operatic extracts by three Italian singers. Chopin was afraid that his playing would be lost in the vastness of the hall. The works played – an Andante Sostenuto, a Scherzo from his Op. 31, and several of his preludes, mazurkas and waltzes – received unanimously glowing reviews in both local and national newspapers. The correspondent of the *Daily News* remarked:

> In these various pieces he showed very strikingly his original genius as a composer, and his transcendental powers as a performer. His music is as strongly marked with individual character as that of any master who has ever lived. It is highly finished, new in its harmonies, full of contrapuntal skill and ingenious contrivance; and yet we have never heard music which has so much the air of unpremeditated effusion. The performer seems to abandon himself to the impulses of his fancy and his feelings, to indulge in a reverie and to pour out unconsciously as it were, the thoughts and emotions that pass through his mind.[26]

For his efforts Chopin received a fee of £60.

Something of his unfortunate manner can be gleaned from his behaviour when visiting a fellow Pole, the physician Dr Adam Lyszczynski, in Edinburgh on his way back to Scotland. Chopin, according to Mrs Lyszczynski, always stayed in bed late, demanded soup in his room and then had his hair curled by his servant – no maidservants were allowed in his room – and the doctor personally had to carry him up and down the stairs. He was now very ill, always shivering and only kept warm when he played the piano. He could not bear to be contradicted, especially by women. Chopin once asked Mrs Lyszczynski to sing but she declined. She later recalled: 'At this he was astonished and quite angry. "Doctor, would you take it amiss if I were to force your wife to do it?" The idea of a woman refusing him anything seemed to him preposterous.'[27]

After this, Chopin stayed at Johnstone Castle near Glasgow, which was the home of another of Jane's sisters, Anne Houston. Like Berlioz, he had a near escape from death when driving in a coach along the coast to visit a neighbouring family. Going downhill, the horses' reins snapped; the carriage was smashed and would have gone over the precipice, only being saved by hitting another tree near the edge. Chopin fortunately was able to scramble out of the wreckage unhurt but shaken. 'I confess that I was calm as I saw my last hour approaching,' he wrote, 'but the thought of broken legs and hands appals me. To be a cripple would put the finishing touch to me.'[28] The house was a convenient base for his Glasgow concert which took place in the Merchant's Hall in the city on 27 September. The matinée was an artistic rather than a financial success: ticket prices were high at a half a guinea. After deducting expenses, Chopin was left with only 50 guineas.

Although he was increasingly in need of rest there was little respite for him. Jane had arranged further country house stays, such as Keir House, Perthshire, which were owned by members of her family. Chopin told a friend that 'as soon as I get a little more used to somewhere I have to move to somewhere else because my Scottish ladies won't leave me in peace, and come to fetch me in order to drive me round to their family'.

One last concert had been arranged in Scotland at the Hopetoun Rooms in Edinburgh on 4 October. It was a lengthy programme, consisting of études, nocturnes, the Grand Valse Brilliante, preludes, ballades, mazurkas and waltzes, and began at 8.30 in the evening. Again the concert attracted critical acclaim. For Chopin it was a disappointment. He informed Adolph Gutman on 16 October: 'I have played in Edinburgh; all the distinguished folk of the region assembled. They say it went off well. There was little success, and a little money.' The tickets were once again half a guinea which acted as a deterrent to concert-goers. It was in order to boost numbers that Jane Stirling bought a hundred tickets. Chopin was not impressed by the level of artistic appreciation of British audiences. Writing to a Paris correspondent on 21 October he remarked:

By 'art' they mean here painting, sculpture and architecture. Music is not an art, and is not called by that name; and if you say 'artist' these English think you mean a painter, sculptor or architect. But music is a *profession*, not an art, and no one ever calls any musician an artist or uses the word in such a sense in print.[29]

Despite his deteriorating health, Chopin continued to accept invitations to the houses of the nobility. He stayed at Lady Belhaven's house at Wishaw, and with the Duke of Hamilton at Hamilton Palace, Lanarkshire. On his way back to Edinburgh in mid-October he caught a chill and remained with his medical friend in Edinburgh. He was now gravely ill, weighing less than seven stone and anxious to escape from the clutches of Jane and her sister. He told Grizymala on 30 October: 'I am not thinking at all of a wife but of those at home, my mother and sisters ... this world seems to slip from me and I forget things. I have no strength. I no sooner recover a little than I sink back lower still ... I am nearer to a coffin than a bridal bed.'[30]

Chopin was relieved to leave for London the following day. He had been found rooms at 4 St James's Place, off Piccadilly, by Prince Czartoryski and his wife. He was seen by a homoeopathic doctor on his arrival and was subsequently visited every day. Chopin was too ill to leave the apartment for the following two weeks. As he feared, Jane Stirling and her sister followed him down from Scotland. Matters were not improved when

19 Number 4, St James's Place, where Chopin stayed for the last part of his 1848 tour

Mrs Erskine tried to convert him to the Church of Scotland, constantly reading the Bible aloud and talking of the next world. Nevertheless Chopin at this time told a friend that if he had his health he would be able to live decently in London by giving two lessons a day to piano pupils.

He had been approached by Lord Dudley Stuart to play at a Grand Polish Ball and Concert on 16 November, the proceeds of which would go to help the plight of Polish refugees. This cause was dear to Chopin's heart and he accepted it. The event was held at the Guildhall, attended by the Lord Mayor and members of the Corporation of London. The main part of the proceedings was the dancing, and the concert, at which a number of artists appeared, was given little prominence, Chopin's name hardly being mentioned in newspaper reports. One of the few surviving accounts stated:

> The people, hot from dancing, who went into the room where he played were but little in the humour to pay attention, and anxious to return to their amusement. He was in the last stage of exhaustion, and the affair resulted in disappointment. His playing at such a place was a well-intentioned mistake.[31]

Chopin had a relapse after the concert and was urged by his doctor to return to Paris as soon as possible. He found it difficult to breathe in the 'beastly London' climate. In spite of his condition he had already agreed to return to England the following year. He left London by train, accompanied by a Polish friend, Leonard Niedzwiecki, and his servant, on 23 November and headed for Folkestone. Shortly after the train had pulled out of the station, Chopin experienced an attack of cramp on his right-hand side below his ribs, but subsequently recovered. After taking lunch at Folkstone they made the Channel crossing to Boulogne and proceeded to Paris the next day.

He remained bitter about his stay in England. When the train had left Boulogne, Chopin, after spending some time looking at the landscape, said to his friend: 'Do you see the cattle in this meadow? *Ça a plus d'intelligence que les Anglais.*' Nevertheless he still had cause to be grateful to his English friends. In the following months, still very ill, Chopin was in a parlous financial state. It was Jane Stirling who anonymously sent a large sum of money to tide him over.[32] The composer died in Paris in the early hours of 17 October 1849 at the age of thirty-nine.

12 Liszt and the wandering years

For many people, the name of Ferencz or Franz Liszt conjures up a picture of a wizened and somewhat forbidding abbé dressed in sober clerical garb. This is of course largely influenced by the photographed portraits of the composer in his later years, and a far cry from the young Liszt who toured Britain during the first half of the nineteenth century.

Liszt was born on the 22 October 1811, at Raiding in Western Hungary, a German-speaking part of the Habsburg Empire. His father, Adam, a talented amateur singer, pianist and cellist, worked on one of the sheep stations on the Esterházy estate. He was soon aware of Franz's exceptional musical gifts, and under his tuition the boy became a formidable pianist, giving his first public concert at the age of nine. Through the financial generosity of Count Michael Esterházy and other aristocrats, the family was able to move to Vienna, where Franz became a pupil of Carl Czerny for piano and Antonio Salieri for composition. Franz gave some successful concerts in Vienna and was supposedly kissed on the forehead by Beethoven after one of them.

Adam decided upon a tour with his son, following in the footsteps of the young Mozart some sixty years earlier. There were successful visits to Pest, Munich, Stuttgart and other cities, and in December 1823 the family arrived in Paris. Besides giving concerts, which were enthusiastically received, he also began to compose an opera *Don Sanche, ou le Château d'Amour*, based on Cervantes's work, which received its performance there two years later. It was in Paris at this time that the Liszts formed a valuable friendship with Pierre Erard of the firm of piano-makers. Pierre's father, Sébastien had been responsible for introducing an improved piano action. When a tour of England was undertaken in May 1824, both Adam and Franz stayed at the Erards' London base at 18 Great Marlborough Street. Pierre had lent the young musician a new seven-octave square piano for the tour, and it accompanied the party to England. This arrangement was beneficial to everyone: the firm enjoyed the publicity for its products, and Franz was happy to play on such a fine instrument.[1]

Opportunities for performance were few at this stage of the London season, and it was only through Adam's canvassing that Franz was able to obtain an engagement to play during the Royal Society of Musicians' annual dinner at the New Argyll Rooms in early June. It was in the same hall that his first public concert took place on the 21st of that month. For the occasion, Adam hired an orchestra conducted by Sir George Smart, as well as some Italian singers and a number of instrumental soloists, who played works for French horn and mandolin; and there were solos by Franz. The occasion attracted a good audience, including Clementi, Cramer and John Field, and the concert went well. Franz played Czerny's variations for piano and orchestra and a set of variations by Winkhler; he also improvised on an aria from Rossini's *Barber of Seville*.

Through the good offices of Prince Paul Esterházy, ambassador to London and the son of Adam's former employer, Franz was invited to Windsor to perform before King George IV and his family. During the two-hour programme, he played pieces by Handel, Mozart and Czerny. The king also presented the boy with a theme for improvisation from Mozart's *Don Giovanni* and was astonished by the boy's virtuosity. An overnight stay in Windsor enabled them to see the sights of the area. Adam wrote later:

> A trip on the Thames surpasses everything. One can see from it what an abundance of water England possesses. Whether we see a village, or a small or large town, everywhere there is wealth, cleanliness and order. Whoever has not seen England has not seen the world's greatest treasure. The people are most agreeable and the countryside is real paradise.[2]

What may surprise the modern concert-goer were the broad musical tastes which were often encompassed within a single programme. The well-known singer John Braham (who was to appear in Weber's opera *Oberon* two years later) gave a benefit concert at the Royal Theatre, Drury Lane, a week after the Windsor visit, and Franz took part in it. Apart from a short opera, *Devil's Bridge*, in which Braham took the leading role, there was a farce, *What Next?* and solo songs such as 'Scots wha' ha'e wi' Wallace bled'. The advertisement announcing the concert stated: 'For this night only, the incomparable Master Liszt has in the most flattering manner consented to display his considerable powers on the new Patent Grand Piano invented by Sébastien Erard.'

A similar picture emerges from the two concerts which he gave in Manchester on 2 and 4 August. Here, he was billed along with another child prodigy, the 'Infant Lyra', a harpist who was not quite four years old. Franz's musical contribution was more substantial: a Hummel piano concerto and Moscheles's *Fall of Paris* for piano and orchestra. Liszt's fame had preceded him and the local papers praised his playing. For the two concerts he was paid a remarkably generous £100, making the visit a worthwhile one. This compensated for the tedious journey from London, which took twenty-four hours. There were no more English engagements and father and son, once again accompanied by Erard's piano, left England for Calais on 12 August.

Less than a year later, Franz and his father paid another visit to England. The tour followed a similar pattern to the previous one; whereas the 1824 tour lasted three months, this one was concentrated into four weeks. Franz appeared again before the king at Windsor, performed at Drury Lane and gave two concerts in Manchester. Franz's skills as a composer as well as an executant were also developing. Apart from his opera, he had had published in Paris and London 1824 *Sept variations brillantes sur un thème de G. Rossini* and in the following year *Huit variations*. His mastery of the keyboard is illustrated in an incident arising at a concert which Liszt gave at a private party on this tour. A flautist, Charles Nicholson, was due to perform his own *Fantasie and variations* with piano accompaniment. The composer Cipriani Potter was due to play the piano part until he discovered that the flute was a semitone flat. There was a deadlock between the two musicians with Nicholson unable to sharpen his instrument, and Potter declared he would not be able to transpose the whole piece. Liszt, who was standing near by, offered to take Potter's place, and performed the transposition at sight.

Like Haydn before him and Mendelssohn and Berlioz after him, Liszt was deeply moved by a performance in St Paul's Cathedral of massed choirs of poor children from free schools. He was later to draw on the experience when he wrote the climaxes of his oratorio *Christus*.[3]

There was a third visit in May 1827. Charles Salaman, the English composer, conductor and pianist, wrote his reminiscences 'Pianists of the Past' some seventy-four years later. In it he recalls as a boy seeing the young Liszt at a rehearsal at the old Argyll Rooms on 27 May. '"Young Liszt from Vienna," said Charles Neate [Salaman's teacher] to me as the slim and rather tall boy ascended the steps leading to the platform. "He is only 15 – a great creature!"' Salaman was anxious to make his acquaintance and was able to visit Franz and his father in Frith Street, and invited them to dine at his house. 'He was a very charmingly natural and unaffected boy,' Salaman wrote, 'and I have never forgotten his joyful exclamation, "Oh, gooseberry pie!" when his favourite dish was put upon the table.'[4] The two youths played some duets and Franz played some of his recently published *Études* Op. 6, which served as a basis later for his *Transcendental Studies*. As a gift, Franz presented Salaman with a version of the Sixth Study in G major. Adam encouraged his son to develop his compositional skills at this time, and Franz wrote a sonata, two piano concertos, a trio, a quartet and a quintet, all of which are now lost.[5]

The climax of the visit was a morning concert at the New Argyll Rooms on 9 June. Posters for the concert recorded Master Liszt in bold letters at their head. As was the custom the programme was of enormous length, encompassing fifteen works, ranging from songs, solo pieces for guitar, horn, viola and flute, piano and vocal duets to a piano concerto. Franz opened the programme as one of four pianists in an arrangement of a Cherubini overture, and his own now lost A minor concerto, which was rapturously received. He rounded off the programme with a rousing performance of his brilliant variations on 'Rule Britannia'.

Well content with the success of the visit, Franz and his father decided that after incessant travel for the last three years, a holiday was called for. They stayed at a hotel in Boulogne, but within a few days, Adam contracted typhoid and tragically died on 28 August. As Liszt's mother, Anna, had not travelled with them to England, Franz not only had to break the news to her, but had to make arrangements for the funeral. These events left a permanent mark on him. Franz became obsessed with death and there are many examples in his compositions, both in their titles and in the frequent use of the *Dies Irae*. Although Franz passed through Boulogne on subsequent occasions, he never again visited his father's grave.

The following thirteen years, before his next visit to England, saw important changes in Liszt's life. Musically, he had been inspired by attending a concert given by the violin virtuoso Niccolò Paganini in Paris in 1831. With his gaunt features, long hair and thin body coupled with a brilliant technique resulting from endless practice, Paganini became a sensation wherever he played.[6] Liszt decide to emulate him on the piano, resulting in similar reactions from audiences and leading to what was widely called 'Lisztmania'. Many of his compositions, calling for brilliant technique, such as the *Années de pèlerinage*, were performed by Liszt at his own concerts. Nevertheless, there were critics who accused him of too much showmanship and vulgarity in his demeanour at the piano, drawing attention to himself rather than the music.

The other major change in his situation arose after his meeting with Countess Marie d'Agoult in 1833. Marie was a beautiful and intelligent woman with a strong character. She set out to change Liszt's image by introducing him to a range of European literature and philosophical ideas, softening his manner and urging him to compose more. Although Marie was married, she and Liszt became lovers and set up home in Geneva in 1835. She bore him three children whilst he travelled around Europe. By 1840 with Marie and the family settled in Paris, Liszt returned to England in the hope of gaining much needed financial success.

His boat landed at Wapping on 6 May 1840 and he was soon engaged in performing, at the Hanover Square Rooms two days later, and on 11 May at a Philharmonic concert. These were not on the whole well received, probably due to the fact that much of the programme comprised his own music, and his ostentatious manner at the piano was seen as an unnecessary distraction. However, he was pleased to be invited to play before the twenty-year-old Queen Victoria and Prince Albert, especially as he had been told that normally she asked for Italian opera singers, rather than instrumentalists. She laughed when Liszt reminded her that she had been present as a small child when he had played before her mother, the Duchess of Kent.[7] There was a further concert with the Philharmonic Society on 8 June and he was soon fêted in high society; particularly by Lady Blessington, at whose home, Gore House, Liszt was introduced to the great and the good.[8]

It was arranged that Marie should join Liszt for the first part of his stay in London. 'I went to Hampstead yesterday morning to find a *ratzenloch* for you. The scenery is delightful. I think you will be happy here. The air is very healthy. It's the highest point in the environs of London, recommended to certain patients (not to consumptives, of course, because there is a sharp breeze there) ... Once or twice a week we shall be able to go on delightful excursions to Richmond, Greenwich, etc.'[9] Liszt was unable to rent a cottage in Hampstead so the couple stayed at the Star and Garter Hotel in Richmond. That there was friction between the two is clear from a note Liszt wrote to her on 20 June. Marie had told Liszt: 'I can do nothing else at this moment, and probably for ever, than live utterly alone.' He replied bitterly to her: 'Yesterday (to recall but one day) for the entire journey from Ascot to Richmond you spoke not a single word to me that was not a wound or an insult.' When they left in mid-July for concerts in the Rhineland and in Russia, it was to be their last tour together, as they were to part for ever in 1843.

One momentous musical innovation was introduced by Liszt during this short stay in London. An advertisement had appeared for a concert on 9 June 1840 with the heading 'Liszt's Pianoforte Recitals'. It consisted entirely of solo piano pieces: the Scherzo and Finale from Beethoven's 'Pastoral' Symphony, Schubert's *Serenade* and *Ave Maria*, and his own *Hexameron*, *Neapolitan Tarantelles* and *Grand galop chromatique*. The term 'recitals' was apparently suggested to him by Frederick Beale, of the firm of music publishers. Liszt had experimented with this format at least a year earlier, and had obviously liked the result. The use of the term 'recitals' rather than 'recital' was explained by Charles Salaman who attended the concert:

> This now commonly accepted term had never previously been used, and people asked, 'What does he mean? How can any one *recite* upon the pianoforte?' At these recitals Liszt, after performing a piece set down in his programme, would leave the platform, and descending into the body of the room, where the benches were so arranged as to allow free locomotion, would move about among his auditors and converse with his friends, with the gracious condescension of a prince, until he felt disposed to return to the piano.[10]

A second concert followed ten days later at Willis's Rooms, consisting of piano works by Handel, Rossini's *William Tell* overture, études and mazurkas by Chopin, and Schubert's *Serenade* and *Erlkönig*: it attracted much critical attention. Thus was born the solo piano recital.

After a brief sojourn on the Continent in July and August, Liszt returned to England. He had agreed to make two national tours as part of a travelling troupe of performers under the direction of Lewis Lavendu, a young music publisher who was also a pianist and a cellist. Others in the party included Lavendu's brother-in-law, Frank Mori, and two singers, Mlle de Varny, who had had some success in opera, and the seventeen-year-old Miss Louisa Bassano.

The party was completed by an interesting and versatile person, John Orlando Parry. It is because of the diaries which he kept of the tours that we know so much about Liszt's part in them. Parry, who had received a formal musical education, initially pursued a singing career but, as one critic commented: 'His face, figure, manner, being and utterance are all against him.' Parry realised that he had the ability to make audiences, including such unlikely people as Chopin and Mendelssohn, laugh and he was able to include in his act various ballads such as *A Wife Wanted* and *The Musical Husband* which he had composed and which he often performed to his own accompaniment. Another of Parry's favourite ditties was his own *Wanted – a Governess* which started, 'A Governess wanted, well suited to fill / The post of tutor with competent skill'.[11] A good description of Parry in action appeared in the *Illustrated London News* in 1849:

> Among the most striking features are his excellent impersonation of a Welsh girl in which he sings a Welsh song with reasonable success; his clever impersonation of an Artist with instantaneous change of costume; and a visit to the Park with drum and fifes and the march of soldiers imitated by rattling the keys ... The bear's rattling on the wires of his den at the Zoological Gardens, and a host of other pleasantries.[12]

Liszt wrote to Marie from Chichester on 17 August, 'my travelling circus begins today'. The itinerary was a punishing one. Within six weeks the troupe had given fifty concerts, often two on the same day. The tour began on the south coast, taking in many of the fashionable towns as far as Bath, and in September they headed north-east, performing at Cheltenham, Leamington, Coventry, Northampton, Market Harborough, Leicester, Derby, Nottingham, Mansfield, Newark and Lincoln, and on to Boston, Grantham, Stamford, Peterborough, Huntingdon, Cambridge, Bury St Edmunds, Norwich, Ipswich, Colchester, Chelmsford and Brighton. They arrived wearily in London, having covered over 1,167 miles.

Liszt was very ill during the early part of the tour, but managed to meet his commitments. He frequently grumbled in his letters to Marie. Writing from Stonehenge on 20 August, he noted: 'England is not like other countries: the expenses are enormous.' Of his companions he complained: 'What is remarkable is that among six such variegated individuals, not a single striking incident comes along, not a single remark worth remembering is made. Every day is like the day before and the day after.'[13] But there were brighter moments. Liszt, like so many other foreign visitors, found the English countryside delightful, and he described Sidmouth and Exmouth in Devon as 'particularly attractive'. Visits to the cathedrals at Chichester, Winchester and Salisbury made a deep impression on him, and at Byron's home at Newstead Abbey he lay on the grass in the bright sunshine feeling overwhelmed by the experience. On the tour, Liszt played a standard repertoire, consisting of the *William Tell* overture, *Marche Hongroise*, *Grand galop*, duets with Mori, and concerti where an orchestra was available.[14]

The party suffered a number of mishaps and disappointments. Early in the tour, the Isle of Wight was on the schedule. The sea was too rough for the piano to be taken to Ryde, and Liszt, after a horrendous crossing, had to perform on an inferior instrument. The size of the audiences varied greatly from place to place. At Bridgewater on 31 August, for example, there were only 30 people, though the next day at Bath there were 280. Concerts given in rural venues posed special problems. At Stamford, the artists were interrupted by pigs squealling during the singing.

A second tour was planned by Lavendu for November 1840. He was well aware that the first tour had created much pressure by having too many performances at different venues, but nevertheless the second tour was an ambitious one. Starting at Reading, then Oxford, Leamington and Birmingham, the party headed north to Chester, Liverpool, Rochdale and Manchester before passing over the Pennines into Yorkshire for concerts at Huddersfield, Doncaster, Sheffield, Wakefield, Leeds, Hull and York. Liszt returned from the Continent in time for the Oxford concert, wearing a spectacular outer garment, described by Parry as 'his great Hungarian coat, composed of skins and ornamented with different coloured feathers. It is a most enormous concern and weighs at least as heavy as three greatcoats.'[15]

By the end of the first week, Lavendu calculated that he had lost £112 even though Liszt and his fellow performers were well received at almost all the venues. In Liverpool, Liszt had to have a tooth extracted, whilst Parry bought him a pair of spectacles. Though much of the travelling was done by road, the recently opened railways were used wherever possible. The party took a train from Leeds to Hull on 11 December – 'rather a long while sitting on the carriage', noted Parry, 'and rather shaky railway ride'. The fifty-seven mile journey took exactly four hours. At the concert in Hull, Liszt accompanied Parry in the latter's poem, *The Inchcape Bell*, which began:

> The storm had passed, and the winds had sung,
>   On the ear scarce a murmur fell
> Save the warning toll from the iron tongue
>   Of the desolate Inchcape Bell.

Although the hall held 800 people there were fewer than 160 in the audience. Unlike the first tour the itinerary extended beyond England. The party crossed to Ireland where they spent nine days in Dublin. On the second day there, 18 December, there was a special concert attended by 1,200 people, including the Lord Lieutenant of Ireland. Liszt had a brand new grand piano from Erard, on which he played Weber's *Konzertstück*, though Parry believed it was the worst Erard he had heard. Liszt's reception was less rapturous than he had expected. Perhaps boredom had begun to set in for he had told Marie at the beginning of the month, 'I am doing nothing but travelling the highroads and doing my tricks for the astonished people'. However, the concert on 23 December was a great triumph. Parry wrote:

> They applauded Liszt to the skies. His *Hexameron* was encored – he played the last two Variations ... Tonight Liszt played for the first time here *extemporaneously*, and a most wonderful performance it was. When Lewis asked the audience if they had any themes ready written, one was handed only, but Mr Pigott gave him the *Russian Hymn* in addition. This was not enough, so after talking to the audience in the most familiar manner and making them laugh very much because he had got no *lively air* to work on, he turned round suddenly and said 'I play de *Wanted Governess*!' And off he started with the *Irish Air* and then the *Russian Hymn* and last my song, which he played most wonderfully, not all the way through, but the Waltz part in the first symphony. He played it in at least 12 different ways and then wound up with the 3 together in a manner truly extraordinary! 'Twas received as it deserved with tumultuous applause.[16]

The party spent a few days at Cork and on New Year's Eve visited the men's and women's wards of the lunatic asylum, Parry in his journal describing in great detail the harrowing condition of some of the 460 inmates 'who stared at us, laughed, howled, grinned, screamed and some made every possible distortion of the body etc.' A foray to Clonmel on 2 January 1841 was unsuccessful as no tickets for the concert had been sold prior to the event. Liszt suggested that the few people who had turned up should come along to his hotel's sitting room, where there was a little Tomkinson piano. Parry recorded: ''Twas like a private Matinée. So funny to see Liszt firing away at *Guilliame Tell* on this little instrument, but it stood his powerful hand capitally.'[17]

After a further visit to Dublin, where Liszt bought two waistcoats of gold cloth, the company performed in Limerick and Belfast before taking a boat to Stranraer in Scotland on 17 January. Concerts followed in Glasgow and Edinburgh. At the latter place 'Liszt frightened the 7 & ½ octave Grand with a *Waltz à la Diable*, which was based on a melody from Meyerbeer's opera *Robert le Diable*. There is an intriguing entry in Parry's diary for the Glasgow concert, where Liszt 'brought in some *very* dashing Scotch girls with him' (where he had been dining). After sight-seeing at Holyrood Palace on 24 January they left Edinburgh to a farewell by a large crowd.

The travelling conditions were formidable. From Edinburgh, the coach proceeded to Dunbar, where they dined and left at 7 p.m. arriving at Newcastle at 9.30 the following morning. Not surprisingly, Parry noted, 'We did not sleep much last night', Liszt had sensibly left the coach at Alnwick putting up at an inn to rest. Further concerts in the north followed at Sunderland, Durham, Richmond and Darlington, and finally at Halifax on 29 January. From Leeds they caught a train back to London. They sat in their own carriage on the train, with their coach on the next truck. A splendid breakfast had been prepared at Derby, then on to Rugby, where they changed on to the Birmingham train, passing through the great Kilsby Tunnel (near Northampton), Tring, Watford Junction and Harrow. 'At quarter to six – to *all* our hearts' content – stopt at Euston Square Grand Birmingham Station.'[18] Parry calculated that the party had travelled 2,222 miles on this second tour.

Liszt had been promised 500 guineas a month by Lavendu, but as the tour had been a financial failure, the former waived his fee.[19] After playing in a 'monster concert' in Hanover Square Rooms on 3 February, Liszt left for Belgium, returning to London from May to July. Most biographies of the composer refer fleetingly to this visit, but it was in fact a fairly substantial one. Liszt wrote to Marie on 14 May 1841: 'I am working like a madman on some tremendous fantasies [for piano], *Norma*, *La Somnambula*, *Freischütz*, *Maometto*, *Moïse* and *Don Juan* will be ready in five or six days. It is a new vein I have found and want to exploit it.'[20]

Apart from a few opportunities for public performances, he also appeared mainly in benefit concerts and for some private soirées as an accompanist.[21] He was now much sought after by society. 'Tomorrow I dine at Chiswick with the Duke of Devonshire,' Liszt wrote. 'Prince Esterházy has asked me to go and dine with him whenever I have nothing to do.' His rare recitals attracted distinguished audiences. One on 13 June was attended by the Duke of Cambridge, the Duchess of Gloucester, the Duchess of Sutherland, Lady Jersey, Lady Carlisle, Lord Ashbourne and the entire Austrian embassy.[22]

He had a narrow escape when his cab overturned, spraining his left wrist. But he was able to give a solo recital in Willis's Rooms on 12 June, and two days later took part in a Philharmonic Society concert in which he played an arrangement for piano of Hummel's Septet. He claimed, however, that he did not need to use his left hand for the work. In reviewing the concert the *Athenaeum* praised Liszt's 'amazing performance . . . played by memory . . . The reception given by the audience will, we hope, open a way to our hearing more master works of the classical composers for the pianoforte, rendered with a like splendour by the same matchless interpreter.'[23] Nevertheless, Liszt's monetary rewards were scant. As he told Marie on the day of the concert: 'This fatal artistic calling is a sore trial to me. My life is as prosaic, harsh and as gloomy as a gambler's, and the game I am playing a long and listless one.'[24] Within a few years he had abandoned his public piano concerts, and devoted himself to conducting and composing. Liszt left England on 2 July, not to return again for another forty-five years.

In the meantime his reputation throughout Europe had reached a high point. Having given up performing in public in 1848, he settled in Weimar. Liszt was closely associated with the championing of Wagner's music, which was greatly admired in England, and audiences were eager to see the by now venerable Abbé, or 'Habby Liszt' as the cabmen affectionately called him.[25] His own music had been heard during his decades of absence through the efforts of one of Liszt's fervent admirers, Walter Bache. Bache had sponsored out of his own funds an annual concert of the composer's works in London.

Liszt's seventy-fifth birthday in 1886 gave rise to many an invitation from European countries where his works were being performed, but it was an acknowledgement of Bache's efforts that the composer decided once again to come to England. Before this Liszt had attended a concert in Budapest in March, receiving an emotional send-off, then to Belgium and to Paris, where he was royally entertained. On 3 April he was met at Calais by Alfred Littleton, of the music publisher Novello, at whose father's home, Westwood House, he was to stay in Sydenham, and the young conductor Alexander Mackenzie. They were joined at Dover by Walter Bache, and the party proceeded to board the train to London. A reception committee awaited him at Victoria Station, but unbeknown to them, the chairman of the London, Chatham and Dover Railway Company had given permission for the boat train to make an unofficial stop at Penge Railway Station, near to Littleton's house. On hearing of this, the reception party rushed from Victoria and intercepted Liszt's party, making their presentation in a crowded waiting room on Penge Station.

The following sixteen days were crammed with so many activities that they would have taxed the strength of a much younger person. Nevertheless, Liszt seemed to thrive on the many celebrations mounted in his honour as well as the adulation he received. Two days after he arrived, on 5 April, he attended a full rehearsal of his oratorio *Saint Elisabeth* at St James's Hall. Some 1,500 people had gathered to catch a glimpse of the great man and he was overwhelmed by the reception he received. The public performance took place the following day. There was a star-studded cast of principals including Albani as Saint Elisabeth. The conductor was Mackenzie, whose main recollection of the performance was when the headgear of one of the female soloists who was of unusual height came into contact with his baton 'with unexpected consequences'.[26] At the end of the performance, the composer was obliged to acknowledge the applause of the audience and the performers by standing in the middle of the orchestra.

Earlier in the day, Liszt had visited the Royal Academy of Music to present a cheque for over £1,000, a sum raised by Bache, to found a Liszt scholarship for promising students. Although he had stated in newspaper interviews before he came to England that he would never perform in public again, he played the piano in private gatherings on a number of occasions. The students were delighted when he gave an impromptu performance of two of his own works. The next day, 7 April, Liszt travelled to Windsor to play before Queen Victoria. It had been nearly five decades since the two had last met, and the queen noted in her journal the great changes in Liszt's appearance from 'a very wild phantastic looking man', to 'a quiet, benevolent looking old Priest, with long white hair, and scarcely any teeth'.[27] Liszt, for his part, described the meeting in a letter the following day: 'Yesterday at 3 o'clock, I was at Windsor, by command of the Queen. She was most gracious this time and conversed in good German: I played her 3 or 4 short piano pieces, including a Nocturne by Chopin.'[28]

It was generally agreed that the climax of the visit was the reception at the Grosvenor Gallery on 8 April, which had been arranged by Walter Bache. Some 400 of the most celebrated representatives of the professions and the arts had been invited to a concert mainly of Liszt's music, for which the performers gave their services. Once again, Liszt obliged the audience by performing a divertissement by Schubert and his own *Hungarian Rhapsody No. 13*. An all-Liszt concert at the Crystal Palace, conducted by Augustus Manns, followed on the Saturday which the composer attended, and on the Sunday he went to Brompton Oratory for the service which included a Mass by Palestrina. The same evening he visited the eighty-eight-year-old Duchess of Cambridge whom he had first met in 1840. By now she was almost deaf but he played two little pieces to her on an upright piano. When he had finished, they both had tears in their eyes.[29] To round off the day, Liszt went on to Marlborough House to have dinner with the Prince of Wales and twenty other guests, again playing the piano for them.

The celebrations were non-stop. 'I'll pass over the invitations to dinner and lunch,' he wrote the following week, 'of which I have been able to accept barely half.'[30] He had an audience with Cardinal Manning and sat for a bust by the eminent sculptor Edgar Boehm, a fellow Hungarian. He attended a 'Monday Pops Concert' at St James's Hall at which Joachim performed, and two days later went to see a play at the Lyceum Theatre. This was the ninety-ninth performance of the stage version of Goethe's *Faust*, in which Henry Irving took the role of Mephistopheles. It was a spectacular production with many innovative visual effects. Liszt was given the royal box and the orchestra played in his honour his *Hungarian March* during the *entr'acte*. At the end of the play, Irving took his guest into the Beefsteak Room where, much to Liszt's delight, he found that his favourite main dish had been provided: lentil pudding, lamb cutlets and mushrooms in batter.[31] Bram Stoker, the creator of Dracula, was among the guests. He noted that Irving and Liszt, through gestures and a few words of each other's language, managed to communicate animatedly.[32]

Amidst the high-level celebrations which accompanied Liszt's visit, he did not lose the opportunity to attend the public recitals on two consecutive days given by his former students, Frederick Lamond, a Scotsman, and Bernhard Stavenhagen, at St James's Hall and Prince's Hall respectively. The latter chose a taxing programme consisting entirely of his teacher's work, a not altogether wise choice, in view of his comparatively little playing experience.

Liszt had intended to leave England for home on 17 April but was obliged to stay on to attend a repeat performance at the Crystal Palace of *Saint Elisabeth*. All of London wanted to be present and Liszt was almost mobbed by a section of the audience as he entered. The critics pronounced the performance of this lengthy and uneven oratorio an artistic triumph. On Sunday evening, 18 April, as Liszt's visit was coming to a close, his host Henry Littleton gave a dinner at his Sydenham house for his old and new friends, including Frederick Beale, Alexander Mackenzie, Henry Irving and Ellen Terry. After dinner Liszt needed little persuasion to play to the assembled guests. Mackenzie wrote of the occasion: 'Those present could truly say that they had heard Liszt, for probably this was the last time he ever ventured on so long and physically exacting a programme: much more than mere flashes of his former supremacy were exhibited that night.' The programme was a generous one; it consisted of Beethoven's Variations in F major, Op. 34, Cramer's Study in G major, two Weber pieces and Bach's Fugue in D major from the first book of the *Well Tempered Clavier*; during this last work, Liszt had a memory lapse but happily improvised until he once more found his place. On Tuesday morning, 20 April, Liszt bade farewell to Littleton and his friends at Herne Hill Station, crossed the Channel and arrived back in Weimar.

Passing through Paris Liszt was reported to be looking remarkable pale and emaciated.[33] However, witnesses such as Mackenzie strongly denied that his London visit shortened his life in any respect. 'Far from harming him, the visit provided the last happy weeks and the final blaze of triumph in a uniquely successful life.'[34] By July, Liszt was a sick man, but insisted on travelling to Bayreuth to lend support to his daughter Cosima Wagner, who was attempting to restore the fortunes of the festival. After attending performances of *Tristan* and *Parsifal*, he developed a high fever, and died on 31 July 1886 at the age of seventy-five.

13 Antonin Dvořák

An English celebrity

One of the most frequent musical visitors to England in the nineteenth century was Antonin Dvořák, who made no fewer than nine journeys. Born in Bohemia in 1841 into a poor family, he claimed that at one stage he had to decide whether to be a musician or a butcher.[1] By the time he received an invitation from the Philharmonic Society of London, in the summer of 1883, to conduct some of his compositions at one of their concerts in the coming season, Dvořák was internationally famous. Many of his works, such as the *Slavonic Dances*, the *Stabat Mater* and his Sixth Symphony, had been performed in England, and there was a growing demand to see the composer in person.

Dvořák accepted the invitation, and accompanied by a pianist friend, Jindrich von Kaan, left Prague on 5 March 1884 on a train which carried him across Europe to Ostend, where he saw the open sea for the first time. He had a life-long love of railways and his three-day journey made him very happy.[2] They were met in at Victoria by Henry Littleton, senior partner in the music publishers, Novello & Co., and the German-born pianist Oskar Beringer. During his time in London he stayed at Beringer's flat in Hinde Street, Manchester Square.

The first rehearsal of the *Stabat Mater* was at the Albert Hall on 10 March, the building being described by Dvořák as one which could comfortably seat 12,000 people. The forty-three-year-old composer was enthusiastically received by the choir:

> When I appeared at the desk, I was welcomed with such a thunder of applause that it took me some considerable time before there was quiet again. I was so deeply touched with the warmth of the ovation that I could not speak a word, and in any case, it would not have been of any use as nobody would have understood me.[3]

The concert itself three days later was an unbounded success. Sir Henry Hadow, in his book *Studies in Modern Music*, wrote: 'His (Dvořák's) reception was one of the most cordial ever offered by our land to a foreign artist. The house was crowded and appreciative; the press for once raised

20 Dvořák on his first visit to England, 1884

a unanimous voice of approbation.'4 The size of the forces used in the work was impressive: 250 sopranos, 160 contraltos, 180 tenors and 250 basses. The string section alone consisted of 92 players. The concert was followed by a dinner party hosted by Littleton, at which almost every musical personality in London was present. The dinner was followed by a selection of Dvořák's vocal and instrumental music, and the party went on until after two o'clock the following morning.

One of the aspects of his visit which most pleased Dvořák was his opportunity to promote Czech music. He was passionately committed to the movement for Czech nationalism, which was spreading rapidly at this time. He was irritated when the English journals described him as 'Herr Dvořák' for this implied that he was of German extraction. His musical output reflected his deep love for his country. At a concert given a week later at St James's Hall, he conducted his *Hussite Overture*, the *Second Slavonic Rhapsody*, and the Sixth Symphony, the last of which included many folk melodies. At a farewell dinner given to Dvořák at the Café Royal, the composer thanked the guests for the warm welcome he had received, and promised to return soon. As he wrote to his father: 'Here in England a happier time ... has begun for me which, I hope, will bear Czech art in general good fruit.'[5] The visit also marked the start of freedom from future financial worries, as Littleton on behalf of Novello had commissioned Dvořák to write another oratorio.

On his return to Bohemia Dvořák lost no time in purchasing a piece of land at Vysoka from his brother-in-law, Count Kounitz. The simple house which he constructed, surrounded by hills and forests, was to be the source of great inspiration to him in his future compositions.[6] He was now able to give more time to his favourite hobby, rearing pigeons, a subject on which he was always willing to wax eloquent.[7]

Within a few months, in September 1884, Dvořák was back in England to celebrate a special occasion. The Three Choirs Festival was to be held at Worcester where, 800 years before, the cathedral had been founded.[8] Dvořák wrote to his father that he had been invited to conduct his *Stabat Mater* at 'the big industrial town of Worchester'. He was accompanied on the journey to England by a music writer, V. J. Novotny, who attended the performance of the work:

> The rendering was excellent, the choir and orchestra were perfectly sure of themselves, and the soloists – Albani, Patey, Lloyd and Santley – had a perfect command of the oratorio style, as, in fact, English singers are unrivalled in this field. The work, admirably performed under the firm confident baton of the Master, made a deep impression on all present.[9]

The *Musical Times* wrote a laudatory review of the performance, calling the oratorio 'one of the greatest compositions of modern times'.[10] Dvořák's fame had spread before him in the town. At the evening concert of secular music later the same day at the Shire Hall, where he conducted his Sixth Symphony, the applause was so overwhelming at his appearance that the performance was unable to start and there was equal enthusiasm displayed between each movement. Dvořák was deeply touched by this reception and wrote the following day: 'Everywhere I appear, whether in the street or at home, or even when I go into the shop to buy something, people crowd round me and ask for my autograph. There are pictures of me at all the booksellers, and people buy them only to have some memento.'[11]

One member of the orchestra who played under Dvořák in the cathedral was the twenty-seven-year-old Edward Elgar. Sharing the third violin desk of the Festival Orchestra, he was in a good position to study both the man and his music. The influence of Dvořák's music on Elgar's own compositions is obvious, and he retained a lifelong fondness for it. After the cathedral performance Elgar told a friend: 'I wish you could hear Dvořák's music. It is simply ravishing, so tuneful and clever and the orchestration is wonderful: no matter how few instruments he uses it never sounds thin. I cannot describe it: it must be heard.'[12]

Although the two men never formally met, there was a fortuitous link which remains one of the most intriguing 'what ifs' in history. Two years later, when Dvořák was conducting his works at the Birmingham Festival, he visited the Oratory, created by Cardinal Newman, in order to attend High Mass. Newman presented the composer with a copy of his poem *The Dream of Gerontius* which he had written two decades earlier. There are two conflicting accounts of Dvořák's reaction to the poem. One was that he left in high glee, stating that it would inspire him to set it to music, the other that Dvořák found the subject too placid and lyrical for his special style.[13] In the former account, the Festival Committee initially suggested that Dvořák should be invited to write a setting for the 1888 festival, but later changed its mind on the grounds that the poem was too Catholic.[14] It was not until 1899 that Elgar was commissioned by the same committee to proceed with the work, which proved to be one of the landmarks in British musical history.

The Philharmonic Society of London had commissioned Dvořák to write a symphony to be played at one of their 1885 season concerts. By 22 December 1884, he was fully occupied with its composition; as he wrote to a neighbour at this time: 'Wherever I go, I have nothing else in mind but my work which must be such as to make a stir in the world, and God grant that it may!'[15] The symphony was completed by the middle of March 1885 and a month later he arrived, with his friend Josef Zubaty, to conduct the work.

The Symphony No. 7 in D minor, which was dedicated to the society, was performed at St James's Hall on 22 April before an enthusiastic audience. It is interesting to note that Dvořák, ever the train-lover, acknowledged that the opening theme of the first movement was inspired by the arrival of a festival express train from Pest to Prague Station. There were two other engagements to fulfil: a concert at which his Piano Concerto was performed, and a choral concert where his minor work, *Hymnus. The Heirs of the White Mountain*, made its British début.

During his month long stay with Henry Littleton in Sydenham, Dvořák was able to sightsee and indulge in the entertainments which the capital city could offer. It is possible that amongst the theatres which he visited was the Savoy, where the current attraction was *The Mikado*.[16] Dvořák enjoyed the open spaces of Hyde Park and Regent's Park, lunched at the Criterion Restaurant and paid a visit to the House of Commons. His friend Zubaty accompanied him to the National Gallery, where Dvořák stood long in silence before a portrait of a Madonna by Raphael: 'At last he began, "You see, that is Mozart. It is so beautifully composed. The landscape behind the throne, you do not know why it is there, but it is lovely and must be like that. In Brussels they have pictures by Breughel, tremendous pictures ... they positively overpower you and you do not realise how small you are – And that is Beethoven."'[17]

Dvořák also took a keen interest in British musical life. He made the acquaintance of a number of composers, becoming a close friend of the Scotsman Alexander Mackenzie. At a banquet to celebrate the 147th anniversary of the foundation of the Royal Society of Musicians of Great Britain, he accompanied the tenor Edward Lloyd in his *Gypsy Melodies*.[18]

Within three months, Dvořák had returned to England to conduct his new oratorio for the Birmingham Triennial Festival. This time he travelled alone, taking a circuitous route. The journey lasted more than forty-eight hours and Dvořák arrived exhausted at Victoria Station, London on 7 August 1885 at six o'clock in the morning. He had been commissioned to write an oratorio for the festival by Littleton and the publisher had also asked Gounod the same year to produce two choral works for the festival. Dvořák was puzzled as to why Littleton had paid Gounod £4,000 for his works and Dvořák only £200 for his oratorio. He protested to Littleton: 'Pray not to pay Mr Gounod who truly does not need it, so immense sums, for what would be left for me?'[19]

It was a hectic schedule. On the day Dvořák arrived in England there was a chorus rehearsal in Birmingham of the work, *The Spectre's Bride*. As there was no local orchestra available, it was necessary for the composer to return to London the following day for the instrumental rehearsals. Henry Littleton had rented a flat in Victoria Mansions, Hove, and took Dvořák to Brighton where, as Dvořák noted, 'the wealthiest London class go in the summer time'. He continued:

> The lovely view of the sea from my room, the sight of thousands of people swarming everywhere, the lovely English women bathing (*and publicly*), there again *men* and *children*, then a countless number of boats large and small, or here a band playing Scottish folk-songs and goodness knows what else besides: everything is enchantingly lovely so that nobody who has seen it can ever forget it.[20]

The following day, the two men returned to London for further rehearsals, and on Friday left Euston for Birmingham. Like Mendelssohn some fifty years before him, Dvořák was impressed with Birmingham. 'I am here,' he wrote to a friend, 'in this immense industrial town where they make excellent knives, scissors, springs, files and I don't know what else, and besides these, music too.'[21] He also admired the patience of the festival audiences. 'It's terrible what the people here manage to do and to stand! There will be eight concerts in all and each will last four to five hours. My day is Thursday 27th at 8 p.m. Please think of me!'[22]

As Dvořák expected after the well-received rehearsals, *The Spectre's Bride* was an unqualified success. 'It really was magnificent,' he told Zubaty:

> I was victorious over all the others, and some of the papers say that no composer had previously gained such a success in Birmingham. The audience was absolutely electrified. Already after Albani's aria there was great applause which continued to increase until the end. It was a din! The constant cries and calls for 'Dvořák' had no end. The orchestra, the choir and the audience were exultant. The female choir surrounded me and all wished to press my hand and congratulate me. I did not know what was happening to me.[23]

A year later, he was pleased to note that 'this work is very popular here. It was probably performed in each town in England'.[24]

Returning home, Dvořák immediately set to work on the Littleton commission, originally agreed to on his first visit to England and for which he was to be paid £1,000. The oratorio, to be performed at the Leeds Festival, was on the Czech historical theme of *St Ludmila*, concerning the conversion to Christianity of Prince Borivoj and his wife, Ludmila, in 1873. When Dvořák left for England in October 1886, he was accompanied by his wife, Anna. He gave an interview for the *Pall Mall Gazette* in which he described his struggle to become a composer. 'And what is your opinion of the English as a musical nation?' asked the reporter. 'Are they so utterly devoid of a sense for music as is generally assumed?' 'Of this I am only an imperfect judge,' replied the composer. 'But as far as my experience of English audiences goes I can only say that people who have not a good deal of love for music in them can hardly sit for four hours closely following an oratorio from beginning to end and evidently enjoy doing it.'[25]

During the rehearsals, Dvořák's shaky English presented difficulties, and Arthur Sullivan, whose own sacred work *The Golden Legend* was also being performed, assisted him by frequently interpreting his wishes to the orchestra.[26] After a fortnight of rehearsals, the first performance of *St Ludmila* took place on 15 October 1886. Although the audience greeted the work warmly, there were some critics who compared it unfavourably with *The Spectre's Bride*. The dull translation from the Czech text was the work of the Rev. John Troutbeck, who had also been responsible for the translation of *The Spectre's Bride*. The oratorio itself, an uneasy compromise between the Handelian style and Czech traditional music, was too long, with the best music occurring in the first half hour.[27]

There was little time for relaxation on the visit. Dvořák travelled with his wife from Leeds to Birmingham to conduct a performance of his D major Symphony. On a day free from rehearsals, they were able to go to Stratford-on-Avon to see Shakespeare's birthplace. The concert was followed by further performances of *St Ludmila* at St James's Hall, London on 29 October and the Crystal Palace on 6 November; they left for Bohemia a few days later.

Although it was some three-and-a-half years before Dvořák next came to England, his music continued to feature prominently in concert programmes. One of his main champions was the conductor Hans Richter. At a Philharmonic Society concert in May 1887, he gave the first British performance of the *Symphonic Variations for Orchestra*, which had been composed a decade earlier. At the first rehearsal, Richter was 'positively carried away. It is a magnificent work ... among the best of your compositions,' he told Dvořák. At the concert a few weeks later it was an enormous success: 'At the hundreds of concerts which I have conducted during my life no *new work* has ever had such a success as yours.'[28]

Shortly before his sixth visit to England Dvořák made the journey to Russia, having been invited there by his new friend Tchaikovsky. The two men had met in Prague where they expressed their admiration for the other's music.[29] While in Russia at the end of February 1890 Dvořák conducted concerts in Moscow and St Petersburg. The following month, he came to London briefly to conduct the first British performance of his Symphony No. 8 in G major, known as the 'English' Symphony. The title is hardly appropriate as it includes many typically Czech tunes. There are three possible explanations: that the name was given as it was published by the English firm of Novello,[30] or that it was an attempt to meet Dvořák's notion of English musical taste,[31] or that it was a deliberate snub to his other publisher, Simrock, who had refused the symphony.[32]

Despite his fame, Dvořák never lost the common touch, constantly remembering his own humble beginnings. In reply to a fulsome letter from a Czech rural choirmaster, he replied:

> I must confess to you candidly that your kind letter took me a little by surprise, because its excessive servility and humility made it seem as if you were addressing some demigod, which of course I never was, am not, and never shall be. I am just a plain Czech musician, disliking such exaggerated humility, and despite the fact that I have moved a bit in the great musical world, I still remain just what I was – a simple Czech musician.[33]

Nevertheless, he was delighted to accept the singular honour the following year, an honorary doctorate of music at Cambridge. Stanford, now Professor of Music at the university, informed him of the Senate's decision, and invited Dvořák and his wife to stay with him, at 10 Harvey Road, Cambridge. He was also invited to conduct a concert sponsored by the Cambridge University Musical Society consisting of his *Stabat Mater* and his Eighth Symphony.

Dvořák and Anna arrived in Cambridge on 11 June 1891. Stanford later commented:

> I heard a noise in the garden in the small hours and saw the pair sitting under a tree in the garden at 6 a.m. He and Brahms must have had in common the gift of being satisfied with from four to five hours of sleep.[34]

The concert in Cambridge Guildhall on 15 June was a notable event, the enthusiastic audience including many undergraduates who were eager to see the great man. The *Cambridge Review* three days later reported that 'Dvořák was himself very pleased with the concert, and thought it the best performance of the *Stabat Mater* that has been given'. Much of its success was due to Stanford's training of the undergraduate choir. The soloists, Albani, Lloyd and Henschel, gave their services without payment.[35] After the concert, when he was entertained to tea, Dvořák astonished the assembled company by consuming a vast quantity of sandwiches, remarking, 'now my stowmack is betterer'.[36]

The degree ceremony at Senate House the following day was witnessed by a large audience. Dvořák was flattered to learn that the only other foreign musician so far honoured was the violinist and composer Joseph Joachim four years earlier. The members of the Cambridge University Musical Society presented Dvořák with a doctor's cap and gown which he wore at the ceremony. The distinguished company of those receiving honorary degrees included the politician, the Marquess of Dufferin and Ava, the Irish historian William Lecky, and Dvořák himself. The greatest applause by the undergraduates was reserved for the composer.

A long speech in Latin by the Public Orator praising his achievements was regarded by Dvořák with detachment. He later commented humorously to one of his composition students:

> I don't like such celebrations. And if it so happens that I must be present at one I am, as it were, on pins and needles. I shall never forget how I felt when they made me a doctor in England: the formalities and the doctors. All the faces so grave and it seemed that none could speak anything but Latin. I listened to my right and to my left and did not know where to turn my ear. And when I discovered that they were talking to me I could have wished myself anywhere else than there and was ashamed that I did not know Latin. But when I look back on it today I must smile and think to myself that to compose *Stabat Mater* is, after all, better than to know Latin.[37]

The occasion, despite his discomfort at the time, remained one of his happiest memories. He proudly took home with him the 'lovely' doctor's cap and gown which are now displayed at the Dvořák Museum in Prague. Three weeks after returning home, he composed his overture *Amid Nature*, which he dedicated to the university.

Because of the success of *The Spectre's Bride* at the 1885 Birmingham Festival the committee was eager for a further oratorio. The composer pleaded pressure of other work and failed to produce any music. However for the festival in 1891, after months of continuous work, Dvořák completed a *Requiem* and came to Birmingham to conduct it. The festival included compositions by Parry, Stanford and Mackenzie. The pianist Adeline de Lara, who met Dvořák during the festival described him as a

> jolly good fellow and at the same time rather quaint. His face was broad, his eyes very bright above a squat nose and a beard which he trimmed very close. With his dark velvet coat he wore a huge silk bow, which seemed out of keeping with the rest of his appearance. He would stroll about with his hands in his pockets, and you could always tell where he was, for he would whistle or hum as he walked.[38]

The performance on 9 October received a mixed reception from the critics, some comparing it unfavourably with other great settings by such composers as Berlioz, Fauré and Verdi. A particularly waspish review was that of George Bernard Shaw. He wrote:

> Dvořák's *Requiem* bored Birmingham so desperately that it was unanimously voted a work of extraordinary depth and impressiveness, which verdict I record with a hollow laugh and allow the subject to drop by its own portentious weight.[39]

This was Dvořák's only appearance in England on the visit as there was urgent business to attend to at home. As far back as 1884 when he was in London, Dvořák had met the American composer Dudley Buck, who invited him to go to America. At the time he had rejected the notion but he finally agreed in December 1891 to become the Director of the National Conservatory of Music of America in New York. For the following three years much of Dvořák's time was spent in the United States.

In November 1895 Francesco Berger, the honorary secretary of the Philharmonic Society, sent Dvořák one of his frequent requests for the composer to visit London and conduct some of his own works. Whilst in New York, Dvořák had begun composing a cello concerto and in accepting Berger's offer agreed to conduct a performance of the new work.[40] As it had been some five years since he was last in England, Dvořák was looking forward to meeting his friends again. Arriving in London in March 1896, he was accompanied by his daughter Otilie; they stayed at the Langham Hotel, just opposite the Queen's Hall, where the concert was to be held. It is recorded that Dvořák, who was prone to making social gaffes, was taking an early morning walk on this visit and was passing the Athenaeum Club in Pall Mall. Assuming that it was a café he entered, sat down and ordered a cup of coffee. He was ejected shortly afterwards.[41]

There were a number of difficulties to be settled before the concert took place. Dvořák had stipulated that his friend Honus Wihan should be the soloist, but the Philharmonic Society had already engaged an English cellist, Leo Stern, for the performance. Dvořák threatened to withdraw the concerto from the concert but later changed his mind.[42] It was a lengthy programme consisting of his Eighth Symphony, the first five *Biblical Songs* and Beethoven's 'Emperor' Concerto as well as the world premiere of the Cello Concerto. The new work was greeted with acclaim as was the rest of the concert.

Dvořák was at the height of his creative powers, although physically he was weary from the pressures of work and travel. The short visit to London lacked much of the spirit of his first encounter twelve years earlier. He wrote to a friend the day before the concert:

> Here the weather is terrible; on Monday there was a great wind, yesterday and today it has rained almost the whole time – one almost despairs, especially when at the same time, one is tormented by cold. Indeed, I could not get a mouthful of good food here – which has never happened to me before – nothing was to my taste. I ate nothing for almost two days, I have only drunk a little coffee – only today and yesterday I was invited to Novello's and so I recovered a little.[43]

Nevertheless, it is clear from his reply to invitations from the Philharmonic Society over the next few years that he fully intended to return to England. He wrote to Berger in December 1899: 'Many thanks for your kindly letter and invitation. Surely I will come to please you and it will be a great pleasure to me to see my good friends in London again.'[44] However, his teaching duties at the Prague Conservatory and his preoccupation in his last years with composing operas, such as *Rusalka*, ruled out further visits. He declared in 1900: 'As you know I never visit London without having a new work for you – but this year I am quite unable to bring something new.' Four years later, on 1 May 1904, Dvořák died suddenly at the age of sixty-two.

14 'This quite horrible city'
Tchaikovsky in London

'What shall I tell you about my journey?' wrote Tchaikovsky to his sister, Sasha, after his return from England in October 1861. 'If I ever started upon a colossal piece of folly, it was this same trip abroad.'[1] This visit of Pytor Ilich Tchaikovsky was not as a musician. He had graduated in law at St Petersburg two years previously and then immediately began work as a clerk in the Ministry of Justice in the city. The abolition of serfdom had recently been promulgated and change was in the air. Tchaikovsky too hoped for a new turn in his career. He had begun serious piano lessons when he was fifteen, composed a song and made a first attempt at conducting a school choir, though without much success. The life of a professional musician greatly attracted him and shortly after becoming a civil servant he began studying thorough bass.

The opportunity to visit England came about through a friend of his father's, an engineer called Vasily Pisarev, who needed an interpreter to accompany him on a tour of western Europe. The two men left St Petersburg in July and travelled to Berlin where Tchaikovsky saw Offenbach's *Orpheus in the Underworld*, then to Hamburg, Brussels and Ostend. They arrived in London on 8 August 1861 and spent the following five days sightseeing. Although he enjoyed visiting Westminster Abbey and the Houses of Parliament, Tchaikovsky's greatest excitement was reserved for a visit to Cremorne Gardens at Chelsea, where lavish entertainments and spectacles were available to the public. 'I've never seen anything like it,' he wrote. 'When you go in it's like something enchanted.' He attended a concert given by the opera-singer, Adelina Patti, who did not impress him, and he made two visits to the Crystal Palace. On one of these, he heard Handel's 'Halleujah' Chorus sung by 5,000 schoolchildren which he found deeply moving. However, the English weather was a matter for constant complaint by the composer on this and subsequent visits. 'London is very interesting,' he told his father, 'but it makes a certain gloomy impression on my soul. The sun is never seen and it rains all the time.' On the other hand: 'The food is very much to my taste. It's simple, even unsubtle, but liberal in quantity and tasty.'[2] Tchaikovsky felt much more at home in Paris, the last call of the tour, seeing operas such as *Il Travatore* and

Les Huguenots but was relieved to return to Russia at the beginning of October.

By the time of Tchaikovsky's next visit to England some twenty-seven years later, he was a celebrated composer. He had abandoned his career as a civil servant two years after his London visit and had taken up music as a full-time student. Among his compositions were *Eugene Onegin*, the ballet *Swan Lake*, four symphonies, three string quartets and orchestral works such as *Romeo and Juliet*, *Francesca da Rimini*, the *1812 Overture*, the *Serenade for Strings* and perhaps the most popular work, his Piano Concerto No. 1 in B flat minor. The tour was undertaken by Tchaikovsky in the belief that, as his works were comparatively little known in the West, a personal appearance might lead to greater popular recognition. The tour was an exhausting one – Leipzig, where he met Brahms and Grieg, Hamburg, Berlin, Prague, where he met Dvořák, and Paris. Here he met Fauré, though Tchaikovsky recorded bitterly that he had not been paid a sou for his conducting efforts.

He left Paris in a snowstorm on 19 April 1888 for the Channel crossing from Calais and boasted that he was the only passenger who was not sea-sick. For his five-day stay in London, Tchaikovsky chose the luxur-ious Hotel Dieudonné in Ryder Street, off Piccadilly, and within walking distance of the St James's Hall where he was to conduct. The two rehearsals had proved to be difficult, partly because of language prob-lems, as Tchaikovsky spoke little English, and partly due to his less than perfect conducting technique. Frederick Cowen, the newly appointed conductor of the Philharmonic Society, eased the situation by acting as interpreter at rehearsals. The players in the orchestra were excellent and performed well for him. Three days later, he conducted a programme which included the *Serenade for Strings* and the *Theme and Variations* from his Third Suite. He wrote to his brother Modest two days later: 'The concert was a brilliant success.'[3] He was called back three times after performing the *Serenade*, and London audiences acknowledged the presence of a gifted musician in their midst.

One pleasant outcome of the concert for the composer was that the press persuaded the sponsors of the concert, the Philharmonic Society, to increase his fees from £20 to £25.[4] Though claiming that London was a dull city, nevertheless he took advantage of its many musical offerings. There were two visits to the ballet, *Enchantment* at the Alhambra and *The Sports of England* at the Empire, Leicester Square. The second ballet depicted various activities, including cricket at Lord's, with female mem-bers of the MCC and the Australian XI, yachting on the Solent, football at the Oval, Derby Day at Epsom, polo at Hurlingham and hunting at Melton Mowbray. Not suprisingly, Tchaikovsky summed up the experi-ence: 'Various goings on. Bored.'[5] He left London 'somewhat ill'; this was due to overindulgence of his favourite dish, macaroni, at Gatti's Restaurant in the Strand, which made a delay of a day necessary in his departure plans for home. Tchaikovsky left England on 24 March, when he headed straight for Tiflis in Georgia.

It was almost exactly a year later that Tchaikovsky returned, if briefly, to England. He had embarked in February 1889 on a second international conducting tour, taking in Germany and Switzerland. He then made a purely private visit to Paris where he saw and ascended the newly-built Eiffel Tower. Arriving in England on 9 April after another rough sea voyage in 'the marvellous steamship *Folkestone*', he once again stayed in London at the Hotel Dieudonné. The following day, he described his reactions to the weather:

> First, I must tell you what a London fog is like. Last year too I had the pleasure of enjoying it every day, but what happened today I would never have thought possible. When I went to the rehearsal in the morning it was foggy as it sometimes is in Petersburg; but when Sapelnikov and I left St James's Hall at 12.30 pm it was pitch dark – just like at 8 o'clock on a moonless autumn night in Petersburg. It made a very strong impression on both of us. Even without a fog I find London very antipathetic. (But for God's sake don't mention this to Miss Eastwood [governess to Tchaikovsky's niece's family].) And now I have the feeling that I am sitting in a dismal underground dungeon – 4.00 pm it is getting somewhat brighter. The extraordinary thing is that this happens in the middle of April; even the Londoners themselves are surprised.[6]

It is little wonder that he recorded in his diary on his last night in London, 'Drunkenness in private'.[7]

The main purpose of the visit was to introduce to an English audience Vasily Sapelnikov. He was a talented pianist whom Tchaikovsky championed, though because of his unprepossessing appearance he was unkindly referred to as an 'ape'. The programme, performed on 11 April, consisted of the First Piano Concerto which, the composer had previously assured the secretary of the Philharmonic society, was 'capable of creating a great impression', and the First Suite. The Society had hoped that the Fifth Symphony, begun in the previous May, would be performed rather than the latter item, but Tchaikovsky pleaded that as yet he was not satisfied with its orchestration. The concert was enthusiastically received, much to Tchaikovsky's satisfaction, especially Sopelnikov's extravagant performance of the concerto; one critic commented that 'if he did not charm the audience, he astonished them'.

There was little time between rehearsals, once more mediated by Cowen, for other activities, but he managed to write, in French, a lengthy letter to Ethel Smyth, one of the earliest English women composers. Tchaikovsky had met Smyth the previous year in Leipzig where she was studying music. They had disagreed on the merits of Brahms as a composer, Smyth

21 The former Hotel Dieudonné, Ryder Street, London, where Tchaikovsky
stayed on three of his visits, 1883–93

staunchly championing his works, Tchaikovsky taking the opposite point of view. Smyth later recalled: 'He would argue with me about Brahms by the hour, strum passages on the piano and ask if they were not hideous, declaring I must be under hypnotic influence, since to admire this awkward peasant did not square with what he was kind enough to call the soundness of my instinct on other points.' Now from London he wrote to Smyth regretting that there would not be time to visit her. 'Let us hope,' he continued, 'that I will return, and my most sincere vow will be to come and see you ... At Hamburg I spent an entire day with your Idol ... Johannes Brahms!! He was charming to me, He is such a sympathetic man, although my appreciation of his talent doesn't correspond with yours.'[8] The following morning, Tchaikovsky entered Sopelnikov's bedroom, kissed the sleeping youth and left the hotel. He reached Marseilles that evening and a fortnight later was once more in Tiflis.

An interesting insight into Tchaikovsky's mind at this time arose from an enquiry made by Carl Rosa, the operatic impresario, shortly after the visit. Rosa asked the composer which of his operas he would consider most suitable for English audiences. In reply, Tchaikovsky suggested *Eugene Onegin* and *The Maid of Orleans*. However, because of Rosa's death shortly afterwards, the matter was taken no further. Another project which Tchaikovsky was contemplating arose out of his discovery of the works of the writer George Eliot towards the end of the 1880s. He had avidly read *Adam Bede*, *Middlemarch*, *Mill on the Floss* and *Silas Marner*, and was particularly fond of *Scenes from Clerical Life*. He mooted the idea of turning the first of the stories from *Scenes*, 'The Sad Fortunes of the Reverend Amos Booth', into an opera but was dissuaded from doing so by Modest who was opposed to the project.[9]

Tchaikovsky's last and most extensive visit to England took place four years later, only five months before his death. In early December 1892, he had received an invitation from the Vice-Chancellor of Cambridge University to come to England to accept an honorary doctorate of music in the following June, to coincide with the fiftieth anniversary celebrations of the founding of the Cambridge University Musical Society. The invitation arrived at a time when Tchaikovsky was depressed at the reception in Russia of his opera *Iolanta*, his ballet *The Nutcracker* and the failure of his E flat Symphony, which became the first movement of his Third Piano Concerto, all combined to leave him a state of creative paralysis.[10] A temporary escape from this situation seemed tempting at the time. Since his previous visit to England, he had completed his Fifth Symphony, the opera *The Queen of Spades* and the ballet *The Sleeping Beauty* and shortly after accepting the invitation to Cambridge, embarked on his Sixth Symphony.

Considering Tchaikovsky's dislike of England, apart from the receptiveness of his music by London audiences, it is surprising that he accepted engagements which would keep him away from home for well over a fortnight. He quickly realised that the visit was a mistake. Leaving St Petersburg on 25 May 1893, he soon wrote: 'Having started on my journey in a happy state of mind, less than an hour later I was attacked by that maddening, indescribable depression which now pursues me every time I go abroad. This continuing mood has not left me for a minute since I left and is an ever-growing *cresecendo*. This is definitely the last time I am going to go abroad.'[11] He landed in England on 29 May and was installed once more at the Hotel Dieudonné, writing the same day to his nephew informing him of his safe arrival in 'this quite horrible city'. He complained: 'I can never find anything here. No men's lavatories, no money exchange offices; it was with difficulty that I found a hat to fit my head.'[12]

Tchaikovsky's fame in England, as in the rest of Europe, had grown remarkably within a few years. His first concert on 1 June, a Philharmonic Society event, attracted the cream of London society as well as many distinguished musicians. His friend Saint-Saëns joined him in conducting their own compositions, in Saint-Saëns's case a concerto and a symphonic poem, and Tchaikovsky conducted his Fourth Symphony. The symphony, although written sixteen years earlier, received its first British performance and was received with loud and sustained applause from the audience but with a somewhat mixed reception from the critics. The final rehearsal for the work had witnessed a total lack of rapport between Tchaikovksy and the orchestra. According to Sir Henry Wood, 'the composer, failing to get the reckless Russian spirit he wanted in the finale of the Fourth Symphony, eventually attained it by exclaiming, "Vodka – more vodka!"'[13] The occasion was only marred by an incident before the concert when Tchaikovsky, unfamiliar with the complex geography of the St James's Hall, lost his way to the back of the stage. He presented himself to the box office to seek assistance, but was only able utter the one word 'Tchaikovsky'. At first mistaken for a member of the public seeking admission, he was informed that there were no seats left for the concert.

There was little time for relaxation as a busy social schedule had been planned for the great man's visit. He and Saint-Saëns were guests of honour at a dinner given at the St Stephen's Club in Westminster, and there were lunch parties, including one with the Stanfords, a visit to the house of the artist Alma-Tadema and invitations to other musicians' houses. George Henschel, the singer and conductor, who had first met Tchaikovsky in Moscow in 1875, was in almost daily contact with him during his stay. He had earlier described him as 'a most amiable, kind, gentle, modest man with just that touch of melancholy which seems to be a characteristic of the Russians'.[14] Now, eighteen years later, Henschel noted that the composer was more inclined to melancholy than ever. 'Indeed, one afternoon during a talk about the olden days in Petrograd and Moscow, and the many friends who were no more, he suddenly got very depressed and, wondering what this world with all its life and strife was made for, expressed his own readiness at any moment to quit it.'[15] On the other hand, he could relax with close friends and preferred an informal to a formal gathering. When he was entertained by Francesco Berger, the secretary of the Philharmonic Society, Tchaikovsky stipulated that there should be 'no party' and 'no evening dress'.[16] He displayed an interest in the development of young musicians and on 9 June, Tchaikovksy unexpectedly visited the Royal Academy of Music. The principal, Alexander Mackenzie, was busy at the time and handed Tchaikovsky the baton for a performance of his First Piano Concerto, to be played by a no doubt nervous student. Recalling Tchaikovsky's lack of success as a conductor at the best of times, Mackenzie later confessed that he had 'unwittingly provided an uncomfortable hour for the composer'.[17]

Tchaikovsky travelled by train from King's Cross on Monday 12 June to Cambridge to fulfil his engagements there. It had been agreed that each of the composers who was receiving an honorary degree should conduct one of their own works with the University Musical Society orchestra, of which Stanford was the conductor. Tchaikovsky was to stay with Frederick Maitland, the president of the society and an eminent academic lawyer. During his three-day stay with the Maitland family, which consisted of his wife, Florence, and two small daughters he was made to feel very welcome and he enjoyed their company. The concert, to be held at the Guildhall, had been arranged for later in the day of his arrival at Cambridge, and it was obvious from Mrs Maitland's observations that the composer was in a nervous condition in anticipation of the ordeal. She decided to use her daughters as a soothing influence. She wrote afterwards: 'I sent them both up to his room to tell him it was time to start for the concert at which he was to conduct his *Francesca da Rimini*. They were in their pink cashmeres with white sunbonnets. He came down with them and was enchanted with them and later on in the day, when he was taking tea, he kissed their hands.'[18]

Francesca da Rimini was the fourth item in a lengthy programme and it was well received. The *Musical Times* called the piece 'a very remarkable and masterly attempt to depict in sound the fate of the ill starred lovers described in Canto V of Dante's *Inferno*'.[19] The local newspaper reported that 'Mr. Tchaikovsky conducted a capital performance and like all the foreign composers, was cheered to the echo'.[20] Such was the importance accorded to the event that the times of the College Boat Races were put back in order not to draw people away from the concert.

At the splendid Jubilee Dinner held at King's College that evening, the young American conductor, Walter Damrosch, found himself seated next to the composer. 'He told me he had just finished a new symphony which was different in form from any he had ever written. I asked him what the difference consisted and he answered: "The last movement is an adagio and the whole work has a programme." "Do tell me the programme," I demanded eagerly. "No," he said, "that I shall never tell."'[21]

The climax of the celebrations occurred the following day, 13 June, with the degree-awarding ceremony. It was a brilliantly sunny and hot day. Apart from the composers, there were a number of other eminent recipients, notably the soldier Lord Roberts of Kandahar, the Lord Chancellor, Lord Herschell, and a wealthy Indian ruler with the awesome title of Sir Takhtsinhji Bhaosinhji, Maharajah of Bhaonagar. Tchaikovsky was impressed with the ceremony surrounding the award. At midday the procession, consisting of the Vice-Chancellor, university officials, heads of houses and the new honorary doctors, made their way to Senate House. Tchaikovsky wrote to his brother two days later:

> A large crowd watched the procession, and an Indian Rajah attracted the greatest attention by the precious stones worth several millions that adorned his dress ... As soon as we were seated, a Latin speech was pronounced in honour of each of us in turn, by the public orator. During this speech one had to stand in front of the rostrum without moving, very difficult. The students who filled the gallery in accordance with centuries-old tradition, during the speeches, screamed, squeaked, whistled, behaved in a scandalous way and you have to suffer all this without a wink ... A solemn luncheon took place at the end of which, again according to ancient tradition, everybody had to drink out of an enormous ancient goblet which is passed along all the tables. Then there was a reception given by the Vice-Chancellor's wife and at four o'clock I left for London.[22]

Despite the arduous nature of the day, Tchaikovsky's engagements were by no means completed. Arriving back at the Dieudonné after 6 p.m., he hastened to a dinner party he was giving for a number of his London friends and then left with Emile Hatzfeld, Tchaikovsky's London escort, for a performance of a new ballet *Chicago* at the Alhambra Theatre, Leicester Square. Set in the grounds of the Chicago Exhibition, the ballet had been the hit of the London season. So delighted was Tchaikovsky with the performance that he afterwards called on the composer-arranger, Jacolin, to congratulate him.[23]

The following morning, Tchaikovsky crossed over to Paris, where he spent a few days recovering from his London and Cambridge exploits. On the following day, 15 June, he wrote: 'Now all is over, it is pleasant to look back upon my visit to England, and to remember the extraordinary cordiality shown to me everywhere, although, in consequence of my peculiar temperament, while there, I tormented and worried myself to fiddle-strings.'[24]

Within two months of his arrival back in Russia, Tchaikovsky told a friend: 'I have finished scoring my new symphony. I have honestly never in my life felt so pleased with myself, so proud, so happy in the knowledge that I really have written something good.'[25] On 28 October, Tchaikovsky conducted the first performance of his Sixth Symphony at St Petersburg. Nine days later, he was dead, either from cholera or, as is more widely believed, by his own hand. According to one source, Tchaikovsky had already accepted the invitation of a friend to stay at his house in England the following year and intended to bring the new symphony for performance by the Philharmonic Society.[26] This was not to be. Francesco Berger summarised the qualities of the composer thus: 'As one who knew and loved him personally, I may venture to say here that in the course of a very wide acquaintance with men and women of mark, I have never met with such a remarkable combination, as in this man, of eminent talent with complete modesty.'[27]

15 Richard Strauss
Trouble with the censor

Few composers can match the record of Richard Strauss, who visited England over a period of almost half a century, from 1897 to 1947. By the time of his first visit, when he was greeted by a gale, Strauss was already an established and successful conductor and composer. Three years before, in 1894, at the age of thirty, he had made his conducting début at Bayreuth after holding other posts in Munich and Berlin. He was already widely acclaimed for his tone poems *Don Juan* (1888), *Tod und Verklärung* (1890), *Till Eulenspiegel* (1894–5) and *Also sprach Zarathustra* (1896).

The visit had come about through a friendship Strauss had struck up with Edgar Speyer, an enthusiastic musical amateur with a taste for modern music. Speyer was a London banker and he first met Strauss at a concert which the latter conducted in Frankfurt towards the end of 1889. Strauss was to make a tour of European countries in 1897 with London as one of the venues. Speyer, who was also chairman of the Queen's Hall Orchestra, was instrumental in presenting the composer to the British public at that venue. On 7 December, in a lengthy programme, Strauss conducted the overture to *Tannhäuser*, the Liebestod from *Tristan and Isolde*, the Good Friday Music from *Parsifal*, Mozart's *Eine kleine Nachtmusik*, *Till Eulenspiegel* and the first British performance of *Tod und Verklärung*. The sponsors of the concert, the Royal Philharmonic Society were, in a typically Straussian manner, informed that the fee offered was too low and that more rehearsal time was needed than had been scheduled.[1] In preparation for the visit, he had taken lessons in English and had the opportunity to use it when he visited the fashionable painters, Sir Edward Burne-Jones and Sir Lawrence Alma-Tadema in their studios during his short stay. Although *The Times* sourly commented on Strauss's 'not very inspiring beat' during the concert, it nevertheless conceded that the performances themselves were of a high order. Indeed, attempts were made to persuade Strauss to conduct thirty operatic performances in London the following year for a sum of 15,000 marks but Strauss's commitments in Munich made this impossible.[2] After his next visit in 1902, Strauss chose amongst his other projects to set to music the poem by Ludwig Uhland, the author of ballads and Romantic poetry, called

Taillefer, after the *jongleur* and troubadour of William the Conqueror. The work never seriously entered the musical repertoire, largely because of its unreasonable orchestral demands – ninety strings, sixty woodwind, eight horns, six trumpets, four trombones and two tubas.[3]

Another famous English connection was forged at this time. Edward Elgar's oratorio *The Dream of Gerontius* had been a dismal failure at its first performance in Birmingham in October 1900 under Hans Richter's direction, mainly due to the lack of rehearsal time, and it seemed doomed to disappear. It was Strauss who, at the Lower Rhine Festival held at Düsseldorf in May 1902, conducted the work and it proved to be a great success. He had already conducted the *Cockaigne* overture and was familiar with Elgar's music. In a luncheon in honour of Elgar after the *Gerontius* performance, Strauss proclaimed him 'the first English progressivist composer'. From this time, *Gerontius*, thanks to Strauss's generosity, came to be recognised worldwide as a masterpiece. It also marked the beginning of a lifelong friendship between Strauss and Elgar, only interrupted by the First World War. The English composer considered Strauss 'a truly great man, somewhat cynical in his music, but a powerful genius', and in a letter to Strauss at the time addressed him as 'Richard Cœur de Lion'.[4] In December the same year, Elgar had travelled to London to hear Strauss conduct the first British performance of *Ein Heldenleben* which he greatly admired.

A much larger-scale Strauss Festival was mounted in London in June 1903 at the old St James's Hall. No less an orchestra than the Concertgebouw from Amsterdam had been engaged, together with its conductor Wilhelm Mengelberg, who was to share the engagement with Strauss. It was the first British festival to be devoted entirely to his music only. The months before had been hectic ones for Strauss. In the previous year, he had started sketching out his large-scale tone poem *Symphonia Domestica*. The work described in explicit detail the daily domestic life of Strauss and his tempestous wife, Pauline, starting with the composer writing at his desk and including a scene at nighttime and love-making. This work occupied him well into 1903. Strauss would from time to time bring Pauline with him. Sir Henry Wood, the conductor of the Queen's Hall Orchestra, found her 'vivacious and somewhat overbearing' but became good friends with the couple. He would escort her on shopping expeditions in the West End, and she once brought blushes to the face of a shopwalker at Dickins and Jones in Regent Street who, on asking her which department she was looking for, answered 'Drawers!'[5]

In the last three months of the year, Strauss made further tours of France, Holland, Germany and Switzerland and returned to Britain in December to conduct concerts in London, Birmingham and Scotland; by the time Strauss reached London for the Festival, his health was deteriorating. After the final concert, Strauss collapsed and was ordered to take an immediate rest. Strauss chose to be in the Isle of Wight, where he had stayed the previous year; he was possibly made aware of it through Elgar, who had spent his honeymoon there. The weather was perfect with blazing hot sun during the four-week period of his convalescence. Strauss was particularly struck by the pleasantness of the English climate; he and his five-year-old son, Bub, particularly enjoyed running about on the hot sand and both going in and out of the sea.[6] The unfinished score of the *Symphonia Domestica* was in his luggage and Strauss was able to complete it during his stay. (Incidentally, the world premiere of this work, which Strauss conducted, took place in Wanamaker's Department Store in New York the following year.)

One aspect of Strauss's compositions which had so far received little attention in England was his operas. He had already written *Guntram* (1894) and *Feuresnot* (1901) and it was almost five years since a new work, the *Symphonia Domestica*, had been heard in a London performance. As Sir Thomas Beecham remarked: 'The town was in just the right mood for a new musical sensation; it expected it and almost decidedly it got it.'[7] This came in the form of Strauss's opera *Elektra* which received its English premiere at Covent Garden on 10 February 1910 in Beecham's first season there. Written the previous year, it had caused a sensation when it was performed in rapid succession in Berlin, Milan, Paris and Vienna. It received nine performances under Beecham's direction and thanks to widespread publicity it was hailed as the success of the season. Strauss himself conducted two performances. To many people, the music was found to be both difficult and unnecessarily dissonant. One eminent British composer, on leaving the theatre, was asked his opinion of it. 'Words fail me,' he replied, 'and I am going home to play the chord of C major 20 times over to satisfy myself that it still exists.'[8]

After the success of *Elektra*, Beecham decided that an even more controversial work of Strauss's should be performed. In 1905, Strauss had set to music Oscar Wilde's version of *Salome* and dedicated it to Edgar Speyer. Arnold Bax, the composer, in his autobiography *Farewell, My Youth* wrote of the premiere in Dresden the following year that Burrian (Karl Burrian, the Czech tenor) 'created a quite horrifying Herod, slobbering with lust, and apparently almost decomposing before our disgusted but fascinated eyes'.[9] The opera also caused a furore in New York, where the Metropolitan Opera withdrew it in the face of public protest after a dress rehearsal and one performance, on the ground of the blasphemous nature of the work. In England, there was a bigger obstacle to overcome, that of the Lord Chamberlain's Office, which exercised censorship in the theatre by granting licences to plays which were not considered morally acceptable. Wilde's play had already been banned in 1892. The main objection now was the appearance of John the Baptist on stage and it was therefore proposed that *Salome* should be trimmed to make it acceptable to the formidable array of objectors to the work.

Beecham recounted later how this was done. It was agreed with the Lord Chamberlain that John the Baptist should simply be called The Prophet and that the more passionate outpourings of Salome were to be toned down. As the opera was to be sung in German, there was comfort to be had in the knowledge that many of the audience would not be following the text too closely. However, a further last-minute setback occurred when objection was made to the decapitated head of John being handed to Salome on a platter and that she was to sing to it in full view of the audience for the last twenty minutes of the opera. However, a compromise was arrived at whereby the platter should be entirely covered by a large cloth, thus destroying an important dramatic element. During the course of the first performance, Beecham noticed a curious change taking place on the stage:

> Gradually I sensed by that telepathy which exists between the conductor of the orchestra and the artists on the stage, a growing restlessness and excitement of which the first manifestation was a slip on the part of Salome, who forgot two or three sentences of the bowdlerized version and lapsed into the viciousness of the unlawful text. The infection spread among the other performers, and by the time the second half of the work was well under way, they were all living in and shamelessly restoring it to its integrity, as if no such things existed as British respectability and its legal custodians.[10]

At the end of the performance, which was greeted with great enthusiasm by the audience, Beecham was horrified to see the Lord Chamberlain's party approaching him. To Beecham's astonishment, the Lord Chamberlain beamed at him and expressed his delight at the performance and thanked the conductor for the way in which he had met their wishes. Beecham concluded: 'To this day I do not know whether we owed this happy finishing touch to the imperfect diction of the singers, an ignorance of the language on the part of my co-editors of the text, or their diplomatic decision to put the best possible face on a dénouement that was beyond either their or my power to foresee and control.'[11] Strauss's already high reputation was enhanced following the production of his new opera *Der Rosenkavalier* in 1911. A year later Frederick Delius remarked, somewhat tongue in cheek: 'I had no idea that any one except myself was writing such good music as this.'

A new departure for Strauss was his venture into the world of ballet. Serge Diaghilev, the great Russian impresario, had persuaded the composer to write a score for the Ballet Russe based on the biblical Joseph story. The outcome was *Josephslegende* first performed at the Paris Opéra in May 1914. It was in every sense a failure, possibly because of Strauss's obvious lack of interest in the medium or the story. Shortly afterwards, he was asked to conduct the ballet in London at a festival of opera and ballet sponsored by Sir Joseph Beecham, Sir Thomas's father. The ballet was performed in June and there were five performances; it was then withdrawn from the repertory and not revived subsequently. Strauss wrote to Hofmannsthal on his return to Garmisch: 'I am back from London where *Joseph* was a great success, in spite of the fact that most of the press was angry and even the sophisticated Englishwomen found the piece indecent.'[12]

Strauss was warmly received in England. On his fiftieth birthday on 11 June 1914, he went to Oxford to receive an honorary Doctor of Music degree from the university, looking splendid in his gown of crimson silk and cream-coloured brocade. The ceremony was followed a few days later by a number of receptions in Strauss's honour. One was at the Grafton Galleries hosted by The Music Club where the chairman, Alfred Kalisch, the music critic and champion of Strauss's music, welcomed such guests as Sir Charles Villiers Stanford and Sir Frederick Cowen. The programme of music which followed the reception had as its title 'The hero's work of peace', a reference to the composer's *Ein Heldenleben*. Among the musical items played on the occasion was his Suite in B flat for thirteen wind instruments conducted by Arthur Nikisch, four songs sung by the soprano Elena Gerhardt, Wagner's *Siegfried Idyll*, and Strauss accompanied Lady Speyer in his E flat Sonata for Violin and Piano.[13] The visit, which had been suggested by Edgar Speyer, ended with a concert on 26 June at which Strauss conducted three of his tone poems and Mozart's Symphony No. 40. At the rehearsal, Strauss spent one hour on his own works and the remaining five hours on the Mozart symphony.[14] Within a few days of this event, Archduke Ferdinand and his wife were assassinated at Sarajevo and by August, England was at war with Germany.

Strauss had gained a reputation as a composer who drove a hard bargain for the performance and commissioning of his works and his general attitude towards money. He complained that Diaghilev had never paid him for the *Josephslegende* score, but more dismaying was the sequestration by the British Government of all German savings in London from 1 August. Strauss had invested a large sum of money, varying in estimates between £50,000 and three times that amount, through Sir Edgar Speyer; now this source of income was denied him. Furthermore, Speyer was accused of collaborating with the enemy and, though cleared, he eventually settled in the United States.[15] In January 1915, Strauss wrote glumly to his librettist Hugo von Hofmannsthal: 'Shall we ever see the Louvre, ever again the National Gallery?'[16] It was not until January 1922 that he was invited back to London where he conducted a programme of his own music in a half-empty Albert Hall. His old friend Edward Elgar gave a luncheon party for Strauss to which he invited a number of promising young British composers, including Arthur Bliss, Rutland Boughton, Arnold Bax, John Ireland and Eugene Goossens. Adrian Boult was also present as well as George Bernard Shaw who, like Elgar, was pleased to renew his acquaintance with Strauss.

As long ago as 1901, Elgar had a discussion with Strauss on the orchestration of Bach organ works and took as an example the Fantasia and Fugue in C minor, BWV 537. The two composers differed in their approaches to the work, Elgar favouring the use of the full resources of a modern symphony orchestra whilst Strauss preferred a more conventional approach. By 1921, Elgar had completed the orchestration of the Fugue and tried to persuade Strauss to do the same for the Fantasia. In the end, Strauss failed to do so, and Elgar completed the work himself in the following year.[17]

Strauss's next visit in April 1926 was an adventure into a new field. The cinema was by now a popular medium of entertainment and the first 'talkie' was in the offing, which would revolutionise the film industry. Strauss agreed to conduct the music for a film version of *Der Rosenkavalier* at the Tivoli Cinema in the Strand. *The Times*'s music critic considered that the film was disappointing but that the music compensated for it. However, there were some technical difficulties which had not quite been overcome. He wrote:

> The reduction of the score to an orchestra of 40 naturally detracted from the richness to which we have been accustomed . . . The performance was adequate in the best sense of the word without attaining a real brilliance. We suppose it is not possible to obtain absolute synchronisation of the music with the action, and must be grateful for the one or two places where a really dramatic effect was obtained by the unanimous entry of a character and a new theme. The audience applauded enthusiastically, but we fancy it was a tribute to the composer rather than to the film.[18]

No more visits were made to Britain for another decade. In 1936, the Dresden State Opera Company gave performances at Covent Garden of Mozart, Wagner and two of Strauss's operas, *Der Rosenkavalier* and *Ariadne auf Naxos*. Strauss conducted the latter opera on 6 November. On the previous day he was present at a concert of the Royal Philharmonic Society where he was presented with its gold medal by Sir Hugh Allen, the director of the Royal College of Music. In his speech of acceptance, Strauss stated: 'For over forty years I myself have been in close touch with the English musical world and have always been particularly happy at the way my works have been taken up in this country. Throughout many years I was in close touch with your great Master, Edward Elgar, and at the present time I have many friends among English musicians.' Strauss then presented the society with the autograph sheet of the manuscript of his first tone poem *Macbeth*.[19] By this time, Strauss had become embroiled in political events in Germany following the coming to power of Hitler and the setting up of the Third Reich. Controversy still reigns over Strauss's actions during the next decade. In November 1933, for instance, he had been made president of the *Reichmusikkammer*, a State music bureau established by Goebbels, the Minister of Propaganda, without being consulted, but had been removed from this office two years later for supporting his Jewish librettist, Stefan Zweig. His own daughter-in-law was Jewish and it has been claimed that he supported the Nazis under protest and that at heart he was not a political animal. On the other hand, there is ample evidence of his anti-Semitic sentiments and he did little to support Furtwängler's protest against the banning of Hindemith's music or to intervene over the dismissal of Jewish musicians from the Berlin and Vienna Philharmonic orchestras. He composed the *Olympic Hymn*, a paean to the new Germany, to open the Berlin Olympics in August 1936 and he was happy to conduct, without a fee, the massed choirs and the Berlin Philharmonic Orchestra in the presence of Hitler and Goebbels. Strauss had been booed at a concert in Antwerp shortly before he came to England in 1936.

When the Second World War ended in 1945 Strauss had, for the second time, lost a large part of his fortune and his wife, Pauline, became ill. He received permission from the American authorities in Austria to leave his home at Garmisch to travel to Switzerland where they subsequently lived in hotels. By 1947 he was in urgent need of money. Alexander Korda, the film producer, made an offer of £20,000 for the film rights of *Salome* and *Der Rosenkavalier*. Strauss declined without hesitation when it became clear that there would be no guarantee that both operas would not suffer cuts or changes.[20]

Ernst Roth, the managing director of Boosey and Hawkes, the music publishers, who had taken over Strauss's major works after the war, devised a plan to help the composer restore his financial position. In May 1947, Roth contacted Beecham, who had recently formed the Royal Philharmonic Orchestra, and the British Broadcasting Corporation to explore the possibility of mounting a festival of Strauss's music in London, the proceeds of which would go to the composer. Strauss himself would come to England specially for the occasion. One obstacle was the political objections which might be raised to such a visit as Strauss had at that stage not been cleared by the denazification authorities. In the event, British government officials were enthusiastic about the plan, granting Strauss the necessary visa and lifting the embargo on payments to enemy aliens for the occasion.

On 4 October 1947, Roth accompanied the eighty-three-year-old composer, boarding an aeroplane bound for London which took off from Geneva airport. It was Strauss's first flight and he enjoyed it like a schoolboy. They were greeted at Northolt airport and later at the Savoy Hotel by hordes of reporters and photographers. During the press interview, he was asked how it felt to be the composer of the *Blue Danube Waltz*.[21]

Another reporter at the end of the interview put the inevitable question, 'Dr. Strauss, what are your plans for the future?' 'Oh,' replied Strauss with a roguish smile, 'to die'.[22] Beecham conducted two concerts at Drury Lane Theatre on 5 and 12 October which consisted of the *Bourgeois Gentilhomme* Suite and three tone poems, *Macbeth*, *Don Quixote* and *Ein Heldenleben*, extracts from the operas *Feuersnot* and *Ariadne auf Naxos*, and a new symphonic Fantasia from his opera *Die Frau ohne Schatten*. This last work was conducted by a former horn-player turned conductor, Norman del Mar, who observed Strauss during his attendance at both rehearsals. Del Mar recalled that during a run-through of the Fantasia: 'He came up to the podium, glumly regarded the score for a few moments, muttered "All my own fault," and went away. Throughout the entire visit he was very terse and uncommunicative, and only twice do I remember him being roused to any liveliness.'[23]

On 19 October, Strauss conducted the recently formed Philharmonia Orchestra at the Royal Albert Hall. Before the concert, Strauss received an ovation from the 7,500 members of the audience. There were two early works, the *Burleske* for piano and orchestra, the *Rosenkavalier* waltzes, *Don Juan*, and the *Symphonia Domestica*. Strauss had flown into a rage on learning of the placing of the *Symphonia* in the second half instead of the first but soon calmed down.[24] During rehearsal, irritated by something which did not please him, Strauss was heard to say: 'No, I know what I want, and I know what I meant when I wrote this. After all, I may not be a first-rate composer, but I *am* a first-class second-rate composer!'[25] A week later he attended two broadcast performances of *Elektra* from the BBC's Maida Vale Studio 1 conducted by Beecham and on 29 October made his final appearance on the podium in England, again at the Albert Hall, when he conducted *Till Eulenspiegel*. Two days afterwards, almost exactly fifty years since his first concert in England, Strauss returned to Switzerland. Before leaving, he once more visited the National Gallery and the Wallace Collection with Dr Willi Schuh, his official biographer. Strauss told his companion that he rated Titian the supreme painter, comparing him to Wagner, and himself to Tintoretto and Correggio, and had planned half a century before to write a 'Picture' Symphony based on mythological and historical subjects.[26]

Earlier in the same year, Strauss had started sketching out a song to a poem by Joseph von Eichendorff, *Im Abendrot* (In the Sunset) in which an old couple look into the sunset and ask 'Is this perhaps death?' After returning from his visit to England, Strauss completed the song and its orchestration on 27 April 1948. Between July and September he completed three more to poems by Hermann Hesse, *Frühling* (Spring), *Beim schlafengehen* (Going to Sleep) and *September*, with one remaining unfinished. Each song was concerned with death and the consolations of old age in a life fulfilled. The *Vier letzte Lieder* (Four Last Songs) were Strauss's farewell to life. In June 1948, whilst writing these pieces, he was cleared by a denazification tribunal and in the following year he returned to his home at Garmisch. He was by now seriously ill and died peacefully on 8 September 1949.

Strauss never heard the Four Last Songs performed but they made one final link with England. On 22 May 1950 at a concert in London conducted by Strauss's friend Wilhelm Furtwängler, Kirsten Flagstad sang them to a rapt audience. Ernst Roth wrote after the performance: 'As the last bar of the last song died away the audience, deeply moved, remained silent for a long time. Strauss had often been reproached for seeking sensation; here was a quiet death and unobtrusive transfiguration.'[27]

16 Bartók and the BBC

The name of Béla Bartók, the Hungarian composer and collector of folk music, tends to conjure up a picture of a withdrawn, uncompromising and unworldly person, steeped in nationalism. What is less well known is the fact that for over thirty years he was a frequent visitor to Britain, making in all twenty tours of varying length. Even more unlikely, Bartók was one of the first visiting composer-executants to make a significant contribution to the broadcasting of contemporary music.

Bartók's first appearance in England, in February 1904, was as a concert pianist. Hans Richter, the conductor of the Hallé Orchestra and a fellow countryman, engaged him to play one of his own recent compositions, *Kossuth*, for piano and orchestra, written whilst still a student at the Budapest Conservatoire. Despite the fact that, as a comparatively un-known artist in this country, Bartók received no fee for the performance, he was happy to return the following year to play two further concerts in Manchester, though by other composers. At one of them, Liszt's *Totentanz*, was not well received by the musically conservative audience. On his first visit, Bartók spent a few days in London and was flattered by the attention which he received. He quickly formed a poor opinion of the English railway rolling stock. He wrote to his mother at the time:

> The carriages on the most unimportant branch line in Hungary are better than the ones here. There is no heating (they merely put a container full of hot water in the carriage) nor head-rests nor arm-rests; the luggage-racks are too narrow. As there are no ash-trays, the floor of the compartments resembles that of pigsties. They do have some lights, surprisingly, and even, here and there God forgive – a communication cord![1]

Although he was not to return for another seventeen years, his reputation as a composer of modern music, such as the opera *Bluebeard's Castle*, composed in 1911, attracted the attention of a number of British musi-cians and critics. One especial champion was Henry Wood, the conductor of the Queen's Hall Orchestra. In September 1914 he performed Bartók's

Suite No. 1 for Orchestra, a rather austere work lasting some forty minutes, at a Promenade Concert. There had been some initial criticism of Wood for including this work in the programme, as the outbreak of the First World War the previous month meant that Bartók was from a country which was an enemy of England. This resulted in some resentment amongst the players in the orchestra. Alfred Brain, an outstanding horn-player and uncle of Dennis Brain, in Wood's words, 'stood up and "went for me". "Surely you can find better novelties than this kind of stuff?" Brain said indignantly.'[2]

It was not until 1920, when the embargo on 'enemy' works was lifted, that Bartók's music was to be heard again in Britain when Wood repeated the Orchestral Suite.[3] His music had been championed during the war by Philip Heseltine, better known by his musical *nom de plume* of Peter Warlock, and a young critic, Cecil Gray. They drew attention to his first two string quartets and other works, and Bartók responded by encouraging Heseltine to arrange a concert tour of Britain.[4] A further possible entrée was provided by the presence in England of two Hungarian contemporaries of Bartók, the sisters Adila and Jelly d'Arányi, both gifted violinists, who had each married and settled there. Bartók readily agreed to compose a violin sonata for Jelly, and he proposed to accompany her in this and other works during his projected visit. Arriving in London in March 1922, Bartók performed his First Sonata with her at a private recital at the residence of the Hungarian *chargé d'affaires* at 18 Hyde Park Terrace on 15 March; it was given a public performance nine days later and was subsequently widely and favourably reviewed in the national press. He was surprised to discover that the English audiences were aware of his music and he was interviewed by the press, speaking a mixture of English, French and German, and was guest of honour at a number of parties.[5]

Bartók was equally gifted as both composer and performer. The conductor Otto Klemperer observed that 'he was a wonderful pianist and musician. The beauty of his tone, the energy and lightness of his playing were unforgettable. It was almost painfully beautiful. He played with great freedom, that was what was so wonderful'.[6] It seemed something of an anti-climax that his first public recital in Britain two days later was a poorly advertised routine weekly concert, consisting of two groups of his own music, to music department students at Aberystwyth University College, Wales.[7] Bartók had been persuaded to play there by Walford Davies, then Professor of Music at the College. Davies had spoken at some length beforehand about the music but was heard to whisper afterwards, 'Baffling, isn't it?'[8] In contrast, their recital at the Aeolian Hall in New Bond Street eight days later was the subject of intense public interest, which resulted in the presence of over twenty leading music critics of the day. Bartók was described by one of them as 'Slight, physically; unassertive yet dignified in manner, his dark eyes often glow with compelling intensity in his sharp-featured face. His hair is white. One feels, however, that he is of the eternally young in heart'.[9] Later, the BBC wanted to broadcast a performance of the new sonata, but as Bartók doubted that the microphone would reflect the correct acoustics, they played instead Beethoven's 'Kreutzer' Sonata.[10]

There is an interesting contrast between Bartók, the by now internationally recognised composer, and Bartók the performer, on his dozen postwar British tours. In the following year, 1923, for instance, he returned twice and gave recitals not only in London, which included a performance of his new Second Violin Sonata, again with Jelly d'Arányi, and other major cities, but also in a series of girls' schools at Malvern, Battle, in Sussex, and Aldeburgh. A tour of northern towns, including, in his words, 'the horrible industrial town of Huddersfield', was less rapturously received. As Hungary had been cut off from advances in Western music during the First World War, Bartók was keen to catch up with the works of such composers of Schoenberg and Stravinsky. Whilst in England, he copied out several pieces by the minor, though popular composer, Lord Berners.[11]

The founding of the British Broadcasting Company (BBC), later the British Broadcasting Corporation, in 1924, led to a fruitful, if often uneasy, partnership between Bartók and the BBC. Committed from its inception to the promotion of music of all kinds and from all periods of time, the company could afford to pay £60 for a London performance compared with a fee of as little as ten guineas for a live recital in the provinces. There was the additional bonus that a broadcast could reach a potential audience of many thousands of listeners. The BBC was established as a corporation in 1927 and in its first year of existence, it broadcast his popular *Romanian Folk Dances*, composed in 1915; Bartók, as performer, was heard on the BBC for the first time in October 1927 playing his recently completed First Piano Concerto, which marked the beginning of a new period in the composer's style.[12] Such was the excitement of the occasion that many distinguished people, including Gustav Holst and Rosa Newmarch, entered the studio against BBC rules to hear the performance. After a second broadcast, public opinion was divided on the merits of his music. In December 1927, the *Radio Times*, the house journal of the corporation, had a long leading article by Percy Scholes headed, 'Is Bartók Mad – or Are WE?' (His considered answer was 'Neither'.) The difficulty of the music lay not only with the listener: Bartók, in performing his own recently composed Piano Sonata at a public performance in London that year came to a complete halt twice, his memory having failed because of the complexity of the music.[13]

The BBC's attitude towards Bartók's music can be gauged from various opinions expressed by other writers, some anonymous, in the contemporary issues of the *Radio Times*. On 1 March 1929, a forthcoming concert drew the following comment:

The rest of Europe knows Bartók better than we may so far claim to do: there, he is one of the dominating personalities of our time, and a visit from him to the London Studios – one for which he takes part as a pianist in his own music – is an event. And however little we may find to enjoy, or even to understand, in his unaccustomed idiom, we BBC listeners can at least be honestly proud of his coming as an event in which we have to share.[14]

In the following January, when Josef Szigeti was accompanied by Bartók in a recital of his own works, a more tolerant approach was apparent:

To our grandchildren, Bartók and the other 'fiery particles' of today may well be the kindly and inspiring friends that Wagner is to us: in the *Radio Times* of 1990, some one may be quoting Bartók, as Wagner is cited here, by way of a sermon on the virtue of tolerance.[15]

And in November the same year, an article summed up the situation which confronted the average British music listener:

Those who still persist in thinking of Bartók as a wild young man, who, with time, will one day learn better, may be reminded that he is nearly 50 years old. He has been writing music for 40 years. No, he is apparently too far gone now to see the error of his ways, and we had better make up our minds to accept him either as he is or not at all. The choice still remains with us.[16]

A landmark in his career, as Bartók acknowledged, was the performance in 1932 in a BBC studio, which he described as 'a kind of a hangar', of the Rhapsody for piano and orchestra with himself as soloist, part of the first orchestral programme devoted entirely to his own works. However, in his solo recitals he included the works of many other composers, such as Kodály, Bach, Purcell and Marcello besides his own.[17] Unfortunately, his percussive approach to playing the piano further alienated listeners. Reviewing in the *Manchester Guardian* the British premiere of Bartók's Second Piano Concerto with the composer as soloist, Neville Cardus, wrote: 'Bartók composes as though he owed the world of music a grudge ... The piano snaps away like a spiteful maiden aunt. It is tedious and crude.' Undeterred, the BBC transmitted on 25 May 1934 from the newly completed Broadcasting House the world premiere of his masterpiece *Cantata Profana: The Nine Enchanted Stags*. This was a work for large forces, requiring two soloists, choir and orchestra with triple woodwind. It was a work close to Bartók's heart, being based on an Hungarian folk song. Most of his visits to London were occupied with work, but occasionally he could find time to be a tourist. In 1932, he took great pleasure in having tea and a plain bun at an ABC Café for the cost of 3d.[18]

Considering Bartók's enthusiasm for broadcasting, it seems strange that in an article entitled 'Mechanical Music', he played down its significance. In it, he conceded that the 'great pedagogical effect of radio music on the broad masses' could be beneficial, but argued that this advantage was neutralised by 'many obnoxious effects'. He continued:

> It can be presumed that radio music makes a great many people superficial and accustoms them to fickleness so far as listening to music is concerned. The reason is that it is very simple to turn the radio knob back and forth, to connect and disconnect it. Furthermore, on account of that, one might undertake other things while listening to the radio, even talk. I am afraid that the broadcasting of serious music for many people is nothing but the caress of a kind of tepid bath, a kind of coffee-house music, a droning in the background so that one can perform other tasks with less boredom and with hardly any attention to the music.[19]

Bartók concluded that 'for the time being, I do not have much faith in its beneficial influence on the masses'.

The 1930s saw the gradual diminution in the broadcasts of Bartók's music and his appearances for the BBC, largely because of the advice given by its influential Music Advisory Committee, which recommended a 'British composers first' policy. An opportunity to broadcast the first world performance of Bartók's *Mikrokosmos*, a novel piano tutor written for the musical education of his son, Péter, played by the composer had already been rejected by the company in March 1926; however, one of his admirers, Kenneth Wright, Assistant Director of Music at the BBC, later secured the first British performance of his Music for Strings, Percussion and Celeste in January 1938. Bartók was not present at the occasion. His last broadcast engagement was on 4 October 1937, when he performed three of the *Mikrokosmos* pieces, together with selections from his forty-four Violin Duos. He was due to perform his Sonata for Two Pianos and Percussion in Paris in February 1939 and offered to follow it with a visit to London, but this was declined.

A more appreciative audience had been found in Scotland. In 1932 and 1933, he had been invited to perform in Glasgow by Erik Chisholm, the pianist and composer, who promoted Bartók's works, at a concert given under the auspices of Glasgow's Active Society for the Propagation of Contemporary Music. Bartók readily accepted and he became a Vice-President of the society. Apart from performing to an enthusiastic audience, he became fascinated by Scottish folk music, listening to recordings of it for many hours as well as enjoying the playing of a bagpiper and he bought a tartan rug. He also performed for the British section of the International Society for Contemporary Music in London and Liverpool. His last visit to England took place in June 1938 when he attended the

Society's Festival. During the course of his visit, he found time to sample London's musical life, including a performance of John Blow's *Venus and Adonis* at the Royal College of Music and a concert of English folk songs and dances at Cecil Sharp House. He told his English publisher, Ralph Hawkes, at the time that 'he had no illusions as to the monetary value of his publications. He never expected the public to like them and play them as he told me so. He remained the epitome of reticence and shyness about his work and remained so until his death'.[20]

Bartók's concerns lay elsewhere in March the following year when Hitler marched into Czechoslovakia. A bitter opponent of the rise of fascism in Europe, he refused to play in Hitler's Germany or Franco's Spain after the dictators came to power. He had already sent his manuscripts to Switzerland for safety and now decided to relocate them in England where he felt they were secure. For a short time they were held here before, like Bartók himself, they crossed the Atlantic in the autumn of 1940 to the United States of America. He died there, dispirited and disillusioned on 20 September 1945.

17 The émigré composers

'His Majesty's most loyal internees'

The coming to power of Adolf Hitler and the National Socialist Party in Germany in 1933 had direct consequences for many of its citizens. Most affected were those of Jewish birth or ancestry, all of whom suffered many hardships, not least the inability to practise their occupations and, worse, imprisonment. From this date onwards, then, there was a steady stream of refugees who travelled to those countries which would take them. The United States of America was the main attraction but had only limited entry. Another democracy which appealed to them, Britain, cautiously welcomed several thousand of them. Amongst them were distinguished composers whose experiences form the basis of this chapter.

Whilst there had long been a tradition of German conductors, singers and pianists being welcomed as visitors to opera houses and concert halls, mainly playing the great German and Austrian classics, the prospect for composers was different. There was a suspicion of dissonant twelve-tone music at a time of conservative musical taste in Britain. Some composers such as Kurt Weill, Ernst Krenek and Hans Eisler came only for a short period, and then moved on to the United States.

A feature of the Nazi persecution was the large-scale exit of university staff and other intellectuals. As Norman Bentwich, writing in 1936 so graphically put it: 'In the academic world there had been nothing comparable to it since the emigration of the Greek scholars on the capture of Constantinople by the Turks in the fifteenth century.'[1] Some 1,200 people were dismissed from their posts, of whom twenty-two were classified as musicologists. England was one of the first countries to come to their aid. In May 1933, the Academic Assistance Council, consisting of distinguished representatives of academia, science and industry, encouraged universities to find openings for exile academics; a similar task was undertaken by the Jewish Professional Committee.

Nevertheless there was a strong undercurrent of anti-Semitism displayed towards the new arrivals between 1933 and 1939. The *Daily Mail* warned of 'misguided sentimentalism' in allowing sanctuary, and in 1938 an MI5 report came before the Cabinet, suggesting that 'the Germans were anxious to inundate this country with Jews, with a view to creating a Jewish problem in the United Kingdom'.[2] There was further unease in some quarters after the *Anschluss* in Austria in 1938 when there was a further stream of exiles. Apart from the language barriers which were encountered, many of the new arrivals also lacked connections in the profession in order to launch their careers.[3] The more fortunate composers were those who had other skills to offer, particularly conducting. Vilem Tausky and Karl Rankl are good examples.

Tausky, born in Czechoslovakia, studied composition and conducting at Brno and Prague. His particular love was opera and in 1924 he conducted a complete cycle of Janáček operas as well as those by a range of other composers. Tausky wrote four operettas which continued to be performed throughout his life, and compositions such as his two cello suites, a symphony and several concertos. After the Nazi occcupation of Czechoslovakia, Tausky escaped to Paris, becoming military bandmaster of the Free Czechoslovak Forces in September 1939.[4] With the collapse of France, he arrived in South Wales on a Yugoslavian coal ship. After the war, he resumed his operatic career, conducting the Carl Rosa Opera, and teaching at the National School of Opera, the Welsh Opera Company and Sadler's Wells. He is probably best remembered now as the conductor of the BBC Concert Orchestra in its long running series, *Friday Night Is Music Night*.

Another composer–conductor of this era was Karl Rankl. Of Austrian birth, he had studied composition with both Schoenberg and Webern and also developed a wide repertoire of opera as chorus master and conductor in a number of leading German, Austrian and Greek opera houses. Shortly before the outbreak of war in 1939 he was at the German Opera House in Prague when Kenneth Wright of the BBC Music Department sent him an invitation to come to England. He accepted but in the following year he was for some time interned on the Isle of Man, but later released. When it was announced in June 1945 that Rankl had been appointed musical director at Covent Garden, there was some opposition to the move. The Incorporated Society of Musicians publicly stated that a foreign music director to Covent Garden should never happen again. Similarly Sir Thomas Beecham argued that Rankl should not have been put in charge and 'proclaimed to the world we could not govern our own musical institutions'.[5] Rankl took over at a time when musical and financial resources were scarce. During the five years he was at the Opera House, Rankl built up an opera company that included a number of British singers and he conducted many fine performances. Nevertheless, he lacked glamour as a conductor and by the time of his departure in 1951 a number of more charismatic guest conductors outshone him.

At the same time as carrying out his operatic work Rankl was busy as a composer. There are eight symphonies to his name, as well as songs and chamber music. It is not surprising, given his background, that he also had aspirations to write opera. The chance came in 1951 with the

Festival of Britain. A competition was organised for composers of opera: not only were there to be awards but there was also a promise that prize winners would have their operas performed. To avoid unfairness, entrants were given pseudonyms. The winners included Rankl and a fellow émigré, Berthold Goldschmidt, as well as two openly communist British composers, Alan Bush and Arthur Benjamin. None of these operas received a performance. Rankl's work, *Deidre of the Sorrows*, based on the legend of the early Irish heroine, was a lyrical work demanding a large orchestra. It still awaits a production.[6] Rankl's subsequent career was as a conductor, first of the Scottish National Orchestra and then the Elizabethan Opera Trust in Sydney.

Rankl was by no means the only émigré to suffer internment during the Second World War. At the outbreak of hostilities there were more than 70,000 Germans and Austrians living in Britain, who overnight became enemy aliens. Out of this total 55,000 were refugees, many of them Jews. There was public disquiet that such a large number could contain pro-Nazi elements, or spies. Measures were quickly introduced to establish three categories of aliens: those to be interned, those to have restricted movements, and those exempt from detention of any sort. With the invasion of Norway and Denmark in April 1940 all aliens came under suspicion, and after the invasion of France and the Low Countries the following month, all German and Austrian males between twelve and sixty were eligible for internment. Some 3,000 were quickly rounded up, and with the growing threat of invasion, many were sent by ship to the Dominions. The camps in England were located in a variety of settings, ranging from Kempton Park Racecourse, a housing estate at Huyton, Liverpool, a series of luxurious hotels in the Isle of Man and disused cotton mills in Bury, Lancashire. It was to these places that several composers were sent.

Typical of the time was the arrest on 5 July 1940 of several distinguished academics holding posts at Oxford University. Many were taken away from their college rooms and sent on a train to an unknown destination. Amongst the party were neurologists, Greek scholars, philosophers, historians, criminal lawyers and the composer, Dr Egon Wellesz, then Fellow of Lincoln College and a former professor at the University of Vienna, whose life will be described later in this chapter. The party arrived at Seaton, Devon, to a camp already holding 400 men, were stripped of their personal belongings and examined for venereal diseases. Wellesz was transferred to Bury and placed in a dilapidated cotton factory where there was little to do, as all books and newspapers were banished. Sleeping arrangements were primitive with rows of individuals lying on palliasses and blankets on the floor. Few dared to undress because of the fear of skin infection from the unwashed blankets.[7] Matters improved for Wellesz when he was transferred to the Isle of Man, where it was possible after dinner every night for lectures and discussions to be held in the common room until 10.15 p.m. in which participants were treated to talks from experts in a range of subjects. There was a series on the interpretation of the *Odyssey*, aspects of metabolism, unemployment and trade cycles and one on pre-history. Wellesz contributed lectures on the genesis of an opera and modern Viennese music.[8] There was also the opportunity for music-making, often by first-rate instrumentalists. The composer Hans Gal wrote music for a review consisting of ten scenes from camp life and called *What a Life!* He had also written previously whilst detained at Huyton his *Huyton Suite*, which was successfully performed after the war.[9]

On the whole, few of the composers who settled in Britain can be said to have made a great impression with their music during their lifetime. Perhaps one of the features of their work which militated against general acceptance was that they were modernists in outlook which clashed with the more conservative tastes of British audiences. As Edward Dent once put it, these lovers of Elgar, Delius and Sibelius were suspicious 'of all those dreadful composers ending in "-er"'.[10] However, there is evidence in the compositions of the émigrés that their music was increasingly influenced by the native style.

Egon Wellesz, born in Vienna in 1885, is a typical example. Born into a wealthy Jewish family, he had a classical education and was inspired to be a composer after having seen Mahler conduct a performance of Weber's *Der Freischütz*. He studied musicology with Guido Adler at the University of Vienna and at the same time became one of Schoenberg's first pupils. His main interest was in Byzantine music, on which he wrote several books during the 1930s and 1940s. Wellesz also adored the operas of Gluck and Handel and in the 1920s composed five operas on classical themes but in a modern style. The advent of the Nazis put an end to his career as an opera composer, though he had planned to write one based on Shakespeare's *The Tempest*.[11]

Wellesz was no stranger to England and was well versed in the music-making here. He had visited Cambridge in 1906 and after the First World War he was a co-founder of the International Society of Contemporary Music, and was responsible for the music of Vaughan Williams, Bliss, Holst and other composers being performed for the first time on the Continent.[12] For his work in promoting English music, Wellesz was awarded an honorary doctorate of music by Oxford University in 1932. Although about this time he converted to Catholicism, Wellesz, who was in Holland in 1938 at the time of the *Anschluss*, decided it would be safer not to return to Austria but to settle in England.

In the following years, because of his international scholarly reputation, he was appointed a Fellow of Lincoln College, Oxford, and in 1947, became Reader in Byzantine Music. As was noted earlier in this chapter Wellesz was interned during the Second World War, and it was thanks to the representations of Vaughan Williams that he was released in the autumn of 1940.[13] Missing his native Austria and because of his stressful personal circumstances, Wellesz felt unable to compose. However in 1943 he resumed writing with his Fifth String Quartet, which was followed by a setting of Gerard Manley Hopkins's *The Leaden Echo and the Golden Echo*. A remarkable aspect of the last quarter century of Wellesz's life was the unexpected burst of musical creativity. In 1945, at the age of sixty, on holiday in the Lake District, he was inspired to write his First Symphony.[14] Another eight symphonies followed, containing music reminiscent of Bruckner and Mahler as well as containing atonal elements. There was also a violin concerto, an octet, five more string quartets, solo vocal works and keyboard pieces; in addition he undertook the writing and editing of books on music and musicology. His affection for Vienna never faded. When he died in 1972 in his ninetieth year, he was buried there.

A fellow Austrian composer–academic, Hans Gal, is less well known. A lecturer in musical theory at Vienna University from 1919 to 1929, he took up the post of Director of the Hochschule für Musik at Mainz. He was celebrated for the five operas which he wrote during this period, and which were performed in many German opera houses. When the Nazis dismissed him from his post in Mainz in 1933, Gal returned to Austria, but within five years he was obliged to flee the country after the *Anschluss*. Gal was not so fortunate as Wellesz had been in gaining a post in Britain. After a spell of internment in the Isle of Man, he resumed his composing, particularly his Second Symphony in 1942. His music is distinctly Brahmsian with an emphasis on melody. Gal obtained a lectureship at Edinburgh University in musical education in 1945, and remained there for the next twenty years until his retirement. He was one of the founders of the Edinburgh Music Festival in 1947. He wrote more than fifty works whilst living in Scotland, including two more symphonies, though few of them subsequently received public performances. It was for this reason that in his later years he turned from the writing of larger ensembles to chamber music, mainly with particular individuals in mind. Gal remained musically active for many years after his retirement, dying in 1987 at the age of ninety-seven.

The path for many other émigré composers was equally difficult. There was a need for adaptability. The Hungarian Mátyás Seiber, born in Budapest in 1905, showed early signs of musical talent. At the age of fourteen, he studied composition at the Budapest Academy of Music and also learned to play the cello. When his *Serenade* for six instruments, written in Hungarian folk music idiom was entered for a music competition in 1925, Bartók walked out when the jury refused to award him a prize.[15] Seiber accepted a teaching post at the conservatory in Frankfurt in 1926, then spent a year playing cello on board a cruise ship; and returned to Frankfurt to found the first course in Europe on jazz theory and practice, which attracted students from many countries. He also became a member of the Lenzewski Quartet.

His time in Frankfurt came to a sudden end in 1933, when he was dismissed from his post. Two years later he came to England. He was unable to find a permanent position and so operated on a freelance basis, turning his hand to a variety of activities. He produced *Rhythmical Studies* for aspiring jazz pianists, a ten-part tutor for the accordion, helped to found the Society for the Promotion of New Music, acted as adviser to music publishers, wrote film music and continued with his composing.

In 1942, he was offered a teaching post in musical appreciation at Morley College, South London, by the composer Michael Tippett. Morley College, a non-vocational adult education institute, mounted courses for mainly musical amateurs, but in his lectures, Seiber relished unravelling for them the complications of twelve-tone techniques. His own works used a combination of this method with overtones of Kodály and Bartók and his beloved jazz rhythms; a good example of this is the *Blues* movement in his Second String Quartet. With his own students, he was an inspiring composition teacher, carefully analysing their work in a dry, matter-of-fact manner.[16]

During the seventeen years Seiber taught at Morley College, he was a prolific composer. He completed a Third String Quartet (*Quartetto lyrico*), and other chamber works and songs, including a setting of Edward Lear's *The Owl and the Pussycat*. In 1956 he had the distinction of having a successful song which entered the Top Ten of the pop charts, called *By the Fountains of Rome*.[17] Towards the end of his life, Seiber collaborated with John Dankworth to write *Improvisations for Jazz Band and Symphony Orchestra*, and an oratorio, *Ulysses*, based on the James Joyce novel, which contained references to old English composers such as Dowland and Tomkins.[18] Film-goers may remember the evocative music which Seiber wrote for the animated cartoon film *Animal Farm* in 1955. That he could easily turn his hand to less serious music-making is borne out in his ready participation in Hoffnung Festival concerts. For the 1956 event, he had planned to write a gargling chorus, a project which was not realised, but in the 1958 concert, Seiber composed and conducted a setting of *The Famous Tay Whale*, a poem by the Scotsman William McGonagall, claimed by the *Guinness Book of Records* as the worst poet in the English language, and declaimed by Dame Edith Evans.[19] Seiber's compositions in his later years, such as his 1960 Violin Sonata, showed his growing mastery of technique. The same year, on a lecture tour of South Africa, on a visit to the Kruger National Park, he was killed in a tragic car accident. Seiber was only fifty-five.

One of the first émigré composers to arrive in England was Franz Reizenstein, who left Germany in 1934. Reizenstein, born in Nuremberg in 1911, had studied composition with Hindemith and piano with Leonard Kreutzer in Berlin. Hindemith considered him to be one of his outstanding students.[20] Reizenstein was fortunate in having relatives in Surrey, and he continued with his studies at the Royal College of Music under Vaughan Williams. He also continued with his piano-playing, taking lessons with

Solomon; this stood him in good stead during the rest of his career as he
was able to earn a living as an accomplished pianist.

Like other émigré musicians Reizenstein was interned in 1939. He was
sent to the Isle of Man where the 'camp' consisting mainly of requisi-
tioned hotels contained a number of creative artists. He featured in 'camp
concerts'. There was much music-making: at one concert he partnered the
violinist Sigmund Nissel (who was to team up with two other internees,
Peter Schidlof and Norbert Brainin to form the basis of the Amadeus
Quartet) in a version of a Bach Violin Concerto.[21] After his release, he
became a railway clerk, being ruled out of army service because of his
poor eyesight. Reizenstein continued to perform as a concert pianist after
the war, forming part of a piano trio.

It was not until comparatively late in his life that he obtained recognised
posts at music conservatories, at the Royal Academy of Music from 1958
and the Royal Manchester College from 1962. In both cases he was a
professor of piano, not composition. To the end of his life Reizenstein
was happy to teach an evening class of budding composers at a music
centre in Hendon.[22] Reizenstein wrote mainly chamber music throughout
his career. The most important phase was from 1947 to 1959, when he
produced amongst other works a piano quintet, his second piano concerto
and the cantata *Voices of the Night*. Like Hans Gal he rejected the serial
music of his contemporaries, adopting a more English lyrical and expressive style. His impressive output of music of every genre included film
scores and incidental music for radio documentaries and plays. Like Seiber
his impish sense of fun is seen at its best in his two contributions to the
Hoffnung Festivals; the *Concerto Populaire*, 1956, featured a concert
pianist, Yvonne Arnaud, battling with the opening of the Grieg Piano
Concerto against the determined interruptions of the orchestra playing
Tchaikovsky's Piano Concerto No. 1. The second Hoffnung Festival
featured Reizenstein's *Let's Fake an Opera* with a cast of singers from
Covent Garden and Sadler's Wells. The libretto by William Mann included
ridiculously juxtaposed excerpts from more than forty operas, which
delighted both Reizenstein and the audience.[23] He continued to compose
and teach until his early death in 1968 at the age of fifty-seven.

Perhaps the most outstanding composer who settled in Britain was
Berthold Goldschmidt who already had an established reputation in
Germany. Born in 1903 Goldschmidt read philosophy and art history at
Hamburg University and then in Berlin. From the age of fifteen he studied
harmony with a friend of Busoni, but turned down a place in Schoenberg's
composition class. Instead, he went to Berlin where he had lessons with
the composer Franz Schreker, who was also head of the Hochschule für
Musik. At the same time he took classes in conducting, for which he had
long harboured a passion. He was also able to gain inside experience of
orchestral playing by establishing himself as a reliable celesta-player. He
took part in the first production of Berg's *Wozzeck* under Erich Kleiber in

1925, and the first Berlin performance of Schoenberg's *Gurrelieder*.[24] At the same time he was appointed Kleiber's repetiteur at the Staatsoper.

The twenties and early thirties were a fruitful era for Goldschmidt. He was becoming recognised both as a composer and a conductor and his works were being performed outside as well as within Germany. His *Passacaglia* for orchestra, First String Quartet and Piano Sonata were frequently played. He was guest conductor to the Leningrad Philharmonic where he met Shostakovich, and worked as musical adviser to Carl Ebert, the intendant, at the Darmstadt Opera from 1927 to 1929. His opera *Der gewaltige Hahnrei* (The Mighty Cuckold) staged by the Mannheim Theatre was due to be performed the following year, but was cancelled when Hitler came to power. Goldschmidt was restricted to coaching Jewish musicians for the Palestine Philharmonic Orchestra and conducting only concerts for a Jewish artists' charity. Shortly after being interrogated by the Gestapo in 1935 Goldschmidt decided to leave for England. He took with him some manuscripts of his works: the rest, left behind, were subsequently destroyed in air raids.

It was eleven years before he secured permanent employment, and he meanwhile continued to compose and teach privately at his Hampstead flat. A performance at Dartington Hall of his Second String Quartet led to a commission to write a ballet score, *Chronica*, for a fellow refugee, Kurt Joos, whose dance company was then based at Dartington. The ballet significantly was based on a parable about a Renaissance dictatorship. From 1944 to 1947 he was full-time music adviser to the BBC's German section of its European Service, selecting appropriate accompaniments to poems read at the end of the political programme.

The following years had their disappointments. Goldschmidt applied to Glyndebourne for the post as chorus master on condition that he might also work as assistant conductor. He had rehearsed the Company's production of Verdi's *Macbeth* for the conductor George Szell, which was to be given at the first Edinburgh Festival in 1947. When Szell disappeared before the performance Goldschmidt took his place with great success. However he was unhappy that former colleagues now working at Glyndebourne, particularly Carl Ebert, were cool towards him, and after two years he left.

Another disappointment was the Arts Council Festival of Britain competition, in which he and Karl Rankl, as mentioned earlier in the chapter, were two of the four prizewinners. His opera, *Beatrice Cenci*, a Renaissance subject to a setting by Shelley, was in a more *bel canto* style than his first opera.[25] Although completed in 1950 it was not staged until forty-four years later.

In spite of these setbacks, Goldschmidt continued to compose. There were three concerti written between 1951 and 1954 for violin, cello and clarinet respectively, which were premiered in BBC studios. He now returned to his old love Mahler, whom Goldschmidt's father had often seen conducting at the Hamburg opera. Goldschmidt conducted the first complete British performance of Mahler's Third Symphony in 1960 and four years later, he collaborated with Deryck Cooke to complete his Tenth Symphony, conducting its first performance also.

Goldschmidt was depressed at the lack of opportunities to have his works performed. William Glock, Controller of Music for the BBC Third Programme, favoured the more *avant-garde* composers, considering Goldschmidt's music too traditional. He lost heart and did not compose for the twenty-four years between 1958 and 1982. At the age of seventy-nine he regarded himself as a forgotten man. But the turning point came in 1983 with a modest performance of his first opera, *Der gewaltige Hahnrei*, which sparked a great awakening of public interest. There were performances of the opera in Berlin in 1992. He travelled to Berlin for a performance some fifty-nine years after its original cancellation there, receiving a rapturous reception when he appeared afterwards on the stage.[26] Many of his works were performed by Simon Rattle and other leading conductors and, most remarkably, two record companies undertook the complete recordings of his works. Goldschmidt began to compose again. His Clarinet Quartet, the Third and Fourth String Quartets and, towards the end of his life, settings of French songs, *Les Petites Adieux* and *Deux nocturnes* are from this period. He continued to write until his death at the age of ninety-three on 17 October 1996.

The émigré composers of the thirties had to overcome many obstacles to enable them to continue with their main vocation. Each solved the difficulty in different ways. All except one, Reizenstein, were over thirty years old and they had to restart their careers. Some stayed loyal to their original style: others, such as Seiber, were profoundly influenced by English music, whilst retaining a Hungarian character.[27] It must also be remembered that there was some support from fellow refugees. Hans Keller, the talks producer for the Third Programme Music Department, who had also been interned on the Isle of Man, commissioned Wellesz to review the first English staging of Schoenberg's *Erwartung* and asked Seiber to review a new biography of the same composer.[28] For many decades, their compositions made little impact on the British musical scene. However, perhaps the great public interest in Goldschmidt's music may herald the start of a revival of the musical contributions of these composers.[29]

Epilogue
Minstrels of the modern age

The first of April 1919 saw the arrival in Liverpool of the Original Dixieland Jazz Band, a quintet of five white American musicians who claimed to be the originators of jazz music. Their appearance at the London Hippodrome a week later marked the first jazz music to be heard in Britain, and caused a huge stir:

> The fever spread throughout the theatre until every last man and woman was on his feet, shouting and clapping in a manner that was peculiarly un-British.[1]

Their performance elicited a variety of responses from critics. One came to the conclusion that 'the best qualification for a jazzist is to have no knowledge of music and no musical ability beyond that of making noises', while another compared the challenging effect their music had to that of Richard Strauss. The classicist Dr Lewis Farnell, Rector of Exeter College, Oxford, was quoted in the *Daily Chronicle* as saying

> Vulgar music might not be as criminal as murder, but it is far more degrading. Our civilisation is threatened by our own inventions, by dreadful noises, our horrible motor traffic, Americanisms and jazz music.

However, the band stayed in London for over a year, appearing regularly at the Palladium and the Hammersmith Palais, and making several recordings for the Columbia label. In the same year, another American band of black musicians, Will Marion Cook's Southern Syncopators, also came to London. This group featured the young clarinet virtuoso Sidney Bechet, one of whose admirers was the Swiss conductor Ernst Ansermet. In his glowing review of the band, and especially of Bechet, he compared their music with Bach's Second Brandenburg Concerto! Both the Original Dixieland Jazz Band and the Southern Syncopators played at Buckingham Palace before the royal family, the future Edward VIII being a particular fan of jazz. Bechet is reported to have described

22 Louis Armstrong in England, *Melody Maker*, 7 October 1933

the Palace as being 'like Grand Central Station with lots of carpets and lots more doors'.[2] He also got into low living ways, and although cleared of attempted rape, he was deported back to the States. However, it was in England that Bechet acquired his trademark straight soprano saxophone.

During the 1920s, jazz became fashionable amongst London's Bright Young Things, but struggled for critical acceptance. Even the legendary trumpeter Louis Armstrong's first London visit in 1932 was given a mixed reception. Armstrong had arrived in London without a musical director, a pianist or even any musical arrangements, but with forty-eight trunks of clothes. Despite the poor quality of the musicians he played with at his Palladium début, his incredible trumpeting ability and creative mastery shone through, for those who had ears for it. There were many who did not, and his appearances have divided opinions as perhaps no other musical visitor ever has. As one critic in the *Daily Herald* put it:

> There have been more arguments over Armstrong than any turn at the Palladium since Gibbon built it. People have called it 'an insult': others have gone every night.[3]

while another compared the revolutionary nature of his music, yet again, with that of Strauss. But Armstrong took to England, revelling in the appreciation he received. During his 1933 visit, he even appeared in a photograph in *Melody Maker* dressed in plus fours and a flat cap.

The year 1933 also saw the visit of Duke Ellington and his Orchestra, whose two weeks at the Palladium was possibly the pinnacle of jazz experience in England thus far. Many claim this was his finest ever orchestra, which included saxophonist Johnny Hodges, trumpeter Cootie Williams and drummer Sonny Greer. The orchestra was number 13 on the bill, with the comedian Max Miller as one of the supporting acts.

The response to Ellington's music, which combined powerful dance beats with excellent orchestration, was ecstatic and also helped establish jazz as music worthy of critical attention. Ellington was amazed how well informed about his music the British audience was, and after a subsequent performance at the Trocadero, then Europe's largest cinema, expressed surprise that the audience were criticised in the press for applauding individual solos. Ellington also gained an audience with Edward Prince of Wales and, at a party given by newspaper magnate Lord Beaverbrook, the prince even played drums with the band. Ellington, affectionately referring to his long-term musical colleague, later praised Prince Edward as 'the Billy Strayhorn of the crown princes'.[4]

Ellington's tour also took the orchestra to Scotland. In an interview he gave with the *Sunday Post*, Ellington compared Scottish bagpipe music with jazz, and saw a relationship between Scottish reels and his own music, expressing a wish to hear a full bagpipe band, and to learn the folk culture of Scotland. He also promised to take back to Harlem at least one haggis.[5]

Ellington's visit was followed in 1934 by those of other jazz stars such as Coleman Hawkins, Cab Calloway and Joe Venuti. Thereafter, a Musicians' Union ban on American musicians prevented many jazz musicians performing in Britain, a state of affairs that continued until the mid 1950s. The outstanding virtuoso pianists Fats Waller and Art Tatum both played in England in the late 1930s, Tatum eluding the ban by appearing only in a Soho nightclub, and Waller by being billed as variety theatre. There were no such problems for European musicians, and the Quintet of the Hot Club of France, which featured guitarist Django Reinhardt and violinist Stephane Grappelli were frequent visitors in the 1930s. At the outbreak of war in 1939 the quintet was in London; Reinhardt fled to France, leaving behind both Grappelli and his guitar.

The ban on American musicians applied only to performance and, in an interesting parallel with Bartók's work for BBC, the great alto saxophonist and multi-instrumentalist Benny Carter was similarly employed. He joined the BBC Dance Orchestra as an arranger in 1936, and worked for them for the next year. He appeared as saxophonist and trumpeter on many broadcasts, including his own composition *Waltzing the Blues*, which was the first jazz composition in three-four time. Carter, one of the longest-living jazz legends, wanted to study composition at the Royal Academy of Music, but was prevented by having to leave the country every three months for immigration reasons.

There were no such problems for visiting American composers. Foremost among these was George Gershwin, who visited England five times during the 1920s. Such was Gershwin's reputation by the time of his first visit in 1923 that on showing his passport to a customs officer on his arrival at Southampton, he was asked 'George Gershwin, writer of "Swanee"?'[6] From this moment, Gershwin was an Anglophile. Gershwin's role in England was that of the superstar composer, overseeing new productions of his musicals and indulging in the social whirl but, like Handel centuries earlier, not as a performer, except at private parties. When Paul Whiteman's orchestra performed Gershwin's *Rhapsody in Blue* at the Albert Hall, Gershwin was in the audience.

He loved England and Englishness, buying his suits in Savile Row, and sporting a bowler hat and umbrella, even adopting an English accent. He became the darling of Mayfair society, and numbered among his circle the actress Gertrude Lawrence, dancer Isadora Duncan and members of the royal family. He was dubbed 'the American Liszt' and dazzled the smart set with his playing. He even received a photograph from the Duke of Kent, the future George VI, with the inscription 'From George to George'.[7]

Gershwin also allowed England to influence his music. His first hit show in London, *Primrose*, captured the spirit of Gilbert and Sullivan, and included song titles such as *Isn't It Terrible What They Did to Mary Queen of Scots?* Later Gershwin was to collaborate with P. G. Wodehouse, and Gertrude Lawrence starred in the show *Oh, Kay!* Like all successful musical visitors, Gershwin adapted to his environment, and in the London production of his Broadway hit *Lady Be Good*, he added a prologue so that the notoriously late-arriving British audience would not miss the entrance of Fred Astaire and his sister Adele. Some years later, he was to write *A Damsel in Distress*, based on a P. G. Wodehouse story, which included the quaintly titled hit song *A Foggy Day in London Towne*.

In the second half of the twentieth century the jet age has enabled all prominent musicians to be musical visitors the world over. No postwar musician of international standing has failed to visit Britain, and necessarily our story comes to an end. The high quality of London recording studios has ensured that many key pop and rock records have been recorded there, and the excellence of session musicians also means that many Hollywood film scores are recorded in London. The burgeoning record industry in London from the 1960s has attracted many rock and pop stars. Perhaps the most interesting personality from the rock world to visit England was the American Jimi Hendrix, arguably the most influential blues and rock guitarist of all time. Hendrix was languishing playing small clubs in New York City in 1966 when Chas Chandler, then the bassist in The Animals, persuaded Hendrix to come to London. At this time London was the hub of activity in pop music, and Hendrix was no doubt attracted by the work of groups such as The Beatles and The Rolling Stones. He was an instant success in England, signing a lucrative record deal and playing venues including the Albert Hall. His group, The Jimi Hendrix Experience, gave free rein to his astounding range of skills, including outrageous showmanship, playing the guitar with his teeth, behind his back, and often damaging or completely destroying the instrument.

For about a year from 1968, his base in London was the attic flat at 23 Brook Street, next door to where more than 200 years earlier Handel had lived the last thirty-six years of his life. Plaques commemorating both

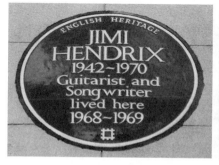 

23 Plaques on 23 and 25 Brook Street, Mayfair, commemorating the residences of Jimi Hendrix and George Frederick Handel respectively

musicians nestle side by side on the front of the Brook Street houses. Hendrix succumbed to a typical 'rock 'n' roll' lifestyle; tragically, in September 1970, at the age of just twenty-seven, he died in a basement flat in Ladbroke Grove, probably after a cocktail of drink and drugs.

The rise of 'world music', in which cultural curiosity vies with an appetite for more and more exotic forms of music to fuel the search for musicians from remote parts of the world, has seen musical visitorism taken to an extreme. World music lays bare the compelling interest in musical visitors which ensures that the music is enjoyed for its foreignness. Britain has been a powerhouse in the development of world music, through the existence of organisations such as the WOMAD festival and Peter Gabriel's Real World. Indeed the term 'world music' was conceived as a result of a series of marketing meetings in a north London pub in the summer of 1987. WOMAD, the World of Music and Dance, first staged in 1982, was inspired by the Drummers of Burundi, a group of drummers from a small village in central Burundi, originally the court drummers for the King of Burundi. The British singer and songwriter Peter Gabriel has also been a key influence, and his Real World records has provided musicians from around the world access to excellent recording facilities since 1989. The number of bands and solo artists from around the world brought to this country increases annually, and through events such as the BBC World Music Awards, world music is perhaps Radio 3's hottest ticket. In the age of the global village, classical, jazz and popular music are all heavily influenced by developments around the world, and world music in turn is influenced by them.

In the twentieth century, jazz, popular and folk musicians became the minstrels of the modern age, playing either their own music or music from an oral tradition. World music has fuelled interest in our own folk culture, and now we can see the native music of the British Isles with a new perspective. We have become musical visitors to our own shores.

Notes

The place of publication is London unless otherwise stated.

Introduction (pages 1–14)

1 Wood, B., 'Pelham Humfrey', in Sadie, S. (ed.), *The New Grove Dictionary of Music and Musicians*, 2nd edn (2001) (hereinafter *Grove*), vol. 11, p. 824.
2 Milhous, J. and Hume, R. D., 'Handel's London – The Theatres', in Burrows, D. (ed.), *The Cambridge Companion to Handel* (Cambridge University Press, Cambridge, 1997), p. 60.
3 Stevens, J., *Music and Poetry in the Early Tudor Court* (Cambridge University Press, Cambridge, 1979), p. 266.
4 Mabbett, M., 'Italian Musicians in Restoration England, 1660–90', *Music and Letters*, vol. 67, 1986, pp. 237–43.
5 Simpson, R., *Carl Nielsen, Symphonist* (Dent, 1952), p. 205.
6 Boyd, M. and Beeks, G., 'Johann Christoph Pepusch', *Grove*, vol. 19, p. 324.
7 Westrup, J. A., 'Foreign Musicians in Stuart England', *Musical Quarterly*, vol. 27, 1941, pp. 75–6.
8 Warrick, D., 'François-André Danican Philidor', *Grove*, vol. 19, p. 560. Among Philidor's operas was a version of Henry Fielding's novel *Tom Jones*.
9 Quoted in Hunter, D., 'Patronizing Handel, Inventing Audiences: The Intersections of Class, Money, Music and History', *Early Music*, vol. 28, 2000, p. 42.
10 Bruckner gave six recitals on the new organ at the Royal Albert Hall in August 1871 and another six at the Crystal Palace later in the month. At the third concert of the latter series, there was an estimated audience of 70,000. Howie, C., 'Bruckner – The Travelling Virtuoso', in Howie, C., Hawkshaw, P. and Jackson, T. (eds), *Perspectives on Anton Bruckner* (Ashgate, 2001), p. 309.
11 Ehrlich, C., *The Piano. A Social History* (Oxford University Press, Oxford, 1990), p. 22.
12 Between 8 June and 23 July, Mahler conducted eighteen performances, fifteen of *the Ring*, two performances of *Tannhäuser* and one of *Fidelio*. Grange, H. L. de la, *Mahler* (Gollancz, 1974), vol. 1, p. 55.
13 Brown, C., *Louis Spohr. A Critical Biography* (Cambridge University Press, Cambridge, 1984), p. 256.
14 Skelton, G. (trans. and ed.) *Selected Letters of Paul Hindemith* (Yale University Press, New Haven, 1995), p. 55.
15 Jones, J. B., *Gabriel Fauré. A Life in Letters* (Batsford, 1988), p. 130.
16 The two programmes are given in full in Hull, A. E., *A Great Russian Tone-Poet, Scriabin* (Kegan Paul, Trench, Trubner, 1916), pp. 64–5.

17 Zemanova, M., *Janacek. A Composer's Life* (Murray, 2003), p. 211.
18 Carner, M., *Puccini, A Critical Biography* (Duckworth, 3rd edn, 1992), p. 104.
19 Tawaststjerna, E., trans. Layton, R., *Sibelius* (Faber and Faber, 1986), vol. 2, 1904–14, p. 106.
20 Bertensson, Leyda, J., *Sergei Rachmaninoff. A Lifetime in Music* (New York University Press, New York, 1956), p. 347.
21 See Fenlon, I. and Keyte, H., 'Memorialls of Great Skill: A Tale of Five Cities', *Early Music*, vol. 8, 1980, pp. 329–34.
22 One writer has pointed out that 'Mendelssohn came [to England] at the right moment: Carlyle was introducing us to Teutonic heroes and to Goethe, and Victoria worshipped the country of her beloved Albert ... Moreover, girls were still taught little but embroidery and the piano and the limpid, uncomplicated *Songs Without Words* were a gift to them as well as to the Queen'. Wilson, F. M. (ed.), *Strange Island. Britain through Foreign Eyes 1395–1940* (Longmans, Green, 1955), p. 187.
23 See Thompson, B., *A Monkey Among Crocodiles. The Life, Loves and Lawsuits of Mrs Georgina Weldon* (HarperCollins, 2000).
24 Kendall, A., *Paganini. A Biography* (Chapell, 1982), pp. 100–9.
25 Cooper, M., *Gluck* (Chatto and Windus, 1935), pp. 46–7. Gluck also collaborated with the actor–manager David Garrick whilst in London.
26 Rimsky-Korsakov, N. A., *My Musical Life* (Knopf, New York, 1923, 5th edn, 1992), p. 41.
27 Rees, B., *Camille Saint-Saëns. A Life* (Chatto and Windus, 1999), pp. 262–4.
28 In 1957, the French composer, Nadia Boulanger, became the first woman to conduct at a Royal Philharmonic concert. Kendall, A., *The Tender Tyrant. Nadia Boulanger, A Life Devoted to Music* (Macdonald and Jane's, 1976), p. 47.
29 May, F., *The Life of Johannes Brahms* (Arnold, 1905), vol. 2, p. 155.
30 Stravinsky wrote a few years later: 'Alas! Patrons of her quality become more and more rare.' Stravinsky, I., *The Story of my Life* (Gollancz, 1936) p. 272.
31 Schmidt, C. B., *Entrancing Muse. A Documented Biography of Francis Poulenc* (Pendragon Press, Hillside, New York, 2002), p. 331.
32 Doctor, J., *The BBC and Ultra-Modern Music 1922–1936* (Cambridge University Press, Cambridge, 1999), p. 234.
33 Butler, E. M. (ed.), trans. Austin, M., *A Regency Tour. The English Tour of Prince Pückler-Muskau Desori, Described in His Letters, 1826–1828* (Collins, 1957), p. 35.
34 Ballam, H. and Lewis, R. (eds), *The Visitors' Book. England and the English, As Others Have Seen Them* (Max Parrish, 1950), p. 95.
35 Osborne, C. (ed.), *Letters of Giuseppi Verdi* (Gollancz, 1971), p. 47.
36 Ibid., p. 167.
37 Ibid., p. 89.
38 Letts, M., *As the Foreigner Saw Us* (Methuen, 1935), p. 84.
39 Ballam and Lewis, op. cit., p. 78.
40 Lesure, F. and Nichols, R. (eds), *Debussy Letters* (Faber and Faber, 1987), p. 160.
41 Bertensson, F. (ed.), trans. Halverson, W. *et al.*, *Edvard Grieg. Letters to Friends and Colleagues* (Peer Gynt Press, Columbus, Ohio, 2000), p. 623.
42 Skelton, op. cit., p. 55.
43 Bailey, K., *The Life of Webern* (Cambridge University Press, Cambridge, 1998), p. 136.
44 Anon., *Letters from Albion to a Friend on the Continent, Written in the Years 1810, 1811, 1812 and 1813* (Gale, Curtis and Kenner, 1814), vol. 1, pp. 97–8.

45 Robson-Scott, W. D., *German Travellers in England, 1400–1800* (Blackwell, Oxford, 1953), p. 11.

46 Ibid., p. 56.

47 Ibid., p. 63.

48 From Richard Flecknoe's *Enigmaticall Characters* of 1658, quoted in Simpson A., '"Of a Petty French Lutenist in England" by Richard Flecknoe', *Lute Society Journal*, vol. 10 (1968), p. 33.

49 *The Weekly Journal* from 1725, quoted in Burrows, D. (ed.), op. cit., p. 47.

50 Flower, D. (ed.), *Voltaire's England* (Folio Society, 1950), p. 163. With some exceptions, such as the field of church music, British society has tended to regard music as a profession not proper for its own people. For example, the fourth Earl of Chesterfield, in a letter to his son in Italy on the Grand Tour, advised him: 'Active participation in painting, sculpture and architecture is approved of, but interest in music is improper and vulgar for a gentleman.' Gibson, E., 'The Royal Academy of Music and its Directors', in Sadie, S. and Hicks, A. (eds), *Handel's Tercentenary Collection* (Macmillan, 1987), pp. 138–51.

51 Carus, C. G., trans. Davison, S. C., *The King of Saxony's Journey through England and Scotland in the Year 1844* (Chapman and Hall, 1846), p. 35.

52 Pückler-Muskau, H. L. H., *Tour of Germany, Holland and England in the Years 1826, 1827 and 1828* (Effingham Wilson, 1832), vol. 4, pp. 218–19.

53 Raumer, F. von, *England in 1835: Being a Series of Letters Written to Friends in Germany* (Murray, 1836), vol. 3, p. 69.

54 Robbins Landon, H. C. and Jones, D. W., *Haydn. His Life and Music* (Thames and Hudson, 1988), p. 125.

55 Raumer, op. cit., p. 206.

56 Howard, P., *Gluck. An Eighteenth-Century Portrait in Letters and Documents* (Clarendon Press, Oxford, 1995), p. 19.

57 Schopenhauer, J. (trans. and ed. Michaelis-Jena, P. and Merson, W.), *A Lady Travels. Journeys in England and Scotland. From the Diaries of Johanna Schopenhauer* (Routledge, 1988), p. 180. Johanna became pregnant on their first tour and her husband seemed anxious to have Arthur born on English soil and so be British.

58 Soligny, Count de V., trans. Patmore, P. G., *Letters on England* (Henry Colburn, 1823), vol. 1, p. 115.

59 Butler, op. cit., p. 89.

60 Weinstock, H., *Vincenzo Bellini. His Life and His Operas* (Weidenfeld and Nicolson, 1972), p. 144.

61 Spiegel, F., *Musical Blunders and Other Musical Curiosities* (Robson Books, 1997), p. 114.

1 'Brothers in the art or science of music' (pages 15–28)

1 Giustinian, S., *Four Years at the Court of Henry VIII*, trans. Brown, R. (Smith, Elder, 1854), vol. 1, p. 86.

2 Ibid., p. 296.

3 Giustinian, op. cit., vol. 2, p. 97.

4 Ibid., p. 136.

5 Ibid., p. 161.

6 Giustinian, op. cit., vol. 1, p. 297.

7 Ashbee, A., Lasocki, D., Holman, P. and Kisby, F., *A Biographical Dictionary of English Court Musicians 1485–1714* (Ashgate, Aldershot, 1998), vol. 1, p. 799.

8 Ward, J., 'Philip van Wilder', *Grove*, vol. 20, 1980, p. 414.

9 Quoted in. Bernstein, J. A., 'Philip van Wilder and the Netherlandish Chanson in England', *Musica Disciplina*, vol. 33, 1979, p. 59.

10 Giustinian, op. cit., vol. 2, pp. 163–4.
11 The list of approximately 350 instruments includes over 70 recorders and a similar number of flutes, as well as keyboard instruments, and a whole host of wind and string instruments, many of them made by the finest foreign craftsmen. See Galpin, F. W., *Old English Instruments of Music* (Methuen, 4th edn, 1965), pp. 215–20.
12 Quoted in Bernstein, J. A. (ed.), *Masters and Monuments of the Renaissance*, vol. 4 (Broude Trust, New York, 1991), p. xxii.
13 Holman, P., *Four and Twenty Fiddlers* (Clarendon Press, Oxford, 1993), pp. 67–8.
14 Ibid., pp. 74–5, 80–1.
15 The information about the origins of the string consort is from Prior, R., 'Jewish Musicians at the Tudor Court', *Musical Quarterly*, vol. 69, 1983, pp. 253–65.
16 Lasocki, D. with Prior, R., *The Bassanos: Venetian Musicians and Instrument Makers in England, 1531–1665* (Scolar Press, Aldershot, 1995), *passim*.
17 Ibid., p. 21.
18 Whose second marriage to Lucretia Bassano, daughter of Anthony, united the two dominant families of wind-players at court.
19 Lasocki with Prior, op. cit., p. 78.
20 Quoted in Lasocki with Prior, op. cit., pp. 35–6.
21 Trombonist and sackbut-player; he has changed his name to Peter Bassano.
22 Kerman, J., 'An Italian Musician in Elizabethan England', *Write All These Down: Essays on Music* (Berkeley, 1994), p. 144.
23 Charteris, R., 'New Information about the Life of Alfonso Ferrabosco the Elder (1543–1588)', *Royal Musical Association Research Chronicle*, vol. 17 (1981), p. 103.
24 Kerman, op. cit., p. 146.

2 The Restoration (pages 29–39)

1 Quoted in Holman, P., *Four and Twenty Fiddlers* (Clarendon Press, Oxford, 1993), pp. 289–90.
2 Quoted in Harley, J., *Music in Purcell's London* (Dennis Dobson, 1968), p. 64.
3 Again from Pepys, quoted in Holman, op. cit., p. 295. Banister later left the Violins, and sometime around 1672 began the world's first series of public concerts.
4 Holman, op. cit., p. 383.
5 See Danchin, P. 'The Foundation of the Royal Academy of Music in 1674 and Pierre Perrin's *Ariane*', *Theatre Survey*, vol. 25, 1984, p. 61.
6 De Beer, E. S. (ed.), *The Diary of John Evelyn* (Oxford University Press, Oxford, 1959), p. 618. She and the Duchess of Cleveland, her predecessor as *maîtresse en titre*, received an annual allowance of £45,000 for themselves and their children.
7 Holman, op. cit., p. 344–5.
8 Ibid., p. 345.
9 Ashbee *et al.*, op. cit., vol. 2, p. 853.
10 Ibid., p. 863.
11 North, R., *Essay of Musicall Ayre*, quoted in Tilmouth, M., 'Nicola Matteis', *Musical Quarterly*, vol. 46, 1960, p. 22.
12 Tilmouth, op. cit., p. 23.
13 De Beer, op. cit., p. 605. Indeed, Matteis's violin itself would have been stupendous, coming from Italy during the golden age of the Cremonese school of violin-makers.

14 Mabbett, M., 'Italian Musicians in Restoration England, 1660–90', *Music and Letters*, vol. 67, 1986, p. 241.

15 Tilmouth, op. cit., p. 23.

16 Ibid., p. 26.

17 Walls, P., 'Nicola Matteis (i)', *Grove*, vol. 16, p. 134.

18 Tilmouth, op. cit., p. 24.

19 Ibid., p. 24.

20 Ibid., p. 32.

21 Purcell might be said to be shedding crocodile tears in his 'Sefuachi's Farewell' at a time when James II's newly opened Catholic chapel was filled with foreign musicians, to the frustration of their English counterparts.

22 Keith, R., '"La Guitare Royale". A Study of the Career and Compositions of Francesco Corbetta', *Recherches sur la Musique Française Classique*, vol. 6, 1966, p. 81.

23 Ibid., p. 81.

24 However, the popular 'Italian Ground', from the second volume of *The Division Flute*, is by Draghi.

25 Quoted in Holman, P., 'Giovanni Battista Draghi', in *Grove*, vol. 7, p. 551.

26 Burden, M., *Purcell Remembered* (Faber and Faber, 1995), p. 36.

27 Ibid., p. 35.

28 For a fuller discussion of foreign influences on Purcell's music, see Burden, M. (ed.), *The Purcell Companion* (Faber and Faber, 1995), pp. 21–7.

29 Matteis, Paisible, and other notable musical visitors are also listed.

30 Burden (ed.), op. cit., p. 44.

31 Ibid., p. 44.

32 Ibid., p. 44.

3 Handel (1) (pages 40–55)

1 Lindgren, L., 'Handel's London – Italian musicians and librettists' in Burrows, D. (ed.), *The Cambridge Companion to Handel* (Cambridge University Press, Cambridge, 1997), p. 78.

2 McVeigh, S., 'London: Musical Life 1660–1800; Concert Life', *Grove*, vol. 15, p. 121.

3 Chetwood W. R., *A General History of the Stage, 1749*, quoted in Simon, J. (ed.), *Handel: A Celebration of His Life and Times* (National Portrait Gallery, London, 1985), p. 77.

4 Mainwaring, J., *Memoirs of the Life of the late George Frideric Handel* (Da Capo Press, NY, 1974, facsimile reprint of 1760 edn, London), p. 5.

5 Deutsch, O. E., *Handel. A Documentary Biography* (Da Capo Press, NY, 1974, reprint of 1955 edn), p. 492.

6 Quoted in Lang, P. H., *George Frideric Handel* (Faber and Faber, 1966), p. 37.

7 Remarkably, for a man of twenty-one, he was accompanied by his own servant, and refused the offer of a generous allowance from the Grand Prince of Tuscany, preferring to draw on his own capital. Relations were perhaps strained between Handel and Ferdinando over Handel's love affair with the singer Vittoria Tarquini, who had also caught the eye of the Grand Prince. This affair is the only record of any such attachment in Handel's life.

8 Mainwaring, op. cit., pp. 65–6.

9 Intriguingly, Scarlatti is rumoured to have left for London in 1719. It has not been confirmed whether he was there, but his presence is possibly witnessed by the fact that one of his operas, *Narciso*, was performed in London in May 1720. Certainly Francesco Scarlatti, Domenico's uncle, was already active in

London concert life; Francesco later moved to Dublin, where he died in 1741. See Boyd, M., 'Domenico Scarlatti', *Grove*, vol. 22, p. 400.

10 Mainwaring, op. cit., p. 53.

11 Lang, op. cit., p. 103.

12 Ibid., p. 104.

13 In his preface to the libretto, Hill expresses the wish 'to see English *Opera* more splendid than her *Mother*, the Italian'. See Price, C., 'English Traditions in Handel's *Rinaldo*', in Sadie, S. and Hicks, A. (eds.), *Handel Tercentenary Collection* (Macmillan, 1987), p. 120.

14 Mainwaring, op. cit., p. 78.

15 Quoted in Simon (ed.), op. cit., p. 77.

16 Quoted in Burrows, D., *Handel* (Oxford University Press, Oxford, 1994), p. 76.

17 Ibid., p. 73.

18 Fewer than 1 per cent of households nationwide had an income of £400 or more. See Hunter, D., op. cit., p. 34.

19 Quoted in Hill, J. W., *The Life and Works of Francesco Maria Veracini* (Ann Arbor, Michigan, 1979), p. 16.

20 Quoted in Careri, E., *Francesco Geminiani* (Clarendon Press, Oxford, 1993), p. 15.

21 Indeed, as a young man leading an orchestra in Naples, his rhythm was so 'wild and unsteady ... that instead of regulating and conducting the band, he threw it into confusion', and he was relegated to playing in the viola section. Ibid., p. 4.

22 From the preface to his *Treatise of Good Taste in the Art of Musick* (1749), quoted in Careri, op. cit., p. 9.

23 Careri, ibid., pp. 28–9.

24 Ibid., p. 32.

25 Part of the original house is now occupied by North London Collegiate School.

26 There had been failed attempts to bring Bononcini to London in 1707, following the success of his *Camilla*, but it was only when Lord Burlington, one of the leading lights of the Royal Academy, heard his opera *Astarto* in Rome in 1719 that Bononcini was finally persuaded to travel to England the following year.

27 Deutsch, op. cit., p. 180.

28 Quoted in Keates, J., *Handel. The Man and his Music* (Gollancz, 1985), p. 114.

29 Ten years later, Bononcini was accused of plagiarism, having passed off a madrigal by Antonio Lotti as his own, and left England for good in October in 1732.

30 See Holman, op. cit., p. 319.

31 See Lindgren, op. cit., pp. 81–2.

32 Quoted in Lindgren, L., 'Nicola Francesco Haym', *Grove*, vol. 11, p. 284.

33 Quoted in Keates, op. cit., p. 91.

34 Perhaps the friction was caused by Senesino's huge success in London. For example John Gay wrote: 'People have now forgot Homer, and Virgil & Caesar ... for in London and Westminster in all polite conversation's, Senesino is daily voted to be the greatest man who ever lived'. Quoted in Keates, op. cit., p. 102.

35 After his retirement, Senesino returned to Italy and built 'a fine house with an inscription over the door to let the world know 'twas the folly of the English had laid the foundation of it'. Simon (ed.), op. cit., p. 121. Farinelli who, in the 1730s was even more fêted and highly paid than Senesino, was said to be earning in the region of £5,000 per season, and for a single benefit performance in March 1735, he earned £2,000.

36 Quoted in Keates, op. cit., p. 88.

37 Ibid., p. 102.
38 Deutsch, op. cit., p. 185.
39 See LaRue, C. S., 'Handel and the Aria', in Burrows (ed.), op. cit., p. 116, and Keates, op. cit., p. 122.
40 From a pamphlet of 1727, quoted in Weber, W., 'Handel's London – social, political and intellectual contexts', in Burrows (ed.), op. cit., p. 46.
41 These three singers were merely the most prominent of two whole generations of mainly Italians who appeared regularly in Handel's operas in London – well over 100 in all. See Lindgren in Burrrows (ed.), op. cit., pp. 82–4.
42 Quoted in Lang, op. cit., pp. 196–7.
43 Quoted in Simon (ed.), op. cit., p. 150.
44 It is interesting to consider the reasons for Handel's failure to set Shakespeare. Perhaps he understood that great plays would not make great operas, and indeed his settings of Haym's more modest librettos proved more successful than those of the more literary Rolli. Perhaps he did not want to subject Shakespeare's plays to the treatment that was required to turn them into opera librettos. Some commentators, especially Lang, compare Handel the dramatist with Shakespeare: maybe Handel saw Shakespeare as some sort of anachronistic 'rival'. Dr. Johnson also made the comparison: 'Handel stands approachless as Shakespeare himself in grandeur and variety' (quoted in Keates, op. cit., p. 313).

4 Handel (2) (pages 56–67)

1 In his years in Italy he was known as Giorgio Federico Hendel.
2 Deutsch, op. cit., p. 191.
3 Lang, op. cit., p. 682.
4 Quoted in Simon, J. (ed.), *Handel: A Celebration of His Life and Times* (National Portrait Gallery, London, 1985), p. 35.
5 Reproduced in Sadie, S., *Handel* (Calder, 1962), p. 156.
6 Burrows, D., *Handel* (Oxford University Press, Oxford, 1994), p. 376.
7 See Riding, J., *Handel House Companion* (The Handel House Trust Ltd, 2001), ch. 2, pp. 23–35.
8 Quoted in Burrows, op. cit., p. 124.
9 Ibid., p. 117.
10 By Handel's friend Mrs Delany, in Deutsch, op. cit., p. 582.
11 See Smith, R., 'Handel's English Librettists', in Burrows, D. (ed.), *The Cambridge Companion to Handel* (Cambridge University Press, Cambridge, 1997), pp. 92–108.
12 Deutsch, op. cit., p. 102.
13 Quoted in Johnstone, H. D., 'Handel's London – British musicians and London concert life', in Burrows (ed.), op. cit., p. 73.
14 Ibid., p. 73. Handel borrowed freely from his own works and from those of other composers throughout his career, a practice which was commented on as early as 1722 by Johann Mattheson, and which has troubled commentators ever since. To some extent, borrowing was common practice at the time, but Handel's case bordered on the extreme, especially at times of stress or illness. See Burrows, op. cit., pp. 46–8. For an interesting theory, that Handel lacked the power of melodic invention, see Roberts, J. H., 'Why did Handel Borrow?' in Sadie, S. and Hicks, A. (eds), *Handel Tercentenary Collection* (Macmillan, 1987), pp. 83–92. In the same volume, George J. Buelow, 'The Case for Handel's Borrowings: The Judgment of three Centuries', pp. 61–82, charts the reception given to Handel's borrowings, which for some nineteenth-century writers became a disturbing moral issue.

15 Quoted in Simon (ed.), op. cit., p. 41. Handel is said to have cut Goupy out of his will after the appearance of the caricature.

16 See Flower, N., *George Frideric Handel. His Personality and His Times* (Cassell, 3rd edn, 1943), pp. 233–58, for a graphic, not to say somewhat fanciful, description of Handel's years of distress. See also Taylor C., 'Handel's Disengagement from the Italian Opera', in Sadie and Hicks, op. cit., pp. 165–82, which shows that it might have been Middlesex himself who finally put paid to Handel's interest in opera.

17 Letter from Jennens to his friend Edward Holdsworth, quoted in Burrows, op. cit., p. 259.

18 Boydell, B., *A Dublin Musical Calendar, 1700–1760* (Irish Academic Press, Dublin, 1988), p. 16.

19 Deutsch, op. cit., p. 537.

20 Johnson also described him as 'A vain fool crazed by his wealth, who, were he in Heaven, would criticize the Lord Almighty'. In 1747, Jennens spent £80,000 just on laying out the grounds of his estate at Gopsall in Leicestershire. However, Jennens was also an avid admirer, collector and student of Handel's music, and commissioned manuscript copies of many scores and parts of Handel's works.

21 Letter to Holdsworth, quoted in Simon (ed.), p. 201.

22 There is a possibility that Mrs Delany's libretto was the one given to Haydn, more than fifty years later, for the composition of *The Creation*. See H. C. Robbins Landon's foreword to *The Creation and The Seasons. The Complete Authentic Sources for the Word-Books* (University College Cardiff Press, Cardiff, 1985), pp. 5–9.

23 Quoted in Sadie, op. cit., p. 135.

24 Horace Walpole dryly observed: 'a spectacle for the proclamation of the peace ... is to open with a concert of fifteen hundred hands, and conclude with so many hundred thousand crackers all set to music, that all the men killed in the war are to be wakened with the crash'. Quoted in Simon (ed.), op. cit., p. 212.

25 Ibid., p. 226.

26 Ibid., p. 249.

27 See Weber, op. cit., pp. 45–54.

5   Wolfgang Amadeus Mozart (pages 68–82)

1 Soloman, M., *Mozart* (Hutchinson, 1995), p. 65.

2 Ottaway, H., *Mozart* (Orbis, 1974), p. 39.

3 Anderson, E. (ed.), trans. Oldman, C. B., *The Letters of Mozart and His Family* (Macmillan, 1938), vol. 1, p. 75.

4 Gutman, R. W., *Mozart. A Cultural Biography* (Secker and Warburg, 1999), p. 181.

5 Anderson, op. cit., p. 65.

6 Deutsch, O., *Mozart. A Documentary Biography* (A. and C. Black, 1965), p. 35.

7 Halliwell, R., *The Mozart Family. Four Lives in a Social Context* (Clarendon Press, Oxford, 1998), p. 91.

8 Keyes, I., *Mozart. His Music in His Life* (Granada, 1980), p. 43.

9 Halliwell, op. cit., pp. 89–90.

10 Gutman, op. cit., p. 192. Leopold nevertheless deplored the fact that many Jews, like Christians, neglected their religion. He also noted that some of the Jews, particularly Portuguese, dressed with Parisian elegance – 'nothing about them resembles a Jew'.

11 Schenk, E., *Mozart and His Times* (Secker & Warburg, 1960), p. 73.
12 Gutman, op. cit., pp. 195–6.
13 Roe, S., 'Johann Christian Bach', *Grove*, vol. 2, p. 414.
14 Gärtner, H., *John Christian Bach. Mozart's Friend and Mentor* (Amadeus Press, Portland, Oregon, 1989), pp. 203, 206.
15 Küster, K., *Mozart. A Musical Biography* (Clarendon Press, Oxford, 1996), p. 19.
16 Terry, C. S., *John Christian Bach* (Oxford University Press, Oxford, 1967), p. 80.
17 Derr, E., 'Some Thoughts on the Design of Mozart's Operas', in Zaslaw, N. (ed.), *Mozart's Piano Concertos: Text, Context and Interpretation* (University of Michigan Press, Ann Arbor, 1990) p. 201.
18 Spaethling, R. (ed.), *Mozart's Letters, Mozart's Life* (Faber and Faber, 2001), p. 307.
19 Schenk, op. cit., p. 71.
20 Gärtner, op. cit., p. 231.
21 Zaslaw, N., *Mozart's Symphonies: Context, Performance Practice, Reception* (Clarendon Press, Oxford, 1989), p. 28.
22 Girdlestone, C. M., *Mozart's Piano Concertos* (Cassell, 1948), p. 387.
23 Deutsch, op. cit., p. 43.
24 Ibid., pp. 95–100.
25 Hyatt King, A., *A Mozart Legacy. Aspects of the British Library Collection* (British Library, 1984), p. 24.
26 Woodfield, I., 'New Light on the Mozarts' London Visit: A Private Concert with Manzuoli', *Music and Letters*, vol. 76, 1995, pp. 189, 195, 204, 207.
27 Anderson, op. cit., pp. 82–3.
28 Spaethling, op. cit., pp. 326–7.
29 Gärtner, op. cit., p. 243.

6 Haydn in London (pages 83–100)

1 Gotwals, V. (ed.), *Joseph Haydn Eighteenth-century Gentleman and Genius* (Madison, Wisconsin, 1963), p. 17 (hereafter Gotwals). (A translation of Haydn's memoirs as narrated to Griesinger and Dies, both first published in 1810.)
2 Robbins Landon, H. C. (ed.), *The Collected Correspondence and London Notebooks of Joseph Haydn* (Barrie and Rockliff, 1959), p. 66 (hereafter *Letters and Notebooks*).
3 Robbins Landon, H. C. and Jones, D. W., *Haydn. His Life and Music* (Thames and Hudson, 1988), pp. 230–1 (hereafter HCRL).
4 Gotwals, p. 119.
5 Ibid., pp. 119–20.
6 *Letters and Notebooks*, p. 112.
7 Ibid., p. 112.
8 Geiringer, K. and I., *Haydn. A Creative Life in Music* (University of California Press, Berkeley, 3rd rev. and enl. edn, 1982), p. 102 (hereafter Geiringer).
9 Gotwals, p. 132.
10 HCRL, p. 234.
11 McVeigh, S., *Concert Life in London from Mozart to Haydn* (Cambridge University Press, Cambridge, 1993), p. 62.
12 Gotwals, p. 131.
13 Ibid., pp. 158–9.
14 Ibid., p. 150.
15 *Letters and Notebooks*, p. 272.

16 Ibid., pp. 254–5.
17 Ibid., pp. 123–4.
18 Ibid., p. 126.
19 Ibid., p. 128.
20 Ibid., p. 132.
21 Gotwals, p. 33.
22 Ibid., p. 130.
23 Geiringer, p. 114.
24 *Letters and Notebooks*, p. 261.
25 Ibid., p. 252.
26 Ibid., pp. 273–4.
27 Ibid., pp. 258–9.
28 Ibid., p. 275.
29 Ibid., p. 275.
30 Ibid., p. 258.
31 Ibid., p. 253.
32 Ibid., p. 262.
33 Ibid., p. 278. In a letter dated January 1792, Haydn writes: 'I am quite well, but am almost always in an "English humour", that is, depressed.' Ibid., p. 126.
34 Ibid., p. 253.
35 Ibid., p. 268.
36 Ibid., p. 288.
37 Gotwals, p. 133.
38 Ibid., p. 152.
39 Haydn said 'I shall be proud to be able to speak of myself as his teacher' (*Letters and Notebooks*, p. 141), and Beethoven was of course keen to have the greatest composer in the world as his teacher. However, it transpired that Haydn returned flawed counterpoint exercises he had set virtually uncorrected, and the lessons lasted only a year.
40 The Venetian Domenico Dragonetti was one of the leading double bass virtuosi in Europe, whose long career in London redefined the role and the perception of the double bass. He performed transcriptions of sonatas by Corelli and Handel on his instrument, and commanded exceptionally high fees when an orchestral player. Dragonetti was a keen collector of dolls, and no doubt was able to share this interest with his friend Haydn, who adored puppets.
41 Gotwals, pp. 167–8.
42 HCRL, p. 249. The concerti grossi of Corelli and Handel and the operas of Mozart are perhaps the only other works that could have hitherto made this claim.
43 *Letters and Notebooks*, p. 300.
44 Ibid., p. 297.
45 Ibid., p. 295.
46 Ibid., p. 304.
47 HCRL, p. 251.
48 Gotwals, p. 34.
49 HCRL, p. 232.
50 *Letters and Notebooks*, p. 291.
51 Ibid., p. 301. John Field, the creator of the nocturne, was only about twelve years old at the time Haydn saw him.
52 Gotwals, p. 30.
53 *Letters and Notebooks*, p. 306.
54 Haydn is credited with about 350 arrangements of Scottish, Welsh and Irish folk songs between 1791 and 1805, many of them commissioned by the Edinburgh publisher George Thomson. Although poets as fine as Robert Burns

provided verses for Thomson, the musical results were mostly disappointing, partly owing to a lack of affinity with the musical character of the song, and partly to Haydn's increasing propensity to 'farm out' these arrangements to his students.

55 *Letters and Notebooks*, p. 124.
56 Gotwals, p. 171.
57 Ibid., p. 23.
58 Ibid., p. 36.
59 *Letters and Notebooks*, p. 164.

7 Interlude (pages 101–104)

1 Plantinga, L., 'Muzio Clementi', *Grove*, vol. 6, p. 40.
2 Craw, H. A., 'Jan Ladislav Dussek', *Grove*, vol. 7, p. 761.
3 See Plantinga, L., *Clementi. His Life and Music* (Oxford University Press, Oxford, 1977), p. 270ff., for a fuller assessment of the work.
4 Beethoven is also said to have preferred his Broadwood pianoforte, which he acquired in 1818, to all others.

8 'That's Weber in London!' (pages 105–118)

1 Benedict, J., *Weber* (Sampson Low, Marston, Searle and Rivington, 1881), p. 8.
2 Ibid., p. 61.
3 Tusa, M., *Euryanthe and Maria von Weber's Dramaturgy of German Opera* (Clarendon Press, Oxford, 1991), pp. 16–17.
4 After some correspondence Weber had received a copy of the score of *Fidelio* from Beethoven himself on 10 April. Albrecht, T. (ed.), *Letters to Beethoven and other Correspondence* (University of Nebraska Press, Lincoln, 1996), vol. 2, p. 238.
5 Saunders, W., *Weber* (Dent, 1940), p. 148.
6 Turner, W. J., *Beethoven. The Search for Reality* (Ernest Benn, 1927), p. 195.
7 Levy, D. B., *Beethoven. The Ninth Symphony* (Yale University Press, New Haven, CT, 2003), p. 20.
8 Von Weber, M. M., trans. Simpson, J. P., *Carl Maria von Weber. The Life of an Artist* (Chapman and Hall, 1865), vol. 2, p. 324.
9 Blainey, A., *Fanny and Adelaide. The Lives of the Remarkable Kemble Sisters* (Ivan R. Dee, Chicago, 2001), p. 35.
10 Weinstock, H., *Rossini. A Biography* (Oxford University Press, Oxford, 1968), p. 135.
11 Ibid., p. 137.
12 Kendall, A., *Gioacchino Rossini: The Reluctant Hero* (Gollancz, 1992), p. 124.
13 Planché, J. R., *Recollections and Reflections* (Tinsley Brothers, 1872), pp. 75–6.
14 Ibid., p. 78.
15 Warrack, J., *Carl Maria von Weber* (Cambridge University Press, Cambridge, 1976), p. 314.
16 Spitta, P., 'Carl Maria von Weber', *Grove*, vol. 27, p. 144.
17 Planché, op. cit., p. 79.
18 Cox, H. B. and Cox, C. L. E., *Leaves from the Journals of Sir George Smart* (Longmans, Green, 1907), pp. 240–1.
19 Weinstock, op. cit., p. 149.
20 Von Weber, op. cit., pp. 427–8.
21 Smart recalled one personal example of this: 'One day, when walking with Weber near Portland Place, a street organ was playing, with false notes, his

celebrated "Huntsmen's Chorus" in *Der Freischütz*. He was very angry, and said, "Why do you allow such compositions to be murdered?" My reply was that I could not help it. "The man," I said, "has the liberty to play the tunes as they are set on the barrell." "Then," said he, "such liberty should not be allowed in any country."' Cox and Cox, op. cit., pp. 247–8.

22 Kemble, F. A., *Record of a Girlhood* (Richard Bentley, 1878), vol. 1, pp. 157–8.
23 Von Weber, op. cit., p. 390.
24 Cox, J. E., *Musical Recollections of the Last Half-Century* (Tinsley Brothers, 1872), vol. 1, p. 234.
25 Warrack, op. cit., p. 354.
26 Planché, op. cit., p. 83.
27 Warrack, op. cit., p. 357.
28 Smidek, E. F., *Isaak-Ignaz Moscheles* (Scolar Press, 1989), pp. 42–3.
29 Von Weber, op. cit., p. 467.
30 Moscheles, C., trans. Coleridge, A. D., *Life of Moscheles* (Hurst and Blackett, 1873), vol. 1, p. 128.
31 Anon., 'Weber in London', *Musical Times*, 1 July 1893, p. 399.

9 Felix Mendelssohn (pages 119–134)

1 Moscheles, C., trans. Coleridge, A. D., *Life of Moscheles*, vol. 1 (Hurst and Blackett, 1873), p. 224.
2 Jourdain, P., 'The Hidden Pathways of Assimilation: Mendelssohn's first visit to London', in Bashford, C. and Langley, L. (eds), *Music and British Culture, 1785–1914* (Oxford University Press, Oxford, 2000), pp. 101–4.
3 Eduard Devrient, Director of Opera at Karlsruhe, who was jointly responsible with Mendelssohn for mounting the performance, described the composer's reactions to it: 'And to think,' said Felix triumphantly, 'that it should be an actor and a Jew that gives back to the people their greatest Christian work.' Devrient, E., trans. Macfarne, N., *My Recollections of Felix Mendelssohn-Bartholdy* (Richard Bentley, 1869), p. 61.
4 Quoted in Nichols, R. (ed.), *Mendelssohn Remembered* (Faber and Faber, 1997), p. 123.
5 Selden-Goth, G. F. M., *Letters of Mendelssohn* (Kraus Reprint Co., New York, 1969), p. 44.
6 Ibid., p. 54.
7 Ehrlich, C., *First Philharmonic. A History of the Royal Philharmonic Society* (Clarendon Press, Oxford, 1995), p. 48.
8 Werner, E., trans. Newlin, D., *Mendelssohn. Image of the Composer and His Age* (Collier-Macmillan, 1963), p. 148.
9 Marek, G. R., *Gentle Genius. The Story of Felix Mendelssohn* (Robert Hale, 1972), p. 166. For an alternative view, see Mercer-Taylor, P., *The Life of Mendelssohn* (Cambridge University Press, Cambridge, 2000), p. 84.
10 Hensel, S., trans. Klingemann, C., *The Mendelssohn Family 1729–1847 from Letters and Journals* (Sampson, Low, Marston, Searle and Rivington, 1881), vol. 1, pp. 213–14.
11 Jacob, H. E., trans. Winston, R. and C., *Felix Mendelssohn and his Times* (Barrie and Rockliff, 1962), pp. 199–200.
12 Hensel, op. cit., vol. 2, 1882, p. 225.
13 Werner, op. cit., pp. 15, 19.
14 Moscheles, C., *Life of Moscheles*, op. cit., p. 267.
15 Mendelssohn was reported to be able to do everything on the organ – except one thing: play the congregation out of the church. 'The more he attempted it, the less they were inclined to go; the more gracefully insinuating his musical

hints, the more delightedly patient they became to remain. It is said that once, when he was playing at St Paul's, the vergers, wearied with endeavouring to persuade the people to retire, resorted at length to the more convincing argument of beating them over the head, and at last cleared the Cathedral.' Blunt, W., *On Wings of Song. Biography of Felix Mendelssohn* (Hamish Hamilton, 1974), p. 174.

16 Werner, op. cit., p. 201.
17 Ibid., pp. 230–1.
18 Ibid., p. 239.
19 Gotch, R. B. (ed.), *Mendelssohn and his Friends in Kensington. Letters from Fanny and Sophy Horsley written 1833–6* (Oxford University Press, Oxford, 1934), pp. 40–1.
20 Ibid., p. 66.
21 Hiller, F. M., trans. von Glehn, M. E., *Mendelssohn. Letters and Recollections* (Macmillan 1874), p. 99.
22 Elliott, A., *The Music Makers. A Brief History of the Birmingham Triennial Musical Festivals, 1784–1912* (Birmingham Library Services, Birmingham, 2000), pp. 6–7.
23 Ward Jones, P., *The Mendelssohns on Honeymoon. The 1837 Diary of Felix and Cécile Mendelssohn-Bartholdy* (Clarendon Press, Oxford, 1997), pp. 86–119.
24 Moscheles, F., *Letters of Felix Mendelssohn to Ignaz and Charlotte Moscheles* (Trübner, 1873), p. 208.
25 Marek, op. cit., p. 293.
26 Ibid., pp. 290–1.
27 Selden-Goth, op. cit., p. 309.
28 Sterndale Bennett, J. R., *The Life of William Sterndale Bennett* (Cambridge University Press, Cambridge 1907), p. 143.
29 Elliott, op. cit., p. 7.
30 Werner, op. cit., p. 462.
31 Moscheles, *Letters*, ibid., p. 275.
32 Polko, E., trans. Lady Wallace, *Reminiscences of Felix Mendelssohn-Bartholdy* (Longmans Green, 1869), p. 15.
33 Seldon-Goth, op. cit., pp. 354–5.
34 The Society, established in 1832, consisted of an amateur orchestra and chorus. From 1836 it was based at Exeter Hall. It gave the first London performance of *Saint Paul* in 1837.
35 Bulman, J., *Jenny Lind. A Biography* (James Barrie, 1956), p. 153.
36 Werner, op. cit., p. 490.
37 Marek, op. cit., p. 317.

10 Berlioz and Wagner (pages 135–148)

1 Cairns, D., *Berlioz*, vol. 2, *Servitude and Greatness, 1832–1869* (Allen Lane, The Penguin Press, 1999), p. 393.
2 Ganz, A. W., *Berlioz in London* (Quality Press, 1950), p. 37.
3 Ibid., p. 42.
4 Quoted in Rose, M., *Berlioz Remembered* (Faber and Faber, 2001), pp. 169–70.
5 Macdonald, H. (ed.), *Berlioz. Selected Letters* (Faber and Faber, 1995), p. 249.
6 Ibid., p. 278.
7 Horwood, W., *Adolphe Sax, 1814–1894. Life and Legacy* (Egon Publishers, Baldock, 1983), p. 43.
8 Ehrlich, C., *First Philharmonic. A History of the Royal Philharmonic Society* (Clarendon Press, Oxford, 1995), p. 4.
9 Ganz, op. cit., p. 123.

10 Quoted in Cairns, vol. 2, op. cit., p. 484.
11 Holoman, D. K., *Berlioz* (Faber and Faber, 1989), pp. 432–3.
12 Macdonald (ed.), op. cit., p. 294.
13 Rose, op. cit., p. 183.
14 Wagner, R., *My Life* (Tudor Publishing Company, New York, 1936), p. 204.
15 Chancellor, J., *Wagner* (Weidenfeld and Nicolson, 1978), p. 58.
16 Hueffer, F. (ed.), *Correspondence of Wagner and Liszt* (Greenwood Press, New York, 1969), vol. 2, p. 102.
17 Barzun, J., *Berlioz and the Romantic Century*, (Gollancz, 1951) vol. 2, p. 111.
18 Hueffer, ibid., vol. 2, p. 104.
19 Quoted in Turner, W. J., *Berlioz. The Man and His Work* (Dent, 1939), p. 280.
20 Wagner, C. (ed. Gregor-Dellin, M. and Mack, D.) *Diaries* vol. 2, *1878–1883* (Collins, 1980), p. 255.
21 Wagner, R., *My Life*, op. cit., p. 628.
22 Cairns, op. cit., vol. 2, p. 570.
23 Macdonald, op. cit., p. 331.
24 Ganz, op. cit., p. 190.

11 Frédéric Chopin (pages 149–158)

1 Kennedy, M. (ed.), *The Autobiography of Charles Hallé* (Elek, 1972), pp. 52–3. The 'perfect freedom' mentioned by Hallé is confirmed in an account written by a contemporary keyboard expert, A. J. Hipkins, who heard Chopin perform in London in 1848: 'Chopin never played his own compositions twice alike, but varied each according to the mood of the moment, a mood that charmed by its very waywardness.' Hipkins, E. J., *How Chopin Played. From Contemporary Impressions Collected from the Diaries and Note-books of the Late A. J. Hipkins* (Dent, 1937), p. 7.
2 Hedley, A. (trans. and ed.), *Selected Correspondence of Fryderyk Chopin* (Heinemann, 1962), pp. 148–9.
3 Moscheles, C. (trans. and ed. A. D. Coleridge), *Life of Moscheles* (Hurst and Blackett, 1873), vol. 2, p. 29.
4 Zamoyski, A., *Chopin. A Biography* (Collins, 1979), p. 145.
5 Sand, G. (trans. and ed. Hofstadter, D.), *My Life* (Gollancz, 1979), p. 235.
6 Jordan, A., *George Sand. A Biography* (Constable, 1976), p. 228.
7 Samson, K. M., 'Freyderyk Francizek Chopin', *Grove*, vol. 5, p. 712.
8 Hedley, A., *Chopin* (Dent, 1947), p. 103.
9 Hedley, A., *Selected Correspondence*, op. cit., p. 315.
10 Samson, J., *Chopin* (Oxford University Press, Oxford, 1966), p. 254.
11 Niecks, F., *Frederick Chopin. As a Man and a Musician* (Novello, 1890), vol. 2, p. 278.
12 Siepmann, J., *Chopin. The Reluctant Romantic* (Gollancz, 1995), p. 209.
13 Murdoch, W., *Chopin. His Life* (Murray, 1934), p. 351.
14 Hedley, *Selected Correspondence*, op. cit., p. 319.
15 Ryals, C. de L. *et al.* (eds), *The Collected Letters of Thomas and Jane Welsh Carlyle* (Duke University Press, Durham, NC, 1995), vol. 23, p. 87.
16 Niecks, op. cit., p. 289.
17 Holland, H. and Rockstro, W. S. (eds), *Memoir of Madam Jenny Lind-Goldschmidt* (Murray, 1891), vol. 2, p. 210.
18 Blainey, A., *Fanny and Adelaide. The Lives of the Remarkable Kemble Sisters* (Ivan R. Dee, Chicago, 2001), p. 238.
19 Niecks, op. cit., p. 286.
20 Samson, J., op. cit., p. 255.
21 Hedley, *Selected Correspondence*, op. cit., p. 330.

22 Murdoch, op. cit., p. 363.

23 Sand, for her part, could write as late as December 1848: 'I still love him as my son, even though he was most ungrateful towards his mother.' Kate, C., *George Sand. A Biography* (Hamish Hamilton, 1995), p. 614.

24 Murdoch, op. cit, p. 364.

25 Brookshaw, S., *Concerning Chopin in Manchester* (privately printed, 1951), p. 12.

26 Ibid., p. 21.

27 Niecks, op. cit., p. 293.

28 Hedley, *Selected Correspondence*, op. cit., p. 342.

29 Ibid., p. 347.

30 Ibid., pp. 350–1.

31 Niecks, op. cit., p. 305.

32 Samson, J., op. cit., p. 259.

12 Liszt and the wandering years (pages 159–171)

1 Watson, D., *Liszt* (Dent, 1989), p. 16.

2 Zaluski, I. and P., *Young Liszt* (Peter Owen, 1992), p. 82.

3 Walker, A., 'Liszt', *Grove*, vol. 14, p. 758.

4 Salaman, C., 'Pianists of the Past', *Blackwood's Edinburgh Magazine*, vol. 152, September 1901, p. 314.

5 Walker, A., *Franz Liszt. The Virtuoso Years, 1811–1847* (Faber and Faber, 1983), vol. 1, p. 121.

6 Beckett, W., *Liszt* (Dent, 1956), p. 11.

7 Williams, A. (ed.), *Franz Liszt. Selected Letters* (Clarendon Press, Oxford, 1998), p. 40.

8 Sitwell, S., *Liszt* (Dover Publications, New York, 1967), p. 97.

9 Williams, op. cit., p. 139.

10 Salaman, op. cit., p. 314.

11 Allsobrook, D. I., *Liszt: My Travelling Circus Life* (Macmillan, 1991), pp. 93–4.

12 Andrews, C. B., and Orr-Ewing, J. A. (eds), *Victorian Swansdown. Extracts from the Early Diaries of John Orlando Parry, the Victorian Entertainer* (Murray, 1933), p. xvii.

13 Williams, op. cit., p. 145.

14 Williams, A., *Portrait of Liszt. By Himself and His Contemporaries* (Clarendon Press, Oxford, 1990), p. 138.

15 Parry, J. O., 'Diaries, Liszt's British Tours of 1840 and 1841', *The Liszt Society Journal*, vol. 6, Spring 1981, p. 6. Ernest Newman pointed out that: 'The quasi-saintly Liszt of the later legend ... has no resemblance whatever to the real Liszt of the end of the 'thirties and the early 'forties. He was in a constantly hectic condition, the result partly of overstrained nerves, partly of excessive indulgence and stimulants and narcotics, partly of the self-disgust that would sometimes take possession of him as he contrasted what he was with what he longed to be.' Newman, E., *The Man Liszt* (Cassell, 1934), p. 87.

16 *The Liszt Society Journal*, vol. 6, Spring, 1981, p. 13.

17 *The Liszt Society Journal*, vol. 7, Summer 1982, p. 17.

18 Ibid., p. 26.

19 Watson, op. cit., p. 59. Writing to a friend in Vienna, Liszt stated: 'I have completed my tour of the three kingdoms (by which I lose, by the way, £1000 sterling net, on £1500, which my engagement brought me).' La Mara (ed.), *Letters of Franz Liszt. From Paris to Rome* (Charles Scribener's Sons, New York, 1894), vol. 1, p. 53.

20 Williams (ed.), op. cit., p. 157.

21 Allsobrook, op. cit., p. 170–8.
22 Williams (ed.), op. cit., p. 161.
23 Newton, D. (ed.), 'From the Musical World', *The Liszt Society Journal*, vol. 9, 1984, p. 18.
24 Williams (ed.), op. cit., p. 161.
25 In April 1865 Liszt had received the tonsure in St Peter's but took no vows of chastity. Perényi, E., *Liszt* (Weidenfeld and Nicolson, 1974), p. 414.
26 Mackenzie, A. C., *A Musician's Narrative* (Cassell, 1927), p. 151.
27 Walker, A., *Franz Liszt. The Final Years, 1861–1886* (Faber and Faber, 1997), vol. 3, p. 486.
28 Williams (ed.), op. cit., p. 937.
29 Sitwell, op. cit., p. 322.
30 Williams (ed.), op. cit., p. 938.
31 Irving, L., *Henry Irving. The Actor and his World* (Faber and Faber, 1901), p. 47.
32 Stoker was fascinated with Liszt's features and borrowed him for his description of Count Dracula. Belford, B., *Bram Stoker. A Biography of the Author of Dracula* (Weidenfeld and Nicolson, 1996), p. 184.
33 Beckett, op. cit., p. 78.
34 Mackenzie, op. cit., p. 141.

13 Antonin Dvořák (pages 172–181)

1 *Pall Mall Gazette*, 13 October 1886, p. 4.
2 Hughes, G., *Dvořák. His Life and Music* (Cassell, 1967). p. 109.
3 Sourek, O., trans. Samsour, R. F., *Antonin Dvořák. Letters and Reminiscences* (Artia, Prague, 1954), p. 74.
4 Hadow, W. H., 'Antonin Dvořák', *Studies in Modern Music*, second series (Sealey, Service, 1923), p. 205.
5 Sourek, op. cit., p. 75.
6 Hoffmeister, K. (trans. and ed. Newmarch, R.), *Antonin Dvořák* (John Lane, The Bodley Head, 1928), p. 40.
7 Hughes, op. cit., p. 111.
8 Boden, A., *Gloucester, Hereford and Worcester. Three Choirs. A History of the Festival* (Alan Sutton, 1992), p. 97.
9 Sourek, op. cit., p. 85.
10 *Musical Times*, 1 Oct 1884, p. 584.
11 Sourek, op. cit., p. 86.
12 Northrop Moore, J., *Edward Elgar. A Creative Life* (Oxford University Press, Oxford, 1964), p. 104.
13 Beveridge, D. (ed.), *Rethinking Dvořák. Views from Five Countries* (Clarendon Press, Oxford, 1996), p. 230.
14 Reed, W. H., *Elgar as I Knew Him* (Gollancz, 1936), p. 59.
15 Sourek, op. cit., p. 87.
16 Hughes, op. cit, p. 116.
17 Sourek, op. cit., p. 140–1.
18 Fischl, V. (ed.), *Antonin Dvořák. His Achievement* (Lindsay Drummond, 1943), p. 37.
19 Elliott, A., *The Music Makers. A Brief History of the Birmingham Triennial Musical Festivals, 1784–1912* (Birmingham Library Services, Birmingham, 2000), p. 17.
20 Sourek, op. cit., p. 95.
21 Ibid., p. 95.
22 Ibid., pp. 95–6.

23 Fischl, op. cit., p. 40.
24 Dvořák, O., *Antonin Dvořák, My Father* (Czech Historical Research Center Inc, Spillville, Iowa, 1993), p. 143.
25 *Pall Mall Gazette*, 13 October 1886, p. 4.
26 Norris, G., *Stanford, The Cambridge Jubilee and Tchaikovsky* (David and Charles, 1980), p. 62.
27 Robertson, A., *Dvořák* (Dent, 1945), p. 53.
28 Fifield, C., *True Artist and Friend. A Biography of Hans Richter* (Clarendon Press, Oxford, 1993), p. 237.
29 Brown, D., *Tchaikovsky. A Biographical and Critical Study* (Gollancz, 1991), vol. 4, pp. 171–2.
30 Robertson, A., 'Dvořák', in Hill, R. (ed.), *The Symphony* (Penguin, Harmondsworth, 1949), p. 316.
31 Hughes, op. cit., p. 140.
32 Clapham, J., *Dvořák* (David and Charles, 1979), pp. 100–2.
33 Clapham, J., *Antonin Dvořák. Musician and Craftsman* (Faber and Faber, 1966), p. 14.
34 Stanford, C. V., *Pages From an Unwritten Dairy* (Edward Arnold, 1914), p. 270.
35 Dibble, J., *Charles Villiers Stanford. Man and Musician* (Oxford University Press, Oxford, 2002), p. 230.
36 Norris, op. cit., p. 64.
37 Sourek, op. cit., p. 142.
38 De Lara, A., *Finale* (Burke, 1955), p. 63.
39 Shaw, G. B., *Music in London, 1890–94* (Constable, 1932), vol. 1, p. 260.
40 Clapham, J., 'Dvořák and the Philharmonic Society', *Music and Letters*, vol. 39, no. 2, 1958, p. 130.
41 Vickers, G., *Classical Music Landmarks of London* (Omnibus Press, 2001), p. 31.
42 Smaczny, J., *Dvořák: Cello Concerto* (Cambridge University Press, Cambridge, 1999), p. 91.
43 Fischl, op. cit., p. 61.
44 Clapham, 'Dvořák and the Philharmonic Society', op. cit., p. 133.

14 'This quite horrible city' (pages 182–190)

1 Tchaikovsky, M. (ed. Newmarch, R.), *The Life and Letters of Peter Ilich Tchaikovsky* (John Lane, 1896), p. 98.
2 Quoted in Brown, D., *Tchaikovsky. A Biographical and Critical Study* (Gollancz, 1978), vol. 1, pp. 55–6.
3 Tchaikovsky, P. I., trans. von Meck, G., *Letters to his Family. An Autobiography* (Dobson, 1981), p. 397.
4 Holden, A., *Tchaikovsky* (Bantam Press, 1995), p. 269.
5 Norris, G., *Stanford, Cambridge Jubilee and Tchaikovsky* (David and Charles, 1980), p. 315.
6 Von Meck, op. cit., p. 420.
7 Tchaikovsky, P. I., trans. Lakond, W., *The Diaries of Tchaikovksy* (Greenwood Press, Westport, CT, 1973), p. 270.
8 Smyth, E., *Impressions That Remained. Memoirs* (Longmans, Green, 1919), vol. 2, pp. 266–7.
9 Brown, op. cit., vol. 4, p. 473.
10 Poznansky, A., *Tchaikovsky. The Quest for the Inner Man* (Schirmer Books, New York, 1991), p. 559.
11 Von Meck., op. cit., p. 541.

12 Ibid., p. 542.
13 Quoted in Holden, op. cit., p. 337.
14 Henschel, H., *When Soft Voices Die. A Musical Biography* (Methuen, 1949), p. 17.
15 Henschel, Sir G., *Musings and Memories of a Musician* (Macmillan, 1918), p. 75.
16 Berger, F., *Reminiscences, Impressions and Anecdotes* (Sampson Low, Marston, 1913), p. 87.
17 Mackenzie, Sir A., *A Musician's Narrative* (Cassell, 1927), p. 186.
18 Quoted in Norris, op. cit., p. 592.
19 *Musical Times*, 1 July 1893, p. 408.
20 Norris, op. cit., p. 394.
21 Damrosch, W. J., *My Musical Life* (Allen and Unwin, 1924), pp. 144–5.
22 Von Meck, op. cit., pp. 544–5.
23 Norris, op. cit., p. 444.
24 Tchaikovsky, M., op. cit., pp. 712–13.
25 Orlova, A., trans. Davison, R. M., *Tchaikovsky. A Self Portrait* (Oxford University Press, Oxford, 1990), p. 403.
26 Berger, F., *97* (Elkin Mathews and Marrot, 1931), p. 162.
27 Ibid., p. 162.

15 Richard Strauss (pages 191–199)

1 Ehrlich, C., *The First Philharmonic. A History of the Royal Philharmonic Society* (Clarendon Press, Oxford, 1995), pp. 194–5.
2 Schuh, W., trans. Whittall, M., *Richard Strauss: A Chronicle of the Early Years, 1864–1898* (Cambridge University Press, Cambridge, 1982), p. 473.
3 Jefferson, A., *The Life of Richard Strauss* (David and Charles, 1973), p. 92.
4 Northrop Moore, J., *Edward Elgar. Letters of a Lifetime* (Clarendon Press, Oxford, 1990), p. 125.
5 Wood, Sir H., *My Life of Music* (Gollancz, 1938), p. 217.
6 Del Mar, N., *Richard Strauss. A Critical Commentary on His Life and Works* (Barrie and Jenkins, 1978), vol. 1, p. 182.
7 Beecham, Sir T., *A Mingled Chime. Leaves from an Autobiography* (Hutchinson, 1944), pp. 89–90.
8 Ibid., p. 90.
9 Bax, A., *Farewell, My Youth* (Longman, Green, 1943), p. 33.
10 Beecham, op. cit., pp. 103–4.
11 Ibid., p. 105.
12 Hammelmann, H. and Osers, E., trans., *The Correspondence of Richard Strauss and Hugo von Hofmannsthal* (Collins, 1961), p. 200.
13 *Musical Times*, 1 July 1914, p. 471.
14 Kennedy, M., *Richard Strauss: Man, Musician, Enigma* (Cambridge University Press, Cambridge, 1999), p. 404.
15 Jacobson, A., *Henry J. Wood, Maker of the Proms* (Methuen, 1994), p. 148.
16 Boyden, M., *Richard Strauss* (Weidenfeld, 1999), p. 233.
17 Northrop Moore, J., *Elgar and his Publishers. Letters of a Creative Life* (Clarendon Press, Oxford, 1987), vol. 1, p. 821.
18 *The Times*, 13 April 1926, p. 12.
19 *Musical Times*, 1 December 1936, p. 1081.
20 Roth, E., *The Business of Music. Reflections of a Music Publisher* (Cassell, 1969), p. 182.
21 Blackwood, A., *Sir Thomas Beecham. The Man and the Music* (Ebury Press, 1994), p. 191.

22 Roth, op. cit., p. 193.
23 Del Mar, op. cit., vol. 1, p. xi.
24 Boyden, op. cit., p. 363.
25 Del Mar, op. cit., vol. 1, p. xii.
26 Wilhelm, K. (ed. Whittall, M.), *Richard Strauss. An Intimate Portrait* (Thames and Hudson, 1989), p. 280.
27 Roth, op. cit., p. 195.

16 Bartók and the BBC (pages 200–205)

1 Demeny, J., trans. West, E., and Mason, C., *Béla Bartók Letters* (Faber and Faber, 1971), p. 37.
2 Wood, H. J., *My Life of Music* (Gollancz, 1938), p. 380.
3 Gillies, M., 'The Orchestral Suites', in Gillies, M. (ed.), *Bartók Companion* (Faber and Faber, 1993), p. 462.
4 For instance, Heseltine had lectured at the Abbey Theatre, Dublin, on 30 May to a large audience and discussed some of Bartók's piano pieces. Writing to Frederick Delius in March 1921, Heseltine commented: 'Bartók is the most loveable personality I have ever met.' Bartók stayed at Heseltine's house in Wales during his 1922 tour. Gray, C., *Peter Warlock. A Memoir of Peter Heseltine* (Cape, 1934), p. 187. For Bartók's influence on Heseltine's musical style, see Collins, B., *Peter Warlock: The Composer* (Scolar Press, Aldershot, Hampshire, 1996), pp. 193–8.
5 Stevens, H., *The Life and Music of Béla Bartók* (Cambridge University Press, New York, 1953), p. 62. In an interview which Bartók later gave to an Hungarian newspaper, he remarked: 'At the end of my violin sonata I was surprised, and almost confused, by the wave of applause rising up to the platform from an English audience which is generally described as cold and reserved.' Quoted in Ujfalussy, J., *Béla Bartók* (Corvina Press, Budapest, 1971), p. 171.
6 Quoted in Milne, H., *Bartók: His Life and Times* (Midas Books, Tunbridge Wells, Kent, 1982), p. 67.
7 Bartók received a fee of £15 for the recital, out of which he paid £5 for a return ticket to London. Moreux, S., *Béla Bartók* (Harvill Press, 1953), p. 139.
8 Parrott, I., 'Warlock in Wales', *Musical Times*, vol. 105, 1964, p. 741. Zoltán Kodály, a close friend of Bartók, writing in 1921, stated that 'people objected to its (Bartók's music) lack of melody, its superabundance of dissonances, its lack of construction, its disorder and incoherence which made it "incomprehensible"'. Quoted in Moreux, *Béla Bartók*, p. 2.
9 *Musical News and Herald*, 19 March 1923, p. 496.
10 Macleod, J., *The Sisters d'Aranyi* (Allen and Unwin, 1969), p. 138.
11 Samfai, L., 'Bartók', *Grove*, vol. 2, p. 212.
12 Króo, G., *A Guide to Bartók* (Corvina Press, Budapest, 1974), p. 133.
13 Gillies, M., *Bartók in Britain. A Guided Tour* (Clarendon Press Oxford, 1989), p. 75.
14 *Radio Times*, 14 February 1930, p. 406.
15 Ibid., 3 January 1930, p. 224.
16 Ibid., 4 November 1930, p. 447. Bartók wrote to his mother in December 1930 in a self-pitying tone: 'The success in London was, it is true, rather big, but just a little *belated* – by some twenty four years.' Quoted in Szigeti, J., *With Strings Attached* (Cassell, 1949), p. 309.
17 From the early 1920s, Bartók had turned to the style of Bach's Italian predecessors and contemporaries for a polyphonic dimension to his compositions. See Suchoff, B., 'The Impact of Italian Baroque music on Bartók's Music',

in Rankl, G. (ed.), *Bartók and Kodály Revisited*, Indiana University Studies on Hungary 2 (Academia Kiadö, Budapest, 1987), p. 196.

18 Kenyon, N., *The BBC Symphony Orchestra* (British Broadcasting Corporation, 1981), p. 87.

19 Suchoff, B. (ed.), *Béla Bartók Essays* (Faber and Faber, 1976), pp. 295–6.

20 Quoted in Gillies, M. (ed.), *Bartók Remembered* (Faber and Faber, 1990), p. 132.

17 The émigré composers (pages 206–214)

1 Bentwich, N., *Refugees from Germany* (Allen and Unwin, 1936), p. 175.

2 Wasserstein, B., *Britain and the Jews of Europe, 1939–1945* (Institute for Jewish Policy Research/Leicester University Press, 2nd edn, 1999), p. 10.

3 Berghahn, M., *German-Jewish Refugees in England. The Ambiguities of Assimilation* (Macmillan, 1984), p. 103.

4 'Vilem Tausky', *The Times*, 18 March 2004.

5 Snowman, D., *The Hitler Emigrés. The Cultural Impact on Britain of Refugees from Nazism* (Chatto and Windus, 2002), pp. 210–1.

6 Foreman, L., 'Karl Rankl', *Continental Britons. The Émigré Composers* (Jewish Music Institute/SOAS, 2002), p. 7.

7 For a first-hand account of life at Warth Mill, Bury, see Mayer, W., 'Internment', in Cesarani, D., and Kushner, T. (eds), *The Internment of Aliens in Twentieth Century Britain* (Cass, 1993), pp. 227–8.

8 Kochan, M., *Britain's Internees in the Second World War* (Macmillan, 1983), p. 133.

9 Seyfert, M., 'His Majesty's Most Loyal Internees', in Hirschfield, G. (ed.), *Exile in Great Britain. Refugees from Hitler's Germany* (Berg, 1984), p. 181.

10 Ambrose, T., *Hitler's Loss. What Britain and America Gained from Europe's Cultural Exiles* (Peter Owen, 2001), p. 127.

11 Ward, P., 'Egon Wellesz: An Opera Composer in 1920s Vienna', *Tempo*, no. 219, 2000, p. 28.

12 Benser, C.C., 'Egon Wellesz', *Grove*, vol. 27, p. 270.

13 Vaughan Williams was Chairman of the Home Office Committee for the Release of Alien Musicians. Vaughan Williams, U., *R.V.W. A Biography of Ralph Vaughan Williams* (Oxford University Press, Oxford, 1964), p. 236.

14 Stevens, L., *Composers of Classical Music of Jewish Descent* (Vallentine Mitchell, 2003), p. 359.

15 Silverman, J., 'Some thoughts on Matyas Seiber', *Tempo*, no. 143, 1982, p. 12.

16 Graubart, M., 'Matyas Seiber: 1905–1960', *The Composer*, vol. 86, 1985, p. 4.

17 Wood, H., and Cooke, M., 'Matyas Seiber', *Grove*, vol. 22, p. 46.

18 For a good assessment of Seiber's output, see Keller, H., 'Matyas Seiber', *Musical Times*, vol. 96, 1955, pp. 580–4.

19 Hoffnung, A., *Gerard Hoffnung* (Garden Press, 1988), pp. 106, 150.

20 Reizenstein wrote a laudatory article on Hindemith's music in *The Listener*, 2 March 1967, p. 304.

21 Snowman, op. cit., p. 109.

22 A description of the Hendon Centre evening class is given by one of the students, in Parfrey, R., 'Night-school Composer', *The Composer*, vol. 31, 1969, pp. 17–19.

23 Hoffnung, op. cit., p. 156.

24 Allison, J., 'Goldschmidt – A Life in Music', *Opera*, vol. 45, 1994, p. 1022.

25 Struck, M., 'Berthold Goldschmidt', *Grove*, vol. 10, p. 105.

26 Drew, D., 'Incognito. Berthold Goldschmidt', *Tempo*, no. 200, 1997, p. 11.

27 Henderson, R. L., 'English by Adoption', *The Listener*, 26 January 1961, p. 201.

28 Garnham, A. M., *Hans Keller and the BBC. The Moral Conscience of British Broadcasting* (Ashgate, 2003), p. 104.
29 See for instance the two concerts devoted to emigrant composers given at the Wigmore Hall, 9 and 17 June, 2002, and the increasing number of broadcasts on Radio 3.

Epilogue (pages 215–220)

1 Godbolt, J., *A History of Jazz in Britain* (Quartet Books, 1984), p. 9.
2 Ibid., p. 17.
3 Ibid., p. 85.
4 Ibid., p. 112.
5 Tucker, M. (ed.), *The Duke Ellington Reader* (Oxford University Press, New York, 1993), pp. 80–1.
6 Jablonski, E., *Gershwin* (Simon and Schuster, 1988), p. 54.
7 Payne, R., *Gershwin* (Pyramid Books, New York, 1960), p. 88.

Bibliography

The place of publication is London unless otherwise stated.

Albrecht, T. (ed.), *Letters to Beethoven and other Correspondence* (University of Nebraska Press, Lincoln, 1996), vol. 2.

Allison, J., 'Goldschmidt – A Life in Music', *Opera*, vol. 45, 1994.

Allsobrook, D. I., *Liszt: My Travelling Circus Life* (Macmillan, 1991).

Ambrose, T., *Hitler's Loss. What Britain and America Gained from Europe's Cultural Exiles* (Peter Owen, 2001).

Anderson, E. (ed.), trans. Oldman, C. B., *The Letters of Mozart and His Family* (Macmillan, 1938), vol. 1.

Andrews, C. B., and Orr-Ewing, J. A. (eds), *Victorian Swansdown. Extracts from the Early Diaries of John Orlando Parry, the Victorian Entertainer* (Murray, 1933).

Anon., *Letters from Albion to a Friend on the Continent, Written in the Years 1810, 1811, 1812 and 1813* (Gale, Curtis and Kenner, 1814), vol. 1.

Anon., 'Weber in London', *Musical Times*, 1 July 1893.

Ashbee, A., Lasocki, D., Holman, P., and Kisby, F., *A Biographical Dictionary of English Court Musicians 1485–1714* (Ashgate, Aldershot, 1998), 2 vols.

Bailey, K., *The Life of Webern* (Cambridge University Press, Cambridge, 1998).

Ballam, H. and Lewis, R. (eds), *The Visitors' Book. England and the English, As Others Have Seen Them* (Max Parrish, 1950).

Barzun, J., *Berlioz and the Romantic Century*, vol. 2 (Gollancz, 1951).

Bax, A., *Farewell, My Youth* (Longman, Green, 1943).

Beckett, W., *Liszt* (Dent, 1956).

Beecham, Sir T., *A Mingled Chime. Leaves from an Autobiography* (Hutchinson, 1944).

Belford, B., *Bram Stoker. A Biography of the Author of Dracula* (Weidenfeld and Nicolson, 1996).

Benedict, J., *Weber* (Sampson Low, Marston, Searle and Rivington, 1881).

Bentwich, N., *Refugees from Germany* (Allen and Unwin, 1936).

Berger, F., *97* (Elkin Mathews and Marrot, 1931).

Berger, F., *Reminiscences, Impressions and Anecdotes* (Sampson Low, Marston, 1913).

Berghahn, M., *German-Jewish Refugees in England. The Ambiguities of Assimilation* (Macmillan, 1984).

Bernstein, J. A., 'Philip van Wilder and the Netherlandish Chanson in England', *Musica Disciplina*, vol. 33, 1979.

Bernstein J. A. (ed.), *Masters and Monuments of the Renaissance*, vol. 4 (Broude Trust, New York, 1991).

Bertensson, F. (ed.), trans. Halverson, W. *et al.*, *Edvard Grieg. Letters to Friends and Colleagues* (Peer Gynt Press, Columbus, Ohio, 2000).

Bertensson, Leyda, J., *Sergei Rachmaninoff. A Lifetime in Music* (New York University Press, New York, 1956).

Beveridge, D. (ed.), *Rethinking Dvořák. Views from Five Countries* (Clarendon Press, Oxford, 1996).

Blackwood, A., *Sir Thomas Beecham. The Man and the Music* (Ebury Press, 1994).

Blainey A., *Fanny and Adelaide. The Lives of the Remarkable Kemble Sisters* (Ivan R. Dee, Chicago, 2001).

Blunt, W., *On Wings of Song. Biography of Felix Mendelssohn* (Hamish Hamilton, 1974).

Boden, A., *Gloucester, Hereford and Worcester. Three Choirs. A History of the Festival* (Alan Sutton, 1992).

Boydell, B., *A Dublin Musical Calendar, 1700–1760* (Irish Academic Press, Dublin, 1988).

Boyden, M., *Richard Strauss* (Weidenfeld, 1999).

Brookshaw, S., *Concerning Chopin in Manchester* (privately printed, 1951).

Brown, C., *Louis Spohr. A Critical Biography* (Cambridge University Press, Cambridge, 1984).

Brown, D., *Tchaikovsky. A Biographical and Critical Study* (Gollancz, 1978–91), 4 vols.

Bulman, J., *Jenny Lind. A Biography* (James Barrie, 1956).

Burden M., *Purcell Remembered* (Faber and Faber, 1995).

Burden, M. (ed.), *The Purcell Companion* (Faber and Faber, 1995).

Burrows, D., *Handel* (Oxford University Press, Oxford, 1994).

Butler, E. M. (ed.), trans. Austin, M., *A Regency Tour. The English Tour of Prince Pückler-Muskau Desori, Described in his Letters, 1826–1828* (Collins, 1957).

Cairns, D., *Berlioz. vol. 2, Servitude and Greatness, 1832–1869* (Allen Lane, The Penguin Press, 1999).

Careri, E., *Francesco Geminiani* (Clarendon Press, Oxford, 1993).

Carner, M., *Puccini, A Critical Biography* (Duckworth, 3rd edn, 1992).

Carus, C. G., trans. Davison, S. C., *The King of Saxony's Journey through England and Scotland in the Year 1844* (Chapman and Hall, 1846).

Chancellor, J., *Wagner* (Weidenfeld and Nicolson, 1978).

Charteris, R., 'New Information about the Life of Alfonso Ferrabosco the Elder (1543–1588)', *Royal Musical Association Research Chronicle*, vol. 17, (1981).

Clapham, J., 'Dvořák and the Philharmonic Society', *Music and Letters*, vol. 39, no. 2, 1958.

Clapham, J., *Antonin Dvořák. Musician and Craftsman* (Faber and Faber, 1966).

Clapham, J., *Dvořák* (David and Charles, 1979).

Collins, B., *Peter Warlock: The Composer* (Scolar Press, Aldershot, Hampshire, 1996).

Cooper, M., *Gluck* (Chatto and Windus, 1935).

Cox, H. B. and Cox, C. L. E., *Leaves from the Journals of Sir George Smart* (Longmans, Green, 1907).

Cox, J. E., *Musical Recollections of the Last Half-Century* (Tinsley Brothers, 1872), vol. 1.

Damrosch, W. J., *My Musical Life* (Allen and Unwin, 1924).

Danchin, P. 'The Foundation of the Royal Academy of Music in 1674 and Pierre Perrin's *Ariane*', *Theatre Survey*, vol. 25, 1984.

De Beer, E. S. (ed.), *The Diary of John Evelyn* (Oxford University Press, Oxford, 1959).

De Lara, A., *Finale* (Burke, 1955).

Del Mar, N., *Richard Strauss. A Critical Commentary on His Life and Works* (Barrie and Jenkins, 1978), vol. 1.

Demeny, J., trans. West, E., and Mason, C., *Béla Bartók Letters* (Faber and Faber, 1971).

Derr, E., 'Some Thoughts on the Design of Mozart's Operas', in Zaslaw, N. (ed.), *Mozart's Piano Concertos: Text, Context and Interpretation* (University of Michigan Press, Ann Arbor, 1990).

Deutsch, O., *Mozart. A Documentary Biography* (A. and C. Black, 1965).

Deutsch, O., *Handel. A Documentary Biography* (Da Capo Press, New York, 1974, reprint of 1955 edn).

Devrient, E., trans. Macfarne, N., *My Recollections of Felix Mendelssohn-Bartholdy* (Richard Bentley, 1869), p. 6.

Dibble, J., *Charles Villiers Stanford. Man and Musician* (Oxford University Press, Oxford, 2002).

Doctor, J., *The BBC and Ultra-Modern Music 1922–1936* (Cambridge University Press, Cambridge, 1999).

Drew, D., 'Incognito. Berthold Goldschmidt', *Tempo*, no. 200, 1997.

Dvořák, O., *Antonin Dvořák, My Father* (Czech Historical Research Center Inc, Spillville, Iowa, 1993).

Ehrlich, C., *The Piano. A Social History* (Oxford University Press, Oxford, 1990).

Ehrlich, C., *The First Philharmonic. A History of the Royal Philharmonic Society* (Clarendon Press, Oxford, 1995).

Elliott, A., *The Music Makers. A Brief History of the Birmingham Triennial Musical Festivals, 1784–1912* (Birmingham Library Services, Birmingham, 2000).

Fenlon, I. and Keyte, H., 'Memorialls of Great Skill: A Tale of Five Cities', *Early Music*, vol. 8, 1980.

Fifield, C., *True Artist and Friend. A Biography of Hans Richter* (Clarendon Press, Oxford, 1993).

Fischl, V. (ed.), *Antonin Dvořák. His Achievement* (Lindsay Drummond, 1943).

Flower, D. (ed.), *Voltaire's England* (Folio Society, 1950).

Flower, N., *George Frideric Handel. His Personality and His Times* (Cassell, 3rd edn, 1943).

Foreman, L., 'Karl Rankl', *Continental Britons. The Emigré Composers* (Jewish Music Institute/SOAS, 2002).

Galpin, F. W., *Old English Instruments of Music* (Methuen, 4th edn, 1965).

Ganz, A. W., *Berlioz in London* (Quality Press, 1950).

Garnham, A. M., *Hans Keller and the BBC. The Moral Conscience of British Broadcasting* (Ashgate, Aldershot, 2003).

Gärtner, H., *John Christian Bach. Mozart's Friend and Mentor* (Amadeus Press, Portland, Oregon, 1989).

Geiringer, K. and I., *Haydn. A Creative Life in Music* (University of California Press, Berkeley, 3rd rev. and enl. edn, 1982).

Gibson, E., 'The Royal Academy of Music and its Directors', in Sadie, S. and Gillies, M., *Bartók in Britain. A Guided Tour* (Clarendon Press Oxford, 1989).

Gillies, M. (ed.), *Bartók Remembered* (Faber and Faber, 1990).

Gillies, M., 'The Orchestral Suites', in Gillies, M. (ed.), *Bartók Companion* (Faber and Faber, 1993).

Girdlestone, C. M., *Mozart's Piano Concertos* (Cassell, 1948).

Giustinian, S., *Four Years at the Court of Henry VIII*, trans Brown, R. (Smith, Elder, 1854), vol. 1.

Godbolt, J., *A History of Jazz in Britain* (Quartet Books, 1984).

Gotch, R. B. (ed.), *Mendelssohn and his Friends in Kensington. Letters from Fanny and Sophy Horsley written 1833–6* (Oxford University Press, Oxford, 1934).

Gotwals, V. (ed.), *Joseph Haydn Eighteenth-century Gentleman and Genius* (Madison, University of Wisconsin Press, 1963).

Grange, H. L. de la, *Mahler* (Gollancz, 1974), vol. 1.

Graubart, M., 'Matyas Seiber: 1905–1960', *The Composer*, vol. 86, 1985.

Gray, C., *Peter Warlock. A Memoir of Peter Heseltine* (Cape, 1934).

Gutman, R. W., *Mozart. A Cultural Biography* (Secker and Warburg, 1999).

Hadow, W. H., 'Antonin Dvořák', *Studies in Modern Music*, 2nd Series, (Sealey, Service, 1923).

Halliwell, R., *The Mozart Family. Four Lives in a Social Context* (Clarendon Press, Oxford, 1998).

Hammelmann, H. and Osers, E. trans., *The Correspondence of Richard Strauss and Hugo von Hofmannsthal* (Collins, 1961).

Harley, J., *Music in Purcell's London* (Dennis Dobson, 1968).

Hedley, A., *Chopin* (Dent, 1947).

Hedley, A. (trans. and ed.), *Selected Correspondence of Fryderyk Chopin* (Heinemann, 1962).

Henderson, R. L., 'English by Adoption', *The Listener*, 26 January 1961.

Henschel, Sir G., *Musings and Memories of a Musician* (Macmillan, 1918).

Henschel, H., *When Soft Voices Die. A Musical Biography* (Methuen, 1949).

Hensel, S., trans. Klingemann, C., *The Mendelssohn Family 1729–1847 from Letters and Journals*, vol. 1 (Sampson, Low, Marston, Searle and Rivington, 1881).

Hicks, A. (eds), *Handel's Tercentenary Collection* (Macmillan, 1987).

Hill, J. W., *The Life and Works of Francesco Maria Veracini* (Ann Arbor, UMI Research Press, 1979).

Hiller, F. M., trans. von Glehn, M. E., *Mendelssohn. Letters and Recollections* (Macmillan 1874).

Hipkins, E. J., *How Chopin Played. From contemporary Impressions Collected from the Diaries and Note-books of the Late A. J. Hipkins* (Dent, 1937).

Hoffmeister, K. (trans. and ed. Newmarch, R.), *Antonin Dvořák* (John Lane, The Bodley Head, 1928).

Hoffnung, A., *Gerard Hoffnung* (Garden Press, 1988).

Holden, A., *Tchaikovsky* (Bantam Press, 1995).

Holland, H. and Rockstro, W. S. (eds), *Memoir of Madam Jenny Lind-Goldschmidt* (Murray, 1891), vol. 2.

Holman, P., *Four and Twenty Fiddlers* (Clarendon Press, Oxford, 1993).

Holoman, D. K., *Berlioz* (Faber and Faber, 1989).

Horwood, W., *Adolphe Sax, 1814–1894. Life and Legacy* (Egon Publishers, Baldock, 1983).

Howard, P., *Gluck. An Eighteenth-Century Portrait in Letters and Documents* (Clarendon Press, Oxford, 1995).

Howie, C., 'Bruckner – The Travelling Virtuoso', in Howie, C., Hawkshaw, P. and Jackson, T. (eds), *Perspectives on Anton Bruckner* (Ashgate, Aldershot, 2001).

Hueffer, F. (ed.), *Correspondence of Wagner and Liszt* (Greenwood Press, New York, 1969), vol. 2.

Hughes, G., *Dvořák. His Life and Music* (Cassell, 1967).

Hull, A. E., *A Great Russian Tone-Poet, Scriabin* (Kegan Paul, Trench, Trubner, 1916).

Hunter, D., 'Patronizing Handel, Inventing Audiences: The Intersections of Class, Money, Music and History', *Early Music*, vol. 28, 2000.

Hyatt King, A., *A Mozart Legacy. Aspects of the British Library Collection* (British Library, 1984).

Irving, L., *Henry Irving. The Actor and His World* (Faber and Faber, 1901).

Jablonski, E., *Gershwin* (Simon and Schuster, 1988).

Jacob, H. E., trans. Winston, R. and C., *Felix Mendelssohn and His Times* (Barrie and Rockliff, 1962).

Jacobson, A., *Henry J. Wood, Maker of the Proms* (Methuen, 1994).

Jefferson, A., *The Life of Richard Strauss* (David and Charles, 1973).

Jenkins, J., *Mozart and the English Connection* (Cygnus Arts, 1998).

Jones, J. B., *Gabriel Fauré. A Life in Letters* (Batsford, 1988).

Jordan, A., *George Sand. A Biography* (Constable, 1976).

Jourdain, P., 'The Hidden Pathways of Assimilation: Mendelssohn's first visit to London', in Bashford, C. and Langley, L. (eds), *Music and British Culture, 1785–1914* (Oxford University Press, Oxford, 2000).

Kate, C., *George Sand. A Biography* (Hamish Hamilton, 1995).

Keates, J., *Handel. The Man and His Music* (Gollancz, 1985).

Keith, R., '"La Guitare Royale". A Study of the Career and Compositions of Francesco Corbetta', *Recherches sur la Musique Française Classique*, vol. 6, 1966.

Keller, H., 'Matyas Seiber', *Musical Times*, vol. 96, 1955.

Kemble, F. A., *Record of a Girlhood* (Richard Bentley, 1878), vol. 1.

Kendall, A., *The Tender Tyrant. Nadia Boulanger, A Life Devoted to Music* (Macdonald and Jane's, 1976).

Kendall, A., *Paganini. A Biography* (Chapell, 1982).

Kendall, A., *Gioacchino Rossini: The Reluctant Hero* (Gollancz, 1992).

Kennedy, M. (ed.), *The Autobiography of Charles Hallé* (Elek, 1972).

Kennedy, M., *Richard Strauss: Man, Musician, Enigma* (Cambridge University Press, Cambridge, 1999).

Kenyon, N., *The BBC Symphony Orchestra* (British Broadcasting Corporation, 1981).

Kerman, J., 'An Italian Musician in Elizabethan England', *Write All These Down: Essays on Music* (Berkeley, 1994).

Keyes, I., *Mozart: His Music in His Life* (Granada, 1980).

Kochan, M., *Britain's Internees in the Second World War* (Macmillan, 1983).

Króo, G., *A Guide to Bartók* (Corvina Press, Budapest, 1974).

Küster, K., *Mozart. A Musical Biography* (Clarendon Press, Oxford, 1996).

La Mara (ed.), *Letters of Franz Liszt. From Paris to Rome* (Charles Scribener's Sons, New York, 1894), vol. 1.

Lang, P.H., *George Frideric Handel* (Faber and Faber, 1966).

Lasocki, D. with Prior, R., *The Bassanos: Venetian Musicians and Instrument Makers in England, 1531–1665* (Scolar Press, Aldershot, 1995).

Lesure, F. and Nichols, R. (eds), *Debussy Letters* (Faber and Faber, 1987).

Letts, M., *As the Foreigner Saw Us* (Methuen, 1935).

Levy, D. B., *Beethoven. The Ninth Symphony* (Yale University Press, New Haven, CT, 2003).

Lindgren, L., 'Handel's London – Italian Musicians and Librettists', in Burrows, D. (ed.), *The Cambridge Companion to Handel* (Cambridge University Press, Cambridge, 1997).

Mabbett, M., 'Italian Musicians in Restoration England, 1660–90', *Music and Letters*, vol. 67, 1986.

Macdonald, H. (ed.), *Berlioz. Selected Letters* (Faber and Faber, 1995).

Mackenzie, Sir A., *A Musician's Narrative* (Cassell, 1927).

Macleod, J., *The Sisters d'Aranyi* (Allen and Unwin, 1969).

Mainwaring, J., *Memoirs of the Life of the late George Frideric Handel* (Da Capo Press, New York, 1974, facsimile reprint of 1760 edn, London).

Marek, G. R., *Gentle Genius. The Story of Felix Mendelssohn* (Robert Hale, 1972).

May, F., *The Life of Johannes Brahms* (Arnold, 1905), vol. 2.

Mayer, W., 'Internment', in Cesarani, D., and Kushner, T. (eds), *The Internment of Aliens in Twentieth Century Britain* (Cass, 1993).

McVeigh, S., *Concert Life in London from Mozart to Haydn* (Cambridge University Press, Cambridge, 1993).

Mercer-Taylor, P., *The Life of Mendelssohn* (Cambridge University Press, Cambridge, 2000).

Milhous, J. and Hume, R. D., 'Handel's London – The Theatres', in Burrows, D. (ed.), *The Cambridge Companion to Handel* (Cambridge University Press, Cambridge, 1997.

Milne, H., *Bartók: His Life and Times* (Midas Books, Tunbridge Wells, Kent, 1982).

Moreux, S., *Béla Bartók* (Harvill Press, 1953).

Moscheles, C. (trans. and ed. Coleridge, A. D.), *Life of Moscheles* (Hurst and Blackett, 1873), 2 vols.

Moscheles, F., *Letters of Felix Mendelssohn to Ignaz and Charlotte Moscheles* (Trübner, 1873).

Murdoch, W., *Chopin. His Life* (Murray, 1934).

Musical News and Herald, 19 March 1923.

Newman, E., *The Man Liszt* (Cassell, 1934).

Newton, D. (ed.), 'From the Musical World', *The Liszt Society Journal*, vol. 9, 1984.

Nichols, R. (ed.), *Mendelssohn Remembered* (Faber and Faber, 1997).

Niecks, F., *Frederick Chopin. As a Man and a Musician* (Novello, 1890), vol. 2.

Norris, G., *Stanford, Cambridge Jubilee and Tchaikovsky* (David and Charles, 1980).

Northrop Moore, J., *Edward Elgar. A Creative Life* (Oxford University Press, Oxford, 1964).

Northrop Moore, J., *Elgar and His Publishers. Letters of a Creative Life* (Clarendon Press, Oxford, 1987), vol. 1.

Northrop Moore, J., *Edward Elgar. Letters of a Lifetime* (Clarendon Press, Oxford, 1990).

Orlova, A., trans. Davison, R. M., *Tchaikovsky. A Self Portrait* (Oxford University Press, Oxford, 1990).

Osborne, C. (ed.), *Letters of Giuseppi Verdi* (Gollancz, 1971).

Ottaway, H., *Mozart* (Orbis, 1974).

Pall Mall Gazette, 13 October 1886.

Parfrey, R., 'Night-school Composer', *The Composer*, vol. 31, 1969.

Parrott, I., 'Warlock in Wales,' *Musical Times*, vol. 105, 1964.

Parry, J. O., 'Diaries, Liszt's British Tours of 1840 and 1841', *The Liszt Society Journal*, vol. 6, Spring 1981.

Payne, R., *Gershwin* (Pyramid Books, New York, 1960).

Perényi, E., *Liszt* (Weidenfeld and Nicolson, 1974).

Planché, J. R., *Recollections and Reflections* (Tinsley Brothers, 1872).

Plantinga, L., *Clementi. His Life and Music* (Oxford University Press, Oxford, 1977).

Polko, E., trans. Lady Wallace, *Reminiscences of Felix Mendelssohn-Bartholdy* (Longmans Green, 1869).

Poznansky, A., *Tchaikovsky. The Quest for the Inner Man* (Schirmer Books, New York, 1991).

Price, C., 'English Traditions in Handel's *Rinaldo*', in Sadie, S. and Hicks, A. (eds) *Handel Tercentenary Collection* (Macmillan, 1987).

Prior, R., 'Jewish Musicians at the Tudor Court,' *Musical Quarterly*, vol. 69, 1983.

Puckler-Muskau, H. L. H., *Tour of Germany, Holland and England in the Years 1826, 1827 and 1828* (Effingham Wilson, 1832), vol. 4.

Radio Times, 14 February 1930.

Raumer, F. von, *England in 1835: Being a Series of Letters Written to Friends in Germany* (Murray, 1836), vol. 3.

Reed, W. H., *Elgar as I Knew Him* (Gollancz, 1936).

Rees, B., *Camille Saint-Saëns. A Life* (Chatto and Windus, 1999).

Reizenstein, F., *The Listener*, 2 March 1967.

Riding, J., *Handel House Companion* (The Handel House Trust Ltd, 2001).

Rimsky-Korsakov, N. A., *My Musical Life* (Knopf, New York, 1923, 5th edn, 1992).

Robbins Landon, H. C. (ed.), *The Collected Correspondence and London Note-books of Joseph Haydn* (Barrie and Rockliff, 1959).

Robbins Landon, H. C. and Jones, D. W., *Haydn. His Life and Music* (Thames and Hudson, 1988).

Robertson, A., *Dvořák* (Dent, 1945).

Robertson, A., 'Dvořák' in Hill, R. (ed.), *The Symphony* (Penguin, Harmondsworth, 1949).

Robson-Scott, W. D., *German Travellers in England, 1400–1800* (Blackwell, Oxford, 1953).

Rose, M., *Berlioz Remembered* (Faber and Faber, 2001).

Roth, E., *The Business of Music. Reflections of a Music Publisher* (Cassell, 1969).

Ryals, C. de L. *et al.* (eds), *The Collected Letters of Thomas and Jane Welsh Carlyle* (Duke University Press, Durham, NC, 1995), vol. 23.

Sadie, S., *Handel* (Calder, 1962).

Sadie, S. (ed.), *The New Grove Dictionary of Music and Musicians*, 2nd edn, (Grove, 2001).

Salaman, C., 'Pianists of the Past', *Blackwood's Edinburgh Magazine*, vol. 152, September 1901.

Samson, J., *Chopin* (Oxford University Press, Oxford, 1966).

Sand, G. (trans. and ed. Hofstadter, D.), *My Life* (Gollancz, 1979).

Saunders, W., *Weber* (Dent, 1940).

Schenk, E., *Mozart and His Times* (Secker & Warburg, 1960).

Schmidt, C. B., *Entrancing Muse. A Documented Biography of Francis Poulenc* (Pendragon Press, Hillside, New York, 2002).

Schopenhauer, J. (trans. and ed. Michaelis-Jena, P. and Merson, W.), *A Lady Travels. Journeys in England and Scotland. From the Diaries of Johanna Schopenhauer* (Routledge, 1988).

Schuh, W., trans. Whittall, M., *Richard Strauss: A Chronicle of the Early Years, 1864–1898* (Cambridge University Press, Cambridge, 1982).

Selden-Goth, G. F. M., *Letters of Mendelssohn* (Kraus Reprint Co., New York, 1969).

Seyfert, M., 'His Majesty's Most Loyal Internees', in Hirschfield, G. (ed.), *Exile in Great Britain. Refugees from Hitler's Germany* (Berg, 1984).

Shaw, G. B., *Music in London, 1890–94* (Constable, 1932), vol. 1.

Siepmann, J., *Chopin. The Reluctant Romantic* (Gollancz, 1995).

Silverman, J., 'Some Thoughts on Matyas Seiber', *Tempo*, no. 143, 1982.

Simon, J. (ed.), *Handel: A Celebration of his Life and Times* (National Portrait Gallery, London, 1985).

Simpson, A., '"Of a Petty French Lutenist in England" by Richard Flecknoe', *Lute Society Journal*, vol. 10 (1968).

Simpson, R., *Carl Nielsen, Symphonist* (Dent, 1952).

Sitwell, S., *Liszt* (Dover Publications, New York, 1967).

Skelton, G. (trans. and ed.), *Selected Letters of Paul Hindemith* (Yale University Press, New Haven, 1995).

Smaczny, J., *Dvořák: Cello Concerto* (Cambridge University Press, Cambridge, 1999).

Smidek, E. F., *Isaak-Ignaz Moscheles* (Scolar Press, 1989).

Smyth, E., *Impressions That Remained. Memoirs* (Longmans, Green, 1919), vol. 2.

Snowman, D., *The Hitler Emigrés. The Cultural Impact on Britain of Refugees from Nazism* (Chatto and Windus, 2002).

Soligny, Count de V., trans. Patmore, P. G., *Letters on England* (Henry Colburn, 1823), vol. 1.

Soloman, M., *Mozart* (Hutchinson, 1995).

Sourek, O., trans. Samsour, R. F., *Antonin Dvořák. Letters and Reminiscences* (Artia, Prague, 1954).

Spaethling, R. (ed.), *Mozart's Letters, Mozart's Life* (Faber and Faber, 2001).

Spiegel, F., *Musical Blunders and other Musical Curiosities* (Robson Books, 1997).

Stanford, C. V., *Pages From an Unwritten Dairy* (Edward Arnold, 1914).

Sterndale Bennett, J. R., *The Life of William Sterndale Bennett* (Cambridge University Press, Cambridge 1907).

Stevens, H., *The Life and Music of Béla Bartók* (Cambridge University Press, New York, 1953).

Stevens, J., *Music and Poetry in the Early Tudor Court* (Cambridge University Press, Cambridge, 1979).

Stevens, L., *Composers of Classical Music of Jewish Descent* (Vallentine Mitchell, 2003).

Stravinsky, I., *The Story of My Life* (Gollancz, 1936).

Suchoff, B. (ed.), *Béla Bartók Essays* (Faber and Faber, 1976).

Suchoff, B., 'The Impact of Italian Baroque music on Bartók's Music', in Rankl, G. (ed.), *Bartók and Kodály Revisited*, Indiana University Studies on Hungary 2 (Academia Kiadö, Budapest, 1987).

Szigeti, J., *With Strings Attached* (Cassell, 1949).

Tawaststjerna, E., trans. Layton, R., *Sibelius* (Faber and Faber, 1986), vol. 2, 1904–14.

Tchaikovsky, M. (ed. Newmarch, R.), *The Life and Letters of Peter Ilich Tchaikovsky* (John Lane, 1896).

Tchaikovsky, P. I., trans. Lakond, W., *The Diaries of Tchaikovksy* (Greenwood Press, Westport, CT, 1973).

Tchaikovsky, P. I., trans. von Meck, G., *Letters to his Family. An Autobiography* (Dobson, 1981).

Terry, C. S., *John Christian Bach* (Oxford University Press, Oxford, 1967).

Thompson, B., *A Monkey Among Crocodiles. The Life, Loves and Lawsuits of Mrs Georgina Weldon* (HarperCollins, 2000).

Tilmouth, M., 'Nicola Matteis', *Musical Quarterly*, vol. 46, 1960.

Tucker, M. (ed.) *The Duke Ellington Reader* (Oxford University Press, New York, 1993).

Turner, W. J., *Beethoven. The Search for Reality* (Ernest Benn, 1927).

Turner, W. J., *Berlioz. The Man and His Work* (Dent, 1939).

Tusa, M., *Euryanthe and Maria von Weber's Dramaturgy of German Opera* (Clarendon Press, Oxford, 1991).

Ujfalussy, J., *Béla Bartók* (Corvina Press, Budapest, 1971).

Vaughan Williams, U., *R.V.W. A Biography of Ralph Vaughan Williams* (Oxford University Press, Oxford, 1964).

Vickers, G., *Classical Music Landmarks of London* (Omnibus Press, 2001).

'Vilem Tausky', *The Times*, 18 March 2004.

Wagner, C. (ed. Gregor-Dellin, M. and Mack, D.), *Diaries* vol. 2, *1878–1883* (Collins, 1980).

Wagner, R., *My Life* (Tudor Publishing Company, New York, 1936).

Walker, A., *Franz Liszt. The Virtuoso Years, 1811–1847* (Faber and Faber, 1983), vol. 1.

Walker, A., *Franz Liszt. The Final Years, 1861–1886* (Faber and Faber, 1997), vol. 3.

Ward Jones, P., *The Mendelssohns on Honeymoon. The 1837 Diary of Felix and Cécile Mendelssohn-Bartholdy* (Clarendon Press, Oxford, 1997).

Ward, P., 'Egon Wellesz: An Opera Composer in 1920s Vienna', *Tempo*, no. 219, 2000.

Warrack, J., *Carl Maria von Weber* (Cambridge University Press, Cambridge, 1976).

Wasserstein, B., *Britain and the Jews of Europe, 1939–1945* (Institute for Jewish Policy Research/Leicester University Press, 2nd edn, 1999).

Watson, D., *Liszt* (Dent, 1989).

Weber, M. M. von, trans. Simpson, J. P., *Carl Maria von Weber. The Life of an Artist* (Chapman and Hall, 1865), vol. 2.

Weinstock, H., *Rossini. A Biography* (Oxford University Press, Oxford, 1968).

Weinstock, H., *Vincenzo Bellini. His Life and His Operas* (Weidenfeld and Nicolson, 1972).

Werner, E., trans. Newlin, D., *Mendelssohn. Image of the Composer and His Age* (Collier-Macmillan, 1963).

Westrup, J. A., 'Foreign Musicians in Stuart England', *Musical Quarterly*, vol. 27, 1941.

Wilhelm, K. (ed. Whittall, M.), *Richard Strauss. An Intimate Portrait* (Thames and Hudson, 1989).

Williams, A., *Portrait of Liszt. By Himself and His Contemporaries* (Clarendon Press, Oxford, 1990).

Williams, A., (ed.), *Franz Liszt. Selected Letters* (Clarendon Press, Oxford, 1998).

Wilson, F. M. (ed.), *Strange Island. Britain through Foreign Eyes, 1395–1940* (Longmans, Green, 1955).

Wood, H. J., *My Life of Music* (Gollancz, 1938).

Woodfield, I., 'New Light on the Mozarts' London Visit: A Private Concert with Manzuoli', *Music and Letters*, vol. 76, 1995.

Zaluski, I. and P., *Young Liszt* (Peter Owen, 1992).

Zamoyski, A., *Chopin. A Biography* (Collins, 1979).

Zaslaw, N., *Mozart's Symphonies: Context, Performance Practice, Reception* (Clarendon Press, Oxford, 1989).

Zaslaw, N. (ed.), *Mozart's Piano Concertos: Text, Context and Interpretation* (University of Michigan Press, Ann Arbor, 1990).

Zemanova, M., *Janacek. A Composer's Life* (Murray, 2003).

Index